A Race with Love and Death

A Race with Love and Death

THE STORY OF RICHARD SEAMAN

Richard Williams

**SIMON &
SCHUSTER**

London · New York · Sydney · Toronto · New Delhi

First published in Great Britain by Simon & Schuster UK Ltd, 2020

Copyright © Richard Williams, 2020

3 5 7 9 10 8 6 4

Simon & Schuster UK Ltd
1st Floor
222 Gray's Inn Road
London WC1X 8HB

www.simonandschuster.co.uk
www.simonandschuster.com.au
www.simonandschuster.co.in

Simon & Schuster Australia, Sydney
Simon & Schuster India, New Delhi

Hardback ISBN: 978-1-4711-7935-8
eBook ISBN: 978-1-4711-7936-5

Typeset in Bembo by M Rules
Printed and bound by CPI Group (UK) Ltd, Croydon, CR0 4YY

In memory of Alan Henry (1947–2016),
colleague and friend

'The potential biographies of those who die young possess the mystic dignity of a headless statue, the poetry of enigmatic passages in an unfinished or mutilated manuscript, unburdened with contrived or banal endings.'

—ANTHONY POWELL, *The Valley of Bones*

'Typical of Drax to buy a Mercedes. There was something ruthless and majestic about the cars, he decided, remembering the years from 1934 to 1939 when they had completely dominated the Grand Prix scene . . . Bond recalled some of their famous drivers, Caracciola, Lang, Seaman, Brauchitsch, and the days when he had seen them drifting the fast sweeping bends of Tripoli at 190, or screaming along the tree-lined straight at Berne with the Auto Unions on their tails.'

—IAN FLEMING, *Moonraker*

CONTENTS

PART THREE (1937–38)

PART FOUR (1938–39)

PROLOGUE

He could see the umbrellas going up again in the grandstands as the rain fell harder, water sluicing across the track, in places forming inch-deep, foot-wide rivers, elsewhere creating a smooth surface as deceptive as ice. The Grand Prix was past the halfway point and he had made it through to the lead.

On a filthy afternoon in the Ardennes, the conditions were as treacherous as they had been when he made his first tentative steps into the sport eight years earlier, barely out of school uniform. But there had been no crowd to speak of on that sodden day in the Malvern Hills, no one to see the 18-year-old make a beginner's mistake. There had been no team manager to offer guidance, no mechanics attending to his car, no young wife watching from the pits, and certainly no national prestige at stake.

No driver likes racing in the rain. Some good ones, champions in other circumstances, can't cope with it. They ease back and wait for the day to be over. Others have a sensitivity that allows them to make the most of the challenge: a light touch on the steering and the throttle, and even greater delicacy on the brakes. In his early days he had made mistakes in the rain, but he had learnt from them and now he was regarded as one of those who possessed the special instinct.

Several of his rivals had already spun off the track and out of the race. His nearest challenger was twenty seconds adrift. He could afford to back off a little and reduce the risk as he sped along the tree-lined road, but that was not in his mind. He still needed to prove himself. His only thought was to press on in the gloom, peering through his visor for reference points – a farmhouse, a road sign, the end of a line of trees – and feeling his tyres search for grip on the wet asphalt. The rain mantling the hills and forests in this corner of Belgium was unlikely to lift in the final hour of the race. As he approached the end of the twenty-second lap, with thirteen to go to the chequered flag, it was all in his hands.

◆

When Dick Seaman died while leading the Belgian Grand Prix that day in 1939, at the age of twenty-six, he was on the brink of taking his place among a generation of British sporting heroes. The others were not hard to identify. Fred Perry, the Stockport-born son of a cotton spinner, became the men's singles champion at Wimbledon three years in a row, from 1934 to 1936, between the ages of twenty-five and twenty-seven. The Russian-born Prince Alexander Obolensky, whose father had been an officer in the Tsar's Imperial Guard, was nineteen when he ran three-quarters of the length of Twickenham one afternoon in 1936 to touch down for an unforgettable try in England's first-ever rugby victory over New Zealand. In 1937 the 21-year-old Stanley Matthews, the wizard of the dribble, scored a hat-trick in England's 5-4 defeat of the formidable Czechoslovaks at White Hart Lane. And in the Ashes series of 1938 the Yorkshire cricketer Len Hutton, aged twenty-two, spent thirteen hours compiling a record 364 runs against Australia at the Oval. Given another season or two, Seaman would surely have joined them.

And yet, five days after his death, the biggest wreath at his funeral came from Adolf Hitler, whose colours he had carried in races across three continents. When he crashed in his Mercedes-Benz, he was admired as the first British racing driver to join one of the two state-sponsored German teams that had established a total domination of the sport. He had emerged from a background of privilege and sophistication, but all his parents' wealth would have been useless without talent and determination as he fought his way to the top.

As the mourners gathered in London, they were headed by the two women between whom he had been forced to choose barely six months earlier: his mother and his wife, united in grief but severed from each other in every other way. And many of those present were shocked by the arrival of the wreath from Berlin. Like Dick's half-hearted Hitler salute at the Nürburgring a year earlier, a reluctant response to the acclaim of a German crowd while surrounded by Nazi uniforms on the victory podium at the moment of his greatest triumph, it stained the reputation of a young man who had now lost the chance to explain himself. Unlike a Hutton or a Matthews, he would have no opportunity to pick up the threads of his sporting career once the war was over. Or, more important, to show which side he was really on.

PART ONE

1911–30

1

A Mayfair romance

The couple who would become Dick Seaman's parents met on a November evening in 1910 at the restaurant of the Savoy Hotel, overlooking the Thames by Waterloo Bridge. William Seaman and Lilian Pearce were the guests of Sir Thomas Dewar, a Scottish whisky distiller and former Member of Parliament. On this evening Tommy Dewar was hosting a table of ten at an establishment where the culinary standards had been set by Auguste Escoffier and diners were expected to wear evening dress.

He was also acting in the role of matchmaker to two friends who had not met before: a man and a woman who had both been widowed prematurely, and whom he seated together. William John Seaman – fifty-two years old, a tall and distinguished figure, albeit bearing some of the signs of recent ill health – was a director of John Dewar & Sons. Seven years earlier his wife had died at their home in Glasgow, leaving him with a 10-year-old daughter. His neighbour at the dinner table, the vivacious Lilian Graham Pearce, was around twenty years his junior; she had lost her husband, a former officer in the Manchester Regiment, to a sudden illness in 1902, barely a year after their marriage. She, too, had been left with a daughter, then still an infant. As she wrote in a memoir many years later, she liked the look of William Seaman straight away, finding him charming and interesting as he told her that he had recently spent several months convalescing on his yacht off the west coast of Scotland after treatment for severe heart problems. Now he was staying briefly in London, at the Berkeley Hotel on Piccadilly, en route to Bournemouth, where he planned to continue his recovery in the company of his valet and his personal physician. Her home, she mentioned, was in Clarges Street in Mayfair, only a couple of minutes' walk from his hotel.

After dinner the party moved on to the Savoy Theatre, where William Seaman thwarted Tommy Dewar's plan to reshuffle his guests by slipping quickly into the seat next to Mrs Graham Pearce. They continued their conversation during the intervals, and he invited her to lunch at the Ritz the following day. When she told him that, alas, a women's lunch party at her club meant she would have to decline, he grimaced and invited her to reconsider, pointing out that it would be his last day in London. He leaned back and put his hand on his heart, leading her to imagine that he might be about to have another heart attack. While protesting that she hated to break an appointment, she finally accepted his invitation and was interested to note the colour return to his cheeks. Their host noticed it, too. 'I asked you to engage this man in interesting conversation,' Tommy Dewar told her, 'not to give him a charge of electricity.'

When she walked up the steps of the Ritz the next day, having been driven the very short distance from Clarges Street, she was surprised to be greeted by William Seaman in morning dress, with a carnation in his buttonhole, looking the picture of health. 'Are you going to a wedding?' she asked, a little mischievously. 'Not today,' he replied, holding her gaze in a way that invited interpretation.

Once they had ordered their lunch, she listened as he told his story. He was an only child, the last heir on his mother's side of a family of Scottish lairds, the Beatties. He had been born in Glasgow, brought up in London, educated at Harrow and

sent abroad to perfect his French and German with a view to
joining the diplomatic service. (There was some family history
involved: a Seaman posted to the British embassy in Paris before
the French Revolution had been the last man out in 1789, taking
the flag with him before the building was padlocked.) Then,
however, a collapse of the family fortunes had derailed all ambitions for any sort of career that required the support of private
means. Instead, at the age of twenty-five, he was redirected into
the world of business, going to work for an uncle, a wealthy
businessman who put him up at his home and took him every
day to his office in Glasgow, where he taught him about the
world of commerce. William Lowrie's company had become
the biggest whisky stockholder in the world; its founder also had
interests in shipping and banking, and he made his nephew an
interesting offer. Whatever you save out of your salary, he said,
I will double the sum, provided that you use it to buy shares in
the company so that one day you can become a director.

Lilian, who had been listening intently as the narrative
unfolded, suddenly noticed that the waiters were resetting the
tables around them, preparing to serve tea. When William
invited her to dinner at the Berkeley, she declined. 'For an invalid,' she told him before being driven home, 'you've had quite
enough social activity for one day.'

◆

At nine o'clock the next morning, a servant answered the
phone at 44 Clarges Street. William Seaman was on the line,
announcing that he now intended to stay in London for a few
more days and repeating his invitation to dinner. That evening
he asked how she planned to spend the winter; she told him she
would be travelling to Cannes for Christmas and then going
on to Egypt. They parted, and the following day he phoned to
say he was not feeling well and planned to leave immediately
for the south coast.

Four days later he was back. He had been bored in

Bournemouth, he told her. Every morning thereafter he called at nine with invitations to lunch, tea or dinner, many of which she accepted. Gradually she learnt more of his life. For all his current wealth, his origins had been modest. His father, also called William, had been born into a fishmonger's family in Spitalfields, in the East End of London, in 1828. As a young man, he had worked as a clerk and a warehouseman and moved to Glasgow, where he and Agnes Beattie were married in 1857, and where their son, the first of their two children, was born the following year. By the time their daughter Florence arrived, in 1867, he had brought his family back to London.

Lilian listened intently as her companion told her how he had moved back to Glasgow, where his childless uncle and aunt had treated him almost as a son; his augmented savings had eventually enabled him to buy shares not just in W. P. Lowrie & Co. but in several of the big distilleries, including Dewar's, Mackie & Co. and Haig & Haig. Having established himself, in 1891 he had married Annabella Gemmell, the daughter of a Glasgow metal merchant, and a daughter, Dorothy, was born the following year. But Annabella's health was poor, and in 1903 she died of peritonitis. Now the widowed William lived in a fine house on Bute Gardens in the Hillhead district, close to the university, and Dorothy, aged seventeen, was travelling in Europe with a governess and a lady's maid before returning to be presented as a debutante at Court.

He also mentioned his yacht, the SY *Titania*, and its permanent crew recruited from the Isle of Skye, on which he and parties of guests cruised up and down the Scottish coast. Lilian listened with equal interest as he described what he had learnt from the great figures of business. There would be many such conversations before, over dinner at Claridge's in the first week of December, barely a month after their first meeting, William Seaman asked Lilian Graham Pearce to marry him.

◆

Her first response was to dismiss the idea completely. He was an invalid, she pointed out. He protested that he felt better when he was with her. Then she announced that there was another reason why they could not be married: she was engaged to a man who was away on business in America and would be returning to London in January. The trip to Cannes was to join his house party. William asked whether, had the circumstances been different, she would have accepted his proposal. She replied that they had known each other for such a short time that she simply didn't know. He left the house and returned to his hotel.

After four days of silence his valet brought a note in which he explained that he had been ill and asked her to visit him. The valet said that on the night of the dinner at Claridge's he had suffered another heart attack while going up in the lift. She went that afternoon and found him in bed, looking ill but perking up a little as they took tea. He asked her to return the next day, and the day after that.

When he returned to the subject of her impending marriage, she told him that the man in question was a widower with a title and an estate and a son to inherit it all. It would be a marriage, she said, with political and social dimensions that she would relish. William pointed out that since there was already an heir, no son she might have could hold out such hopes. She thought this suggestion betrayed his regret at his own lack of a son to whom he could pass on his wealth. When he persisted, she told him that she was simply not his type – too modern, too energetic. 'In fact,' she remembered, 'I did everything I could to make him see that it would never do.'

Perhaps she did. More probably they were reeling each other in. 'Such protestations, such entreaties, such arguments,' she recalled. But before long he was helping her to write a letter to an address in America, explaining her change of heart. Her visits to the South of France and Egypt were cancelled, and a new set of plans took their place.

◆

First the engagement ring was chosen, and pearls for the bride's necklace were sized, graded and strung. The yacht was brought down from Scotland to Southampton, where it was overhauled and refurbished to her taste. The couple visited the showrooms of the Daimler Company Ltd on Pall Mall to order their wedding cars, with bespoke upholstery to match the bride's dress. Since 1902, Daimler had supplied motor vehicles to Britain's royal family, and to those of Russia, Germany, Sweden, Japan, Spain and Greece.

Both parties agreed to dispose of their respective houses in Glasgow and London and to find somewhere in the country, perhaps not far from Portsmouth, where the *Titania* could be kept in readiness. Their friend James Buchanan, another distiller, suggested that the wisest course might be to rent a property, and mentioned a place near his own in West Sussex. Standing just north of the road between Arundel and Chichester, 70 miles from London, and built around 1800, Aldingbourne House had been the home of the younger brother of the Duke of Norfolk, whose family seat was at Arundel. The estate included stables and yards, ornamental and kitchen gardens, a lodge, a park and a great deal of farmland.

Announced in March, the wedding was to take place on 1 June. In the little time available, a trip to Paris had to be made in order to select the bride's trousseau. Lilian, her maid and an elderly chaperone stayed at the Hôtel Meurice on the Rue de Rivoli while William – who no longer needed to travel with a doctor – was with his valet at the Ritz, close by in the Place Vendôme. Every morning of their stay he sent her a card, flowers and a present before she went shopping. Soon there were orders for shimmering paillette dresses from the houses of Worth and Doucet, day dresses from Patou, yachting dresses from Paquin, 'tailormades' (suits) from Creed, ostrich-feathered picture hats from Maria Guy and Caroline Reboux, and jewels from Van

Cleef & Arpels. They dined at Maxim's and visited the Casino de Paris. At the theatre they saw the great performers of the day: Mistinguett, Sacha Guitry and the dancer Cléo de Mérode, a legendary beauty. 'Paris was indeed itself,' Lilian recalled.

Back in London she took a suite at Claridge's, where she made her last-minute arrangements. On the eve of the wedding, while she was preparing for a celebratory dinner with friends, her maid announced that Mr Seaman wanted to see her in the living room. She went in. He placed a box and a long envelope in her hands. The box contained a diamond tiara, which he invited her to put on. The long envelope contained a different sort of gift: several certificates for large blocks of shares in the great Scottish companies with which he was connected. This was his way of presenting her with a marriage settlement, while avoiding negotiation. Then, as she remembered, he looked at the tiara and told her that he hoped she would have a son, and that one day his wife would wear it.

They were married at St Paul's Church, Knightsbridge. On a bright day, the bride was accompanied on the car ride to the church by her 9-year-old daughter, Vahlia, who had been given the day off from Roedean, her boarding school in Sussex. Afterwards they returned to Claridge's for the reception, where Tommy Dewar made an entertaining speech. This, he said, was the last time he was ever going to introduce any of his widows to any of his friends. It always led to trouble.

◆

When it came to filling in the marriage certificate, the new Mrs Seaman took some interesting liberties. Her name appeared on the form as Lilian Mary Graham Pearce. Her age was given as twenty-nine. Her father's name was entered as 'Charles Taplin', and his rank or profession as 'Gentleman'. In fact she had been born Lilian Mary Tuplin, not Taplin, and after the death of her first husband, Captain Graham Ravenhill Pearce, she appro-priated his first name and surname as a combined, and rather grander, surname for herself and her daughter. She was not twenty-nine but thirty-three, having been born on 16 January 1878 – and not in Norfolk, as she sometimes claimed, but at 8 Crown Place, off Aldgate in the City of London, a quarter of mixed repute once known as Old Jewry. Her father's name was Thomas Tuplin; Charles was the last of his three forenames. His position in society was not, in the accepted sense, that of a gentleman.

Thomas Tuplin had been born in 1839 in a Lincolnshire village called Moulton. A farm labourer's son, he worked there as a butcher, the trade he pursued after moving to London. By 1875 he was serving with the City of London police, eventually reaching the rank of sergeant. In 1880 he married Susannah Pearce, the daughter of a South Norfolk beer-house keeper, although they had already described themselves as man and wife on the birth certificates of Lilian and her brother Frederick, who had been born in 1875. Susannah had two older children with no father's name on their birth certificates, both of them initially taking her surname: Anna Maria (later known as Madge), born in 1869 in Norfolk, and Louise, born in London in 1873. In 1884 Susannah had her last child, a daughter called Ellen, with Thomas in London; all five children took the Tuplin name, but only the last had been born in wedlock.

By then Thomas Tuplin had taken his family to live at 60 Fenchurch Street, barely a stone's throw from their former home but a little further from the low-life of Aldgate and Whitechapel. A 17-year-old girl was employed to help Susannah with the children. A short walk away was Liverpool Street station, with services to Suffolk and Norfolk, enabling Susannah to maintain links with her family.

Thomas was forty-five when he died of an abdominal tumour. In the final stages of his illness he had gone to his in-laws' home in the rural South Norfolk village of Alburgh, and was buried there. The final line on his tombstone in the churchyard of All Saints – *His end was peace* – suggests the ordeal he had endured. He left Susannah the sum of £368 2s. 11d. and five children, aged between one and sixteen, to bring up alone in London.

◆

Lilian Tuplin's ambition helped her to rise above that mundane background. Throughout her life she was avid for knowledge about royalty and the aristocracy, the houses they lived in, the paintings they bought and the clothes they wore, and she was keen on the sort of travel that would teach her more. Most of all, she was alert to opportunities. By the time she made the leap from police sergeant's daughter to infantry officer's wife, she had acquired the social equipment that obscured her origins.

She was twenty-three years old when, on 30 March 1901, she presented herself at the British consulate in Marseille to become the second wife of Graham Pearce, a widower nineteen years her senior. The son of Ravenhill Pearce, a doctor with a prosperous practice in Brighton and Hove, he had seen action in the Egyptian War of 1882 but had retired from the army before his first marriage, at Le Havre in 1895, to Alice Brooks, a divorcée. On the certificate of that marriage he gave his rank as major, although mentions in the *Army & Navy Gazette* place him no higher than captain; such self-awarded 'promotions' on returning to civilian life were by no means uncommon. After eight months of marriage, Alice died the following April.

Graham's marriage to Lilian was ended after only fourteen months by his own death. Their daughter had been born three months earlier, in Ceylon, after which the family returned to England to live at 33 Sydney Street in Chelsea. Graham was forty-four when he died in 1902, leaving his estate – £5,072 gross, £2,226 net (just over a quarter of a million pounds today) – to his widow, who was soon amending her surname.

When Lilian Graham Pearce met William Seaman, she was mixing in high society and living in Mayfair with a butler, a housemaid, a kitchen maid and a cook, and had acquired the occasional habit of entering 'Alburgh, Norfolk' as her birthplace on official documents. A more attractive place of origin, perhaps, with its apple orchards, its fields of wheat and its sixteenth-century manor house, than the teeming, fog-shrouded Aldgate of the 1870s, whose public order Sgt Thomas Tuplin had been pledged to preserve.

◆

At Claridge's, the newly married couple put their signatures to rewritten versions of their respective wills in an upstairs room before saying farewell to their guests and leaving for their honeymoon. They were driven to Dover, where they were saluted by the uniformed crew, about twenty strong, as they boarded the *Titania* before setting off along the English Channel towards Cornwall.

At the beginning of July they disembarked in Portsmouth and were driven up to London. There they were joined by their daughters before setting off for Scotland, where the yacht would meet them on the Clyde. Mrs Seaman visited the impressive offices and warehouses of W. P. Lowrie & Co. in Glasgow, marvelling at the success of her husband's patron and nodding her agreement as she listened to William and his fellow directors lamenting the heavy taxation and the 'prohibitive' excise duty levied on the goods that had made their considerable fortunes.

Back in West Sussex, they could settle into their new home, with its squads of servants, cooks, gardeners, coachmen, farm labourers and a new head chauffeur, Henry Wood, to look after the Daimlers. The couple blended quickly into local society, and after a busy Christmas they greeted 1912 by heading for the South of France, stopping off en route in Paris, where Lilian ordered a new wardrobe. In Cannes they stayed at the Carlton, the grandest hotel on the Croisette, opened the previous year. For three months they made the most of the Riviera's warm winter climate, motoring to Monte Carlo, Menton, Cap Martin and elsewhere, entertaining friends and enjoying the sights.

They were back at Aldingbourne when, one evening late in June, as they sat together in the library after dinner, Lilian told her husband that she was expecting a child, and that she was certain it would be a son.

2

Country life

Since her doctor told her that an active mother was more likely to give birth to a boy, Lilian Seaman continued to accompany her husband to the events of the summer season: the rowing at Henley, the racing at Goodwood, the yachting at Cowes, and a trip to Deauville, where they moored the yacht. At Aldingbourne House, a nursery suite was filled with clothes and toys. Christmas passed, and in the first month of 1913 a platoon of nurses arrived to take up residence.

At dinner on the evening of 3 February, she began to feel that the birth was imminent. She later reported that, as word spread, people from the estate's cottages and farms made their way to the great house, waiting for news. It came in the early hours of the following morning, with the safe delivery at home of a boy: Richard John Beattie Seaman, normal and healthy in every respect, already seeming to his mother to possess virtues of virility, resolution, character and determination. She was dozing when, at eight o'clock, she was woken by the bells of St Mary's, the parish church, carrying clear across the fields, ringing to celebrate the birth of a child at the great house for the first time in living memory.

Named by his father after a friend who had died young, the infant Richard was christened on 2 April beside the church's twelfth-century marble font. Afterwards the Seamans' guests returned to the house for a party with speeches and a band hired from London. The following week the 2-month-old infant was being taken around the schools of Aldingbourne and the other nearby farming villages, where slices of his magnificent christening cake were distributed to the local children.

◆

It was the last full year before the world changed. There were ripples on the surface, events that indicated imminent disruption to the status quo, from the near-riot with which a Parisian audience greeted the premiere of Igor Stravinsky's *Rite of Spring* to the death of the suffragette Emily Davison under the hooves of the King's horse during the Epsom Derby. Trouble was reported in the Balkans and in Ireland, where 15,000 men had joined a republican militia. But in 1913 the lives of the wealthy and privileged were still unblemished either by the wholesale slaughter of their young sons or by the sense of threat that would emerge when opposing ideologies redefined the tone of the century.

The following summer was one of the loveliest in memory, a season of sun-kissed cricket festivals, gymkhanas and tennis parties, when the possibility of war seemed like just another game waiting to be mastered: 'Never such innocence, / Never before or since,' as the poet Philip Larkin would write. Before Dick could walk, he was being taken on board the *Titania* for weekends on the Solent. At Deauville he played on the beach and was wheeled in his perambulator up and down the promenade by his nurse. He was an active child from the start, and before long he had developed a fondness for sitting in the front seat of one of the family's Daimlers, sandwiched between his nurse and the chauffeur.

He was eighteen months old on the day when the Belgian government's invocation of a treaty of 1839 brought Britain into war against Germany. Enthusiastic crowds poured into the streets of London. Some were repeating the view, ascribed to Field Marshal Sir John French, that it would be over by Christmas; such optimism was not shared by the recently appointed Secretary of State for War, Lord Kitchener, who asked for 100,000 volunteers to form a new army. In the City of London there were long queues outside banks as people tried to exchange their cash for gold.

On that very date – Tuesday 4 August 1914 – Dick's parents had organised one of the last garden parties of the season, with a military band to provide the music. Even in bucolic West Sussex, the atmosphere was febrile. Lilian Seaman remembered the spreading of rumours: the pier at Southsea had been blown up during the night, Russians had landed in the north, the Kaiser was at the head of his army marching for Paris, and so on. At the end of the party the band played 'God Save the King', inducing in the hostess the feeling that they had delivered 'an inner rallying call to the nation'.

And that, to all intents and purposes, was an end to the unfettered social life of the Seamans and their circle for the next four years. By the end of the month, British soldiers were suffering a bloody defeat at Mons. As the first shots were fired between British and German warships off Heligoland in the North Sea, the SY *Titania* was laid up in Southampton, later to be requisitioned for postal deliveries between England and France. And that was the last the family saw of the vessel. William Seaman may not have greatly mourned its loss; by the war's end he would be sixty years old, his precarious health deteriorating.

◆

While Dick was still learning to walk and talk, his half-sisters were growing up. In August 1915 Dorothy married Charles Walter deBois Maclaren, a young diplomat, in Glasgow; afterwards the couple left for Bitlis in eastern Turkey, where the groom had been made the vice-consul of the British legation.

When 15,000 Armenians were murdered in the city by Turks, the Maclarens were quickly reposted to Rasht, the capital of the province of Gilan in Persia and the headquarters of a band of anti-monarchist guerrillas, the Jangali Movement.

It was there that the first of their three daughters was born, in September 1916. Two years later Charles Maclaren was captured by the Jangalis and apparently tortured. After his release the British writer, traveller, Arabist and diplomatic officer Gertrude Bell recorded in her diaries a scandal in Tehran involving her riding companion Sir Walter Barttelot, the British military attaché, who was 'murdered in his bed by a jealous husband'. A Mrs Maclaren, she noted, had returned home. The family was indeed soon back in Scotland, where Charles Maclaren joined his father's publishing firm.

Vahlia, Dick's other half-sister, had been a boarder at Roedean, on the outskirts of Brighton, since the autumn of 1911. Founded in 1885, the school's purpose was to prepare young ladies of good breeding for admission to the new women's colleges at Cambridge University. Vahlia sang and played the piano, received good marks for French conversation, and particularly enjoyed the chance to act. The school magazine described her as 'a most amusing Miss Pole' in *Scenes from Cranford*, and spoke of her Ghost in *A Christmas Carol* as making 'everyone shiver as she came in rattling her chains'.

In the late summer of 1915 the Seamans decided that Aldingbourne was too near to the vulnerable south coast – and in particular to Portsmouth harbour, a naval base, and to the army barracks at Southsea – for their continued peace of mind. Kentwell Hall in Suffolk seemed to be at a safe distance. Next to the village of Long Melford, it was a sixteenth-century mansion surrounded by a moat, built on 5,000 acres of land mentioned in the Domesday Book as the location of a manor house and given in the mid-thirteenth century by King Henry III to his half-brother, Sir William de Valence. The estate passed through various hands until being sold to a family who eventually let it to tenants – including, in October 1915, the Seamans: William, Lilian, Dick, and Dick's pekinese dog.

The magnificent red-brick house, with its tall, twisted chimney stacks and mullioned windows, stood at the end of a long straight drive, bordered by lime trees, with swans in the moat, a dovecote, an ornamental garden to one side, stables and servants' quarters. The kitchen wing was presided over by an aged resident housekeeper, Mrs Curroll, who complained immediately to her new mistress about the difficulty of obtaining female staff of the necessary calibre. She herself had gone into service at a time when maids were expected to start a full day's work at 5 a.m. Nowadays, she said, girls wanted to work from 9 a.m. to noon; they had been spoiled, she alleged, by 'high heels, silk stockings, dancing and the cinema'. There was, Lilian Seaman agreed, much truth in what she said.

Their first winter in Suffolk was a severe one. Dick's best Christmas present was a toy car, which he pedalled around the corridors until the risk of accidents with servants carrying trays became apparent. The nurse who had accompanied him from Sussex was replaced in February 1916 by a French nursery governess. That was the month when wealthy families were asked by the National Organising Committee for War Savings to close part of their homes, gardens and greenhouses in order to free their staff for more necessary work. The committee also criticised the 'selfish, thoughtless extravagance' of people who kept chauffeurs and used motor cars for pleasure, and asked for less extravagance in women's dress.

The family had moved to East Anglia to escape the war, but a few months before their arrival a Zeppelin airship had crossed the Norfolk coastline to drop bombs on King's Lynn, 50 miles away, killing twenty people. The Seamans complied with the instruction to maintain a blackout of all the house's many windows at night, but late one night in October 1916, when William was away on business, Lilian, Dick and the French mademoiselle were alarmed by the noise of bombs going off. It turned out that they had fallen harmlessly on a nearby wood, but the force of the explosions had been sufficient to break crockery in the house and skew pictures on the walls.

Soon after Dick's fourth birthday a tutor was engaged to supplement the lessons given by the governess. There was also the arrival of a pony, Black Bess, to add to the list of things with which, as his mother related, the boy kept busy: 'Gamekeepers and guns, reaping and haymaking seasons, fruit picking in the orchards, walnut picking and pickling in October, young pheasants hatching out, fishing and boating, he took a keen interest in it all.'

The family still made frequent visits to London, where Dick had his hair cut at Harrods, and eventually they decided that a house in town would be a sensible acquisition. They settled on the purchase of 3 Ennismore Gardens, in an elegant terrace just off Princes Gate, close to Hyde Park and Knightsbridge. There was a large communal garden – almost a small park – to the rear, and a mews running down the side, containing stables that could be converted into garages and chauffeurs' quarters.

They were at Kentwell Hall on 11 November 1918, when the armistice was declared, marking the end of a war that had killed around 10 million, almost a million of them from Britain and its colonies. Across the country blackout curtains came down, the masking was removed from street lights, there was dancing in town and village squares, and licensing laws were ignored. As they listened to the bells of Long Melford church ringing across the park, the Seamans could rejoice that, unlike so many, their family had survived and emerged intact into a world that had changed in ways no one could yet comprehend.

3

Safe and sunlit

Two months after the armistice, the Seamans were able to move into Ennismore Gardens, where number 3 had been redecorated and filled with furniture and paintings. Now there was no shortage of children deemed suitable for him to play with on the lawns behind the house, and a new tutor arrived to help prepare him for the experience of formal schooling.

He was six years old when he was taken for his first day at the establishment founded by Mr C. H. Gibbs in a house at 134 Sloane Street. This was no more than a twenty-minute walk away, although to begin with he was delivered in the morning – wearing a grey knickerbocker suit with a cherry-red cap and matching tie – by his governess, the two of them driven by the chauffeur, who returned to pick the boy up at the end of the school day.

Charles Henry Gibbs was a pioneer of sympathetic pre-preparatory schooling for children between the ages of six and eight. He was also something of a character. The actor and writer Peter Ustinov, another pupil, remembered him as 'extremely cordial, and also extremely absent-minded ... a charming old gentleman, in spite of his belief in corporal punishment and the sanctity of the Boy Scout movement'.

English, French, Latin, maths, algebra, geography and history were on the curriculum, and several times a week the boys would be taken to Barnes, where they played cricket in the summer and football in the winter at a sports ground set up for employees of Harrods. To the pupils, the school offered an idyllic experience. 'Everything within this academy was safe, and sunlit,' Ustinov concluded. 'Nobody questioned the rectitude of King or Country, and both Jesus and the Boy Scout seemed in place, as indeed did those portions of the map coloured red.'

Dick's predecessors at the school included the film director Anthony Asquith and the novelist Anthony Powell. Among his contemporaries were Jo Grimond, later to lead the Liberal Party, and John Profumo, whose career as a Conservative cabinet minister would be ended by a scandal involving a young woman and a Russian diplomat.

Before long Dick persuaded his parents to let him travel to Sloane Street and back alone with the chauffeur, minus his mother or the governess. Once he had settled in, he was even granted his wish to go to and from home on the bus, as some other pupils did. On his return he would sometimes disappear into the mews to spend time with his father's employees, among the family's Daimlers.

◆

That summer at Kentwell Hall, having watched horses being ridden in Hyde Park, Dick drove his pony and trap with renewed enthusiasm. In autumn and winter he looked forward to the pheasant shoots, those days when large numbers of men arrived and tables were set up for lunch, laden with steak and kidney pie, chicken casserole, and apple and blackberry pudding. Rather less to his parents' delight, the 6-year-old also ventured outside one September morning with a loaded shotgun, pulling the triggers on both barrels before being disarmed by horrified gamekeepers. According to his mother, he responded to their threats of exposure to his father with the precociously cunning suggestion that he might in turn report their failure to keep the gunroom locked.

Among the regular summer visitors to Kentwell was Alexander Bull, the son of the rector of a nearby village, on holiday from his job as a master at Hildersham House, a prep school in Broadstairs, Kent. Bull took an interest in young Dick, testing his rudimentary Latin and suggesting to his parents that Hildersham House might be a good option for the next stage of his education. The Seamans took his advice, and it was arranged that Dick would begin there at the start of the summer term in 1921. A trunk was bought, nametapes were sewn into all the garments of the specified uniform, and at Easter the family gathered in Suffolk for a last weekend before his departure. But on the Monday, only a few hours before he was due to return to London and prepare for his first term at boarding school, Dick came down with scarlet fever.

After a convalescence that kept him at home until half-term, his delayed departure from Ennismore Gardens for Kent, wearing his new tweed knickerbocker suit, provided a dramatic memory for his mother: 'He came down the stairs and was very quiet and composed, but felt the strain of saying goodbye to all those assembled in the hall to see him start off on his new life. The outdoor manservants stood outside and even their wives had walked up to see him go, and nearly all were in tears or on the verge. They felt his leaving very keenly.'

She might not have been exaggerating by much. In a great house, bonds of loyalty and affection could unite those above and below stairs, crossing – if certainly not erasing – class barriers, particularly in the case of children. And the experience of leaving home at the age of seven or eight, to be thrust into a completely unknown society often lacking in any semblance of the warmth and comfort experienced in the family environment, could be a cruel one. Those outside the system often found it difficult to comprehend. The best that could be said was that it sometimes developed a sense of independence and self-reliance in a child. But it was always a wrench.

4

Away from home

The special train from Victoria ended its 70-mile journey at Broadstairs station, a short walk from Hildersham House. For Dick, this day in the spring of 1921, in the middle of the Easter term, was a first encounter with the place where he would spend the next five years. For the other pupils in his year, who had started there in September, alliances would already have been formed and rituals established. To join part of the way through the school year would not have been the easiest experience for a boy of eight.

At the end of their walk along a country lane, Dick found his home for the next five years: a dark, imposing, L-shaped building set back from the road, behind a half-moon drive and a well-kept lawn. Built in 1870, its main three-storey structure contained the classrooms; the side block held the dormitories for the sixty pupils. To one side stood an ancient flint-walled barn used as a shooting range. In the extensive grounds behind the main building were pitches for cricket, rugby and football, and a squash court.

The returning pupils and the new boy were greeted by the headmaster, Arthur Snowden, the elder son of the school's founder, the Reverend Harcourt Snowden. Arthur's younger brother, also called Harcourt, had been killed by a sniper's bullet in January 1915 while serving in France. A plaque commemorating his life had been installed by his parents on the wall of the church where the pupils were taken each Sunday.

◆

By the 1920s, Broadstairs had become to the education of boys between the ages of eight and thirteen what Lausanne was to finishing schools for young women. Parents appreciated the direct rail link to London, as well as the healthy air and relative remoteness of the little fishing port on the Kent coast. On Sundays, as Dick and his fellow Hildersham pupils walked in crocodile formation down the high street of St Peter's-in-Thanet, past its shops, post office and pub to the parish church, they would be joined by the pupils of several other similar schools, including St Peter's Court, where King George V and Queen Mary had sent the three youngest of their five sons, the Princes Henry and George (the future Dukes of Gloucester and Kent) and John, whose epilepsy forced his withdrawal after a single term and who died at thirteen.

As a boy, Arthur Snowden had gone from Hildersham House to Rugby School, where he captained the first XI. Sport was an important feature of life at Hildersham, the school following the maxim of *mens sana in corpore sano* borrowed from the poet Juvenal by the English philosopher John Locke for prominent mention in *Some Thoughts Concerning Education* in 1693. The moral and spiritual dimension of the boys' education was to be reinforced in the year after the young Seaman's arrival by a new member of staff, the Rev. Gerald Parker, a young clergyman who left a curacy in Swindon to accept a post as teacher and chaplain at Hildersham House. Dick responded to his mentoring, and the two would correspond for the rest of his life, long after Gerald Parker had left Broadstairs to become the rector of two country parishes in the Cotswolds. At his next school, and in his professional career, Dick was never averse to seeking advice from older and more experienced men whose views he respected; later there would be older women who supplied advice and support in the matter of his emotional life.

During his first year at the school, his parents visited for the summer garden party and sports day. Dick took part in various races and the tug o' war and was, in his mother's view, 'in great form', keen to tell them about his new life and new friends. A few weeks later they met him at Victoria station at the start of the summer break, buying toys at Harrods before setting off for Suffolk. For the 8-year-old, the holidays would be largely spent in the garages and stables at Kentwell Hall, watching the chauffeurs and coachmen go about their work.

◆

The next year, however, would mark a change in their lives. Early in 1922 William Seaman's health started to deteriorate once more, and a doctor told them that living in the country, with frequent journeys to London and elsewhere on business, was no longer a sensible idea. After seven years there, they drove out of the gates of Kentwell Hall for the last time and headed back to Ennismore Gardens.

Another kind of change, one that may have been designed to please Lilian, had already been made. On 7 February 1922 an item in the *London Gazette* announced: 'Notice is hereby given that WILLIAM JOHN BEATTIE SEAMAN, of Ennismore Gardens, London S.W., Esquire, lately called William John Seaman, has (according to the desire of his late uncle, Patrick Todd-Beattie) assumed the surname of Beattie in addition to his surname of Seaman and intends henceforth upon all occasions and at all times to sign and use and to be called and known by the name of William John Beattie Seaman in lieu of his former name of William John Seaman, and that such intended change of name is formally declared and evidenced by a deed poll under his hand and seal, dated the 28th day of January, 1922, duly executed and attested, and enrolled in the Central Office of the Supreme Court of Judicature on the 3rd day of February, 1922.'

With all due respect to the wishes of a late uncle, it is not hard to divine here the influence of a woman who had amended her own name after her first husband's death, along with that of her daughter. Now that she had moved into a more elevated social world, the desire of the former Lilian Tuplin to consolidate her position could easily be understood – particularly since her second husband's name had already been bestowed on her son, who would now be able to make legitimate use of its inclusion in a compound surname, should he so wish – which, as it turned out, he generally did not. His mother, however, invariably opted for the double-barrelled form, with hyphen. Henceforth she would be known as Lilian Beattie-Seaman.

As far as William's health was concerned, the doctor's prognosis was not entirely gloomy, and there was little resistance to recommendations including cruises to healthy climates and winters in the South of France. That summer Dick accompanied his parents on a cruise to Scandinavia; the following February, William and Lilian sailed to Algiers, taking Vahlia, now aged twenty-two, with them. Dick – sometimes obliged to remain at school during the holidays while his parents took their winter breaks in the Mediterranean – was not appreciative.

◆

With one year left at Hildersham House, Dick began to suggest to his parents that they should consider taking another country house. At school he would have seen many of his friends going off to such homes at the end of every term. Although he enjoyed many aspects of life in London, he was missing the open air and the countryside, the company of farmhands, gamekeepers and coachmen, and the freedom of a large estate: all the things that would appeal to a 12-year-old boy.

His mother tried to deflect his argument by countering that it was now hard to find servants for such establishments, and that many big houses were being demolished through the economic impossibility of keeping them going. He argued his case so persistently, however, that they went to inspect one of them: Weald Hall, an ivy-clad Tudor manor house set amid rolling Essex countryside, 25 miles from London. With around twenty bedrooms, a Norman church in the gardens, a deer park and a lake, it had a history that included visits by the future Queen Elizabeth I and her elder half-sister and rival, the future Queen Mary I, as children. The estate had been in the hands of the Tower family since 1759. Its present owner, Christopher Tower, was ten years old; he had inherited it after his father's death in the war, and the estate's trustees had been letting it out. In the summer of 1925, William Seaman signed an agreement to take it over.

The young owner continued to live in the smaller Dower House with his widowed grandmother, a *grande dame* whose portrait by John Singer Sargent hung in the entrance hall. His mother had remarried and was with her new husband, a diplomat, on his posting to the embassy in Rio de Janeiro, with their infant son. Christopher had stayed in England for his schooling; he was destined for Eton, followed by Cambridge and a distinguished career as a poet.

Dick and Christopher, two years apart in age, became friends and played together in the school holidays. Now, too, Dick was old enough to join the guns at the shooting parties, proving himself to be a useful shot and given a place at the lunches in the gamekeeper's lodge. He took his mother on shopping expeditions to nearby Brentwood in a pony and trap, but it was in the lanes around the estate that she suspected Charles Clifford, the successor to Henry Wood as the family's principal chauffeur, of teaching her persuasive son to drive a motor car. The boy had, after all, been refused nothing.

5

The Seaman Special

William Seaman had assumed that his only son would follow his own path by going on to Harrow School, but the advice of Hildersham's headmaster persuaded him otherwise. Rugby School was Arthur Snowden's alma mater, and that of his father, brother and son. He promoted its principles so effectively that in the autumn of 1926, at the age of thirteen and a half, Dick found himself heading for the Midlands.

He was arriving at a school that had given its name to a game that had become widely adopted by other public schools. But Rugby's deeper significance to the world had sprung from its most celebrated headmaster, Dr Thomas Arnold, whose philosophy could be boiled down to the two words that came to summarise the public-school ethos of Victorian and Edwardian England: 'muscular Christianity'. They were the foundation of a world in which, as one historian put it, your Englishman went through the world 'with rifle in one hand and Bible in the other'. And probably with cricket bat and rugby ball in his steamer trunk, too.

Dr Arnold devised a set of educational priorities: 'First moral and religious principle, second gentlemanly conduct, third intellectual ability.' His reign at Rugby lasted only fourteen years, until his death at the age of forty-seven in 1842, but even the iconoclastic Lytton Strachey, assessing Arnold in *Eminent Victorians*, admitted that 'by introducing morals and religion into his scheme of education, he altered the whole atmosphere of public-school life', hitherto 'a system of anarchy tempered by despotism'. After Arnold, Strachey remarked, 'no public school could venture to ignore the virtues of respectability'.

Those virtues were broadcast still further by the success of *Tom Brown's School Days*, first published in 1857 as written by 'An Old Boy of Rugby', later revealed to be a former pupil named Thomas Hughes. The author's semi-fictionalised portrait of the school, via the story of a troubled pupil who is mentored by another boy and in turn gives help to a frail younger one, became highly successful around the world, persuading its readers to see the British public-school system as imbuing its products with boldness, courage and a sympathy towards those less able or fortunate: the very qualities supposedly required, in fact, to rule an empire that circled the globe.

Among the book's admirers was Pierre de Coubertin, the son of an aristocratic French family, who read it at the age of twelve. The young Baron de Coubertin visited Rugby twice, in 1883 and 1886; combined with an interest in the culture of the Ancient Greeks, the school's example led him directly to the creation of the first Olympic Games of the modern era, held in Athens in 1896.

◆

Dick's boarding and tuition fees at Rugby were just over £200 a year (about £12,000 today), and on arrival he settled into Molony's House, an imposing red-brick building at 3 Hillmorton Road, set back behind a large enclosed garden. The housemaster was the Rev. B. C. Molony, a parson's son and Old Rugbeian, a scholarship boy who had gone on to Trinity College, Cambridge, where he graduated in mathematics in 1914. Brian Molony had been mentioned in despatches as an infantry captain on the Western Front in 1917, and returned to Rugby in 1919. He was ordained as a priest in 1921 and, at the age of thirty-three, had just taken over the house when Dick arrived.

In the school chapel, which Arnold had made the centre of the school's life (and under whose flagstones he had been interred), the 600 pupils heard sermons preached by his latest successor. Another former pupil, Dr W. W. Vaughan, had returned in 1921 to take over a school whose roll call of former pupils lost in the Great War numbered more than 350.

As the boys of Molony's House walked to the daily morning prayers in the chapel, they passed the end-of-terrace house at 5 Hillmorton Road where Willie Brooke, a master at the school, and his wife Ruth had brought up their four children in the last years of the nineteenth century. Rupert, the second of their three sons, attended Rugby and became England's most celebrated war poet before dying in 1915, at the age of twenty-seven, of sepsis from a mosquito bite in transit to the Gallipoli landings. Eventually a marble plaque was installed on the south wall of the chapel, bearing a bas-relief of the poet and his most famous poem, the one that begins: 'If I should die think only this of me: / That there's some corner of a foreign field / That is forever England.'

◆

At Rugby, Dick would form two important friendships. One was with Antony Dewhirst Cliff, whom he had known slightly at Hildersham House and with whom he now found himself sharing a study. After Tony Cliff's father had been killed in the Great War, he had been brought up in North Yorkshire by his mother. In the 1890s a wealthy uncle had bought the Crayke estate on the edge of the North York Moors; he was childless, and his plan was to bequeath it to his young nephew. Soon Dick and Tony added a third friend: Rainald 'Ray' Lewthwaite, a member of an old Cumbrian family. The Lewthwaites'

Broadgate House, built in 1820, was set in 550 acres of land outside the village of Millom.

They called themselves the Three Musketeers and, like most boys of their era, age and class, they were obsessed by speed. Speed in the air, speed on water, and particularly speed on land. To their generation, motor racing was a new and thoroughly modern sport, an expression of the latest technology, its evolution occurring before their eyes. The very first motor race, from Paris to Rouen and back, had taken place in 1894, and the first Grand Prix was held at Le Mans in 1906. The big races now drew huge crowds of the curious and the smitten. To British boys, the glamour was made more potent by the French, German and Italian names of those who dominated the sport: manufacturers such as Renault, Mercedes, Alfa Romeo, Maserati and Bugatti, drivers with names like Lautenschlager, Boillot, Benoist, Ascari and Divo. These men raced mostly on circuits made up of public roads running from town to town and village to village, all temporarily closed for the purpose. In Britain, racing on public roads was banned. Brooklands, a purpose-built autodrome, had opened in 1907, but otherwise competition was restricted to hill-climbs and speed trials, although that did not stop enthusiastic amateurs tinkering in their garages, producing their 'specials' from bits and bobs of existing cars and home-made parts.

Thanks to an allowance from his parents, Dick was able to subscribe to the magazines that appealed to enthusiasts, such as *The Motor*, a weekly, and a monthly newcomer, *The Brooklands Gazette* (later to become *Motor Sport*), which offered race reports from exotic places like Monza and Montlhéry alongside advertisements for MGs and Bugattis. In his first year at Rugby, he might have also read a serial titled 'The Speed Kings', written by John Hunter and published in *Chums*, a popular weekly newspaper aimed at schoolboys. Devoted to stories by such authors as Robert Louis Stevenson, W. E. Johns and Edgar Wallace about the exploits of soldiers, sailors, aviators ('How I

Flew from New York to Paris!' by Captain Lindbergh), pirates, explorers and sportsmen, *Chums* was suffused with patriotism and echoes of Empire, and entirely free from the distracting presence of girls. In 'The Speed Kings' he would have followed the fictional adventures of two English boys named Tony and Dick who banded together to create a British racing team with the aim of beating the continentals, a Union Jack flying from the bonnet of their car as they overcame their rivals' dastardly tricks. Inspired by all this, in his spare time – and perhaps while sitting through the lessons that bored him – he began doodling pictures of a racing car he called the 'Seaman Special'.

It was an age of early motoring idols, and Dick would have admired such British speed demons as Malcolm Campbell, George Eyston and Sir Henry 'Tim' Birkin, all war veterans now risking their lives on the circuits. He would have learnt of the victories of William Grover, the Anglo-French driver who raced under the name 'Williams', disguising his identity from his family as he won the inaugural 'race around the houses' at Monaco in 1929. Dick's personal hero, however, was Major Henry O'Neil de Hane Segrave, the foremost British racing driver of his era. Dick absorbed the details of Segrave's life, starting with his birth in Baltimore, Maryland, in 1896 to an American mother and an Irish father, his upbringing in Ireland and his Eton education. At eighteen Segrave was commissioned into the army; two years later he transferred to the Royal Flying Corps. He was wounded both on land and in the air before the war ended. At Brooklands in 1921, at the wheel of a French Darracq, he won the first long-distance race to be held in Britain. Two years later, driving a Sunbeam at Tours, he became the first British driver to win a Grand Prix. In the year of Dick's arrival at Rugby, Segrave set the first of several speed records on land and water.

All this was of much greater interest than anything the boy was being taught in the classroom. Although far from unintelligent, Dick was never remotely outstanding in academic

terms, a failure that seemed to indicate a simple lack of application. His preferred reading included the comic novels of
P. G. Wodehouse, particularly the Jeeves and Wooster series.
Otherwise, apart from speed, his main preoccupation was with
food, an interest that an English boarding school of the 1920s
might not have been best equipped to satisfy.

Rugby's pupils were expected to distinguish themselves in
life, preferably in the service of the nation. During his first term
Dick would have read the notices in the school magazine, *The
Meteor*, congratulating former pupils on their recent distinctions.
Two had become aides-de-camp to the King, while another
had gained the Sword of Honour at Sandhurst, one of many
Rugbeians to go on to military careers.

The world as it appeared to boys of Dick's generation could
be glimpsed in the issues put before the school's debating
society. Sometimes amusingly frivolous ('This house believes
the Cinematograph is a political, social and moral danger to
society'), they could also reflect the turbulence created by
the sanctions imposed on the Great War's losing side, and the
feverish anxiety surrounding the spread of Bolshevism. Mass
unemployment was already a reality and the Wall Street crash
was just over the horizon. During Dick's first weeks, the motion
was proposed that 'In the opinion of this house the present
situation is the result of democracy'. After one speaker claimed
that 'the lower classes should not be given complete liberty to
get what they want, as they do not know what they want', the
motion was carried. 'This house believes that England needs
a Mussolini', however, was defeated. Given his interest in cars
and motorbikes, Dick would have been among the unusually
large audience who gathered in November 1929 to debate the
motion that 'This house considers that competition in speed
and distance, involving risk to human life, should be declared
illegal'. One speaker argued that 'a man who shows sufficient
talent to be able to drive at high speeds ought to use his life, not
throw it away'. A dissenter spoke on behalf of progress: 'Only

pioneers incur risk. Practice makes perfect, and posterity will be grateful to them.' Another argued: 'It is the object of men to contribute to the fame of their country.' The motion was crushed by seventy-six votes to twelve.

At some point during their time at Rugby, the Three Musketeers managed to acquire a couple of motorbikes: a BSA and a Rover, the latter fitted with a sidecar. This was without their parents' knowledge and quite against the school's rules, which allowed boys to own nothing more powerful than a bicycle. Having found somewhere in the town where they could hide the illicit machines, they stole out for rides into the Warwickshire countryside at weekends.

Dick's parents paid regular visits for half-term, speech day, the school play and the annual cricket match between the first XI and an old boys' team, for which Arthur Snowden would return from Hildersham House. These weekend reunions of the Seaman family often included drives in the Daimler, during which Dick was allowed to take the wheel. 'Looking back in after-years there seem no days like those days,' his mother wrote of their visits, 'and the longing and regret that we did not make more of them, and value them more, while they were there. Afterwards, when sorrow and tragedy comes, and loneliness is our lot, and memories our only solace, such days of happiness seem almost unbelievable.'

◆

During Dick's summer holidays his parents sent him to France to spend the summer improving his command of the language – and, collaterally, to acquire his habit of using a piece of bread to mop up his food, which, as Ray Lewthwaite pointed out, tended to raise eyebrows at English dinner tables. On the first visit they accompanied him from Victoria to Paris on the *Golden Arrow*, a boat train restricted to passengers travelling first class. A train from Paris took them south to Blois, in the department of Loir-et-Cher, and Dick's ultimate destination: the Château de

Nanteuil, a modest country house near the village of Huisseau-sur-Cosson, where several other English public schoolboys were quartered with the same intention.

He would return there the following year, and for one or two more summers after that, taking the opportunity as he grew older to travel up to Paris and explore the city's attractions. A clue to what he and his friends got up to came during the last of those trips, when his mother arranged to meet him in Paris at the Hôtel Meurice. Very quickly she discovered that her teenaged son now knew his way around the city far better than she did. Having dutifully escorted her to various couturiers, he persuaded her to break her habit of dining in her hotel by joining him and a group of his friends at his favourite restaurant, located on the heights of Montmartre amid an altogether more raffish ambiance.

The bistro of La Mère Catherine had been open for business since 1793 in the Place du Tertre, just below the basilica of Sacré-Cœur. Dick loved the food they served in large quantities – soupe à l'oignon, magret de canard, tarte tatin – and surprised his mother once the meal was over by joining the dancers moving in lines around the tables in the square. What he and his friends don't know about Paris, she thought to herself, clearly wasn't worth knowing. She may even have wondered if his familiarity with a *quartier* close to the cabarets and night clubs of the Place Pigalle had led to an education in matters other than French cuisine.

It might also have been on nights out in Montmartre, while admiring girls with bobbed hair and dropped-waist silk dresses, that Dick first encountered jazz, which had caught on with the Parisian public. For some English schoolboys with a distaste for authority in the 1920s, the cultivation of an interest in American dance music was one means of mildly rebellious self-expression.

A few public schools even banned the playing of jazz records, leading the *Melody Maker*, the weekly paper devoted to such music, to fulminate: 'Prohibition is just about the most dangerous device that any institution can employ to check the conduct of a community. Therefore when certain of our public schools issue fiats to their pupils barring hot jazz, it can lead to those dangers of insubordination exemplified in illegal whiffing of Woodbines behind the woodshed. Do they honestly think that Duke Ellington, a humble disciple of Delius, is a black ogre conspiring to demoralise the youth of Great Britain?'

◆

As with many public schools, the Officers' Training Corps was a significant feature of life. There were lectures on military themes, such as one on 'High Speed Flying' by Squadron Leader Augustus Orlebar, an Old Rugbeian who had shot down Lothar von Richthofen, brother of the Red Baron, and had recently set a world airspeed record of 357mph in a Supermarine seaplane. When Major-General Charles Bonham-Carter arrived to make the official summer inspection of the OTC in 1929, he assessed the drills and exercises before delivering a summary lent poignancy by hindsight: 'Cadets are receiving a valuable grounding, which should materially shorten the period of training necessary to fit them to hold a commission later on, should the need arise.'

Dick's keenness on the OTC was not matched by his enthusiasm for the team game through which the school had achieved worldwide renown. Although he had shown some promise at Hildersham House, the birthplace of rugby football found him losing interest. While Ray Lewthwaite worked his way up to the first XV, also shining at squash and hockey, Dick made little impact. He played hockey for his house, but only twice were his contributions deemed worthy of mention, when he scored his team's goal in a 4-1 defeat at the hands of Kittermaster's and then, more happily, a hat-trick in an 8-1 win over School House's B team. He would have had more fun in the early weeks of 1929, during an unusually harsh winter, when Dr Vaughan allowed the boys to devote the first lesson of Monday afternoons to skating on the flooded and frozen fields by the River Avon.

During Dick's last year *The Meteor* recorded the success of a fellow pupil, one J. F. Dugdale, in the school's art exhibitions. John Dugdale's choice of subjects included a seaplane, a motor-cyclist (described as 'an effective study of speed') and 'one poster of a racing car which was very successful, although of a difficult subject'. That shared interest in speed and racing machines would lead Dugdale and Seaman to a later crossing of paths.

◆

In Dick's final term, an outing to the RAF base at Upper Heyford in Oxfordshire enabled members of the OTC to admire an exhibition of stunt flying by the dashing pilots of Blackburn Lyncocks, a nimble single-seater fighter. His last OTC camp was spent at the army barracks in Strensall, in North Yorkshire, where rain fell so hard on the moors that a route march had to be abandoned. 'During lunch wet clothes were put in a drying room which caught fire,' one of the boys wrote, 'and despite fire engine and human chain with buckets, incinerated everything except some boots and pieces of equipment and the Sgt-Major's buttons.'

In those last months, Dick would have read of the exploits of Woolf Barnato, the heir to a South African gold and diamond mining fortune, who raced his Bentley Speed Six against the famous Blue Train, the express that took British holidaymakers from Calais to Cannes and back. Barnato, already twice a winner in the 24 Hours of Le Mans, successfully bet £100 that not only would he beat the train from Cannes to Calais but that he would be in his London club by the time the express arrived at the English Channel. Dick would also have learnt of the death of his hero, the recently knighted Sir Henry Segrave, during a record attempt in his speedboat, *Miss England II*, on Windermere. With his first two runs, Segrave averaged 98.76mph – a new world record. On the third run, attempting to break the 100mph barrier, his boat disintegrated. Of the crew of three, the chief engineer was killed, while the mechanic survived with a broken arm. Segrave regained consciousness long enough to ask about his men, and to be told that he had already broken the record, before succumbing to bleeding in his lungs. A tragic end, but not one to deter a 17-year-old with his own visions of heroism.

That summer, Dick's maternal grandmother, Susannah Tuplin, died at the age of eighty. She was buried in Alburgh, her tombstone standing between that of her husband, Sgt Thomas Tuplin, and another marking the grave of her parents. The row was completed by the tombstone of her youngest child, Frederick, Lilian's only brother, who had died in 1908, aged thirty-two.

At the start of the autumn term, *The Meteor*'s first issue of the new academic year contained a rare printed acknowledgement of Dick's presence at Rugby. In the column headed VALETE – 'Farewell' – the name R. J. B. Seaman made its last appearance. He had moved on, leaving only the lightest of footprints.

PART TWO

1931–36

6

Princes and spies

Probably to no one's great surprise, Dick failed his first attempt at the Cambridge entrance examination, and in the autumn of 1930 he was sent to Orpington in Kent for residential private study with a tutor to prepare him for another try. The initial failure was not in line with William Seaman's expectation that his son would enter the diplomatic service, the career he would have chosen for himself had circumstances not diverted him into the world of business. The other possibility, in his father's view, was a law degree followed eventually by a seat in the House of Commons. Either path would have represented a natural transition for a young man of independent means and no great sense of vocation. But the months in Orpington were themselves interrupted by an unexpected opportunity.

The Seaman family's large circle of acquaintances included Francis Bradley-Birt, a diplomat and writer married to a cousin of Winston Churchill. Although Bradley-Birt's career had begun in the Indian civil service, his interests and his connections had carried him into the orbit of the crowned – and some no longer crowned – heads of Europe. It was during a visit to the exiled Kaiser Wilhelm II, the last German emperor, in Holland that he learnt of plans for a London visit by Crown Prince Rupprecht of Bavaria in the first week of February

1931. The son of Ludwig III, the King of Bavaria, Rupprecht had commanded his own large group of the Imperial German Army with distinction on the Western Front, ignoring the high command's desire for a scorched-earth policy as defeat loomed and the retreat began. In 1918 his father abdicated and Bavaria became a republic, denying Rupprecht the succession. During the rise of the National Socialist Party he resisted Hitler's attempts to woo him with promises of a royal restoration; now he hoped to win British support for the creation of a constitutional monarchy. Bradley-Birt told William and Lilian Seaman that Rupprecht would need an aide-de-camp and equerry during his visit, and suggested that young Dick might enjoy the experience.

The Prince and his party stayed at the Ritz, where various politicians and dignitaries attended a lunch given for him by Lilian Seaman on the day of his arrival. There was much to discuss about the situation in Germany, where the Nazi Party had secured 107 seats in the Reichstag in the recent election. 'As the ladies of the party curtsied to the Crown Prince, and the men bent low over his hand,' the delighted hostess wrote, 'it almost appeared safe to assume that things would be well again between England and Germany, and peace and friendliness would be assured for many years to come.' Later in Rupprecht's stay, Lilian took him to Her Majesty's Theatre to see Noël Coward's hit musical *Bitter Sweet*, then nearing the end of its West End run. Afterwards she went home while the Prince's party, including his young aide-de-camp, moved on to the fashionable Embassy Club on Old Bond Street; in his sixty-first year, Rupprecht danced until two in the morning and remarked that the experience reminded him of his bachelor days.

The visit included a weekend outside London. First came Oxford, and an official reception with lunch at St John's College, where Rupprecht was toasted as 'the King' in unlikely but amusing recognition of an ancient Jacobite claim for his ancestors as the true monarchs of England. At Windsor Castle, however, the Crown Prince visited the royal apartments like any foreign tourist. He had put in a formal request for an audience with George V but, despite extending his stay to ten days, his wait was to be in vain.

According to his mother, Dick coped easily with the ceremonial duties. He liked Rupprecht and was much in favour, not surprisingly, of his succession to the crown. Two years later, the election of Hitler as Chancellor of Germany would put an end to all that. The new leader would no longer require the fig leaf of association with a vanished regime.

◆

Dick's months of additional studies in Orpington paid off with success in the Cambridge exam. First, however, came a Mediterranean cruise with his parents in the summer of 1931, visiting Gibraltar, Naples (climbing Vesuvius and examining Pompeii with particular interest), Venice (where he was moved by a waterborne funeral procession on the Grand Canal), and Athens. Somewhere they might have met up with Vahlia, his half-sister. Since leaving Roedean at sixteen she had spent much of her time abroad, and in 1931 she was preparing for her only recorded appearance as a professional actress, in a French film called *Azaïs*. In the supporting role of Lady Hamilton, Vahlia was described as 'a star of tomorrow' by the critic of *Le Matin*, but she would not manage to transform that promising debut into the career of which she may have dreamed when making an impression in *A Christmas Carol* at Roedean. Her stepfather had long since grown exasperated with the constant need to fund her way of life, halting the injections of cash with which he had supplemented those provided by her mother.

That spring they gave Dick his first car: a low-slung Riley Nine Speed Model. Perhaps they thought that its little four-cylinder 1.1-litre engine was not powerful enough to get him into trouble. But in July he paid a visit to the hill-climb competition at Shelsley Walsh, a 1,000-yard course in Worcestershire, on the edge of the Malvern Hills, where competitions had first been held in 1905. There he watched a wealthy young American, Whitney Straight, winning his class in a similar Riley, and his imagination was fired.

In September, before going up to Cambridge, he was back at Shelsley for the Midland Automobile Club's autumn meeting, this time as a participant. With his car bearing the racing number 13, he was faced with the daunting prospect of heavy rain falling on a short but winding ascent with an average gradient of 10 per cent. According to the report in *Motor Sport*, the number of spectators was reduced by the unpleasant weather, but 'those who braved the elements were treated to an excellent display of driving [and] not a few hectic moments'. One of those moments was experienced by the driver entered as R. J. Beattie Seaman, who appeared in the results as coming second of only two entrants in the 1100cc sports-car class, behind T. B. Wood in another Riley. But whereas the winner's time was given as 58.4 seconds, Seaman's was recorded as exactly twenty seconds slower. If that suggests some sort of mishap on the way up, perhaps a spin on the wet track, it would be no surprise, given that the 18-year-old was making his competition debut in such awkward conditions.

The fastest time of the day, forty-six seconds dead, was recorded by Raymond Mays, an established master of Shelsley, in his supercharged Vauxhall-Villiers. Mays was thirty-two years old and already a figure of vast and varied racing experience. Educated at Oundle School and Christ's College, Cambridge, he habitually wore bespoke silk racing overalls ordered from his Jermyn Street shirt-maker. Even as a schoolboy Mays had shown a keen interest in style: it pleased him, he would recall, when scruffy boys were told off. In the vile conditions at Shelsley that day, the well-prepared Mays had a team of mechanics and friends with buckets of water and scrubbing brushes ready to remove the paddock mud from his car's tyres before the start. Dick had no such assistance, and no experience of competing in such unhelpful conditions – or any conditions at all.

The next issue of *Motor Sport*, containing the magazine's first mention of Seaman in the results from that afternoon, also included a report on the international hill-climb at Mont Ventoux. This was a real mountain, the Giant of Provence, 13.5 miles of ascent with no protection from precipitous drops, a contest won by the German ace Rudolf Caracciola in a 7-litre Mercedes-Benz whose supercharger howled as it raced along the twisting ribbon of shale leading up to the bald mountain's 6,200ft summit: a national hero in a machine and a setting that inspired awe. It was a long way from an English teenager in his first car, fumbling his way up a slippery strip of asphalt in the Malvern Hills.

◆

On 1 October 1931 Dick was admitted to Cambridge as a pensioner – a fee-paying student – at Trinity College, where his fellow undergraduates, 300 of them, included his Rugby pal Ray Lewthwaite. Eventually they would be joined by Tony Cliff, who had stayed on an extra year at school. Dick was studying French and Italian. Ray was studying law and planning to join the army. Tony had been intending to study law or medicine, but his plans changed when he was bequeathed the Crayke estate after his uncle's death. Now he was studying agriculture in order to learn how to run his sudden inheritance. They were reunited at Cambridge's biggest and richest college, founded by Henry VIII in 1546, its alumni including the physicist Isaac Newton, the poet Byron, and the Duke of York, the future George VI, who had gone up in October 1919 and spent a year studying history, economics and civics without staying on to take a degree.

This was a bigger world, but Dick's upbringing had given him a social confidence invaluable in such an environment. Neither would he be overawed by the imposing Tudor-Gothic architecture of Trinity. The honey-coloured stone towers and ivy-covered walls of the Great Court, the vaulted ceiling and stained-glass windows of the dining hall, and the Wren Library, its walls covered with the fine woodcarving of Grinling Gibbons, were not so far removed in style and scale from the Elizabethan splendour of Kentwell and Weald Halls, with their minstrels' galleries and warrens of rooms, their lawns and streams and moats.

His first Cambridge lodgings were at 16 Trinity Street, in the city's medieval heart. Owned by the college, the house was next door to an old coaching inn, the Blue Boar. He was given a room on the second floor by Mr and Mrs Armes, who lived in the basement in conditions, as Dick's mother would note, of Dickensian disorder. Beneath Dick on the first floor was a fellow student, William Alexander Evering Cecil, the 3rd Baron Amherst of Hackney. For a while Mrs Armes got away with charging each of the young men for a whole half-pound of butter every day, to go with their single slice of bread at break- fast. 'It was,' Lilian declared with acid distaste when Dick told her of the deception, 'an experience I had not been privileged to meet with in life before.'

Dick's new home was no more than 50 yards from the col- lege's Great Gate. The Master of Trinity was J. J. Thomson, an eminent physicist and a Nobel Prize winner for work that would lead to the discovery of the electron. Not noted for con- cern with sartorial matters, the Master had once been mistaken for a tramp. Dick's tutor, responsible for his moral and spiritual welfare, was John Burnaby, a classicist and theologian who had served at Gallipoli and on the Western Front. The son of a clergyman, Burnaby would eventually take holy orders himself and become the university's Regius Professor of Divinity; for Dick, he carried on a strain of pastoral care that had begun at Hildersham House with Gerald Parker and continued at Rugby with Brian Molony.

Fellow students at the college included some who would

become notorious decades hence, such as Guy Burgess, studying history and very keen on fast cars (according to his biographer, he had 'missed hardly an issue of *The Autocar* since he was nine years old'), and Kim Philby, studying economics, both of them a year older than Dick. His exact contemporaries included John Cairncross, studying French and German, and Victor Rothschild, the 3rd Baron Rothschild, who drove a Bugatti, played first-class cricket and entertained his friends with his expertise as a jazz pianist. Among the junior research fellows was Anthony Blunt, who had returned after graduating in modern languages the previous year.

Blunt, Burgess, Cairncross and Rothschild were members of the Apostles, a long-established group of Cambridge intellectuals who met once a week and whose previous generations included the poets Tennyson and Brooke, the philosophers Bertrand Russell and Ludwig Wittgenstein and the economist John Maynard Keynes. The continuing reverberations of the Wall Street crash of 1929 led the group to intense discussion of the crisis of capitalism. Gradually their thinking began to be dominated by a study of Marxism and a particular enthusiasm for the progress of communism in the Soviet Union, leading some of them, including Blunt, Burgess and Cairncross, to become significant figures in a network of spies who would pass information to Moscow throughout the Second World War. Rothschild, who had once given Blunt and Burgess a lift from Cambridge to Monte Carlo in his Bugatti, would head MI5's wartime explosives and sabotage section.

Burgess and Blunt were linked by their homosexuality as well as their political convictions. Seaman appeared unsusceptible to seduction on either front, although he would have been unlikely to escape the attention of the 'moist-eyed Cambridge dons gazing Housman-like at unattainable athletic limbs', in the words of the historian Hywel Williams. He rowed with the First Trinity Boat Club, his height and weight – half an inch under 6ft 3 and 13 stone – making him ideally suited to handling an oar in the fiercely contested Bumps races on the River Cam. He also competed at Henley Regatta, where the First Trinity eight – with Dick in the number four seat – failed to make it through the qualifying round of the Ladies' Cup in 1932, beaten by Oriel College, Oxford. A year later they narrowly lost a heat of the Thames Cup to the Americans from Hun School of Princeton, with Dick at number six. His fellow crew members included Edmund Wigram, a future member of the 1936 Everest expedition, and Dickie Newbery, who would shoot down ten V1 'doodlebugs' while leading a Spitfire squadron in 1944. Dick also joined the university's burgeoning automobile club, whose members drove fast cars while thinking about how to acquire even faster ones. He would take his rowing no further; the cars were a different matter.

◆

After his first experience of competition at Shelsley Walsh, he entered the Riley in three more events over the next six months. All of them were trials: unglamorous but highly competitive contests, held mostly in the winter months, in which competitors drove their cars over specified routes on public roads, required to undertake a mixture of challenges, including standing starts, brake tests and steep hills, within strict time limits. The first two, either side of Christmas 1931, were organised by the Motor Cycle Club. In the London–Gloucester Trial, from Staines to Birdlip, he was unclassified, but in the Exeter Trial, from Virginia Water to Shaftesbury, he won a premier award. The third, the Colmore Trial, organised by the Sutton Coldfield and North Birmingham Automobile Club, took place in February 1932 and saw him win a second-class award over a demanding course on a day when the organisers sprinkled salt to disperse the snow.

That same month he wrote to Thomson & Taylor, a firm of race-tuning specialists at Brooklands, enclosing a handwritten proposal – complete with diagrams – for a more powerful

crankshaft design for the Riley engine. A reply from the engineer Reid Railton, another Old Rugbeian, indicated several
flaws and pointed out that to build a satisfactory engine to such
a specification would cost between £300 and £400, which was
more than the existing car had cost new. Dick took it no further,
but the exchange indicated that he was keen on investigating
ways to improve the performance of his cars, even if the theory
and the diagrams were almost certainly not his own work.

The solution came on his nineteenth birthday, when his
parents presented him with a new MG Magna to replace the
Riley. Whether they realised it or not, the 2-litre, six-cylinder
Magna – which cost them £285 – was ideal for a young man
intending to take his next step in motor sport. 'A fascinating
car to drive,' *Motor Sport* said in its road test report, praising its
'extreme handiness and excellent acceleration' up to a top speed
of 70mph. Dick's Magna made its competition debut on the
last weekend of March in the Land's End Trial from Virginia
Water to the tip of Cornwall. In a gruelling event with many
demanding climbs on gravel roads, he won a silver award.

The next step was more ambitious. The week-long
International Alpine Trial was held in high summer, over a
route running from Munich to San Remo. Organised by the
automobile clubs of Switzerland, Italy, Austria, Germany and
France, it was, *Motor Sport* declared, 'the world's most severe
trial'. It had caught the imagination of Dick's compatriots: the
Magna was one of five MGs among the forty-three British
entrants in a field of 107 cars. The extent of the challenge
became clear on the opening day, when a 230-mile route
included a 5,700ft pass in the Hohe Tauern mountains. Over
the following six days Dick's little car met the challenges of the
Sella, the Pordoi and the Falzarego passes in the Dolomites, the
Stelvio – with its forty-nine hairpins – in the Italian Alps, and
the Petit Saint-Bernard, the Galibier and the Lautaret in the
French Alps.

It was spectacular and it was fun. *Motor Sport*'s correspondent called it 'quite the most enjoyable affair it is possible to imagine. To begin with, people were so extremely courteous and helpful to the competitors. The Italian customs officials and police treated the whole trial as a race, and villages and towns could be taken at what would have been a disgraceful speed had not smiling and delighted policemen been holding up all the cross traffic.' Although Dick failed to win an award, merely finishing would have felt like an achievement.

◆

His exemplar in motor sport was a fellow undergraduate whom he had glimpsed during his first visit to Shelsley Walsh the previous summer. Whitney Straight was already marked out as a figure of special attributes and resources. Three months older than Dick, this strikingly handsome and charismatic figure had been born in New York, the son of Dorothy Payne Whitney, a joint heir to a family fortune amassed through oil, tobacco and – in particular – a notorious railroad scam masterminded by her father in the early 1900s. Dorothy's first husband, Major Willard Straight, was a man of high ambition; he had attended a military academy, studied architecture at Cornell University, covered the Russo–Japanese war as a Reuters correspondent in 1904, worked as an investment banker, and served the State Department as a consul in Korea, Cuba and Manchuria. He and Dorothy were married in 1911 and Whitney was born the following year. In 1914 the Straights, now living between a Fifth Avenue mansion and the Whitney home in Old Westport, Long Island, had founded *The New Republic*, a political magazine. Willard died in France during the great flu epidemic of 1918 while serving with the US Army, leaving Dorothy with three children.

Two years later she met Leonard Elmhirst, the son of a Yorkshire parson. Elmhirst had spent time in Bengal with the spiritual guru Rabindranath Tagore, and his desire to make the world a better place resonated with the young widow, who was uncomfortably aware of the way her family's wealth had been amassed at the expense of others. They were married in 1925 and moved later that year to England, realising their dream of founding an establishment where people could cultivate the land and learn together, exploring art and philosophy in an enlightened, self-governing environment. This was Dartington Hall, the fifteenth-century centrepiece of an 800-acre estate in rural Devon, and it was where Whitney Straight and his younger siblings were allowed to develop their divergent talents and proclivities, absorbing the latest developments in dance and drama and listening to such visiting lecturers as Bertrand Russell and Aldous Huxley while failing to learn much about spelling or algebra.

Whitney was studying Moral Sciences at Cambridge, and an exhibition of his photographs had been mounted by the Cambridge University Camera Club, but his true interests lay in the world of cars and aeroplanes. At sixteen he had taught himself to fly, and on his seventeenth birthday he became the youngest licensed pilot in England. Before going up to the university he bought himself the Riley that Dick had seen him driving at Shelsley Walsh, but his ambitions quickly surpassed the car's abilities, and in March 1932 he drove a Bugatti in the British Automobile Racing Club's Easter Monday meeting at Brooklands, finishing in a dead heat for victory in the Mountain Handicap. By the Whit Monday meeting he had graduated to a year-old Maserati – a supercharged 2.5-litre, eight-cylinder Grand Prix model formerly owned and campaigned by Tim Birkin – and the following Easter he used the black-painted car to win the Mountain Handicap.

He had been allocated digs at 32 Trinity Street, almost directly opposite Dick's lodgings, and the two became good friends. In order to circumvent a rule forbidding first-year students from having their own cars at Cambridge, Whitney kept an 8-litre Bentley coupé elsewhere in the town, quartered with a chauffeur named Dewdney, who doubled as a kind of racetrack valet. Straight also owned a light aeroplane, which he flew from the grass runway of Cambridge's small airfield at Fen Ditton. According to a profile in the *Illustrated News*, 'he had an attractive modern manner of leaving a lecture at Cambridge at one o'clock and flying to Brooklands to take part in a race that began at half past two'. Dick was impressed enough by Straight's accomplishments – and, perhaps, by his general panache – to spend part of his holidays taking flying lessons at Heston aerodrome, west of London.

Music was another shared interest. Straight played the alto saxophone and had led his own band. For their generation, opportunities to hear real jazz were increasing. When Louis Armstrong gave a concert in Cambridge during Dick's last year at the university, a small group of undergraduates – including Geoffrey Green, studying classics and later to become the football correspondent of *The Times*, and Billy Griffith, a future secretary of the Marylebone Cricket Club – smuggled the great New Orleans trumpeter into their college rooms after curfew for a session of drinking and conversation that lasted until dawn.

7

The Straight syndicate

Two years after inviting Dick to accompany Crown Prince Rupprecht on his visit to London, Francis Bradley-Birt made another intervention in the lives of the Seaman family. According to Lilian, it was while dining with them at the Ritz that Bradley-Birt was told of Dick's response when asked by his mother what he would like for his twentieth birthday. A country house, he said, perhaps light-heartedly. Bradley-Birt lived at Birtsmorton Court, a medieval house near Malvern. He was able to tell Lilian of a large property called Pull Court, not far from his own home and newly on the market.

She claimed to have resisted the idea, pointing out to Dick that higher taxes and death duties were bringing the era of the country house to a close, and adding that her husband's health was now in real decline, requiring occasional stays in nursing homes. That was the reason they had left Weald Hall, only 25 miles from London, some time earlier. All her friends, she said, were moving from their big houses into modern service flats. But her son persisted. Service flats, he said, were places to commit suicide in.

He drove her up to Worcestershire in one of the Daimlers – a 120-mile journey taken 'at racing speeds', she remembered. With nineteen rooms on the ground floor alone and enough bedrooms for a regiment, Pull Court was, Dick claimed, the ideal place for all the furniture and the many paintings that had filled their earlier country houses, and for which there was no space in London. The wood panelling, the stained-glass windows, the chapel and the galleried hall impressed them. So did the 3 acres of kitchen garden, a cider press, a slaughter-house, facilities for carpenters and a blacksmith, extensive cellars, cowsheds, an ice house, a laundry, a timber yard, oak horseboxes in which to stable hunters, and a pair of splendid iron gates brought from Tewkesbury Abbey, now leading on to a magnolia walk.

His mother continued to protest. But eventually, as in so many of her dealings with him, she capitulated. Since her husband, aware of his own frailty, had given her complete control of the family's finances, she was able to sign the necessary deed of conveyance. Together she and Dick hatched a plan to live in one of the cottages until the main house had been refurbished.

Several decades later, Ray Lewthwaite told a rather different story. The acquisition of Pull Court, he claimed, was entirely the idea of Mrs Seaman, who wanted her son to inherit a country seat and thus to join the landed gentry – or, if her account of the Beattie family history was to be believed, to rejoin it. In Lewthwaite's memory, Dick had no interest in the place. If so, he seemed able to fool his mother very effectively.

Pull Court had been the home of the aristocratic Dowdeswell family, whose sons had held the parliamentary seat of Tewkesbury on behalf of the Conservative Party for much of the eighteenth and nineteenth centuries. Rebuilt several times, it now existed in its Tudor form: a large and handsome building in pale stone, looking out over rolling farmland in the Vale of Gloucester, between the Cotswolds and the Malvern Hills, with the River Severn winding along the edge of the property. After 400 years of Dowdeswell occupation, the direct line had died out and a nephew of the last occupier had sold the whole estate, including several farms, to a consortium of investors headed by the economist John Maynard Keynes. They broke it up and sold its constituent parts, with the house and its outbuildings and immediate grounds – including a farm, several cottages, a bathing pool, woodland, and a front lawn shaded by large cedar trees – as a separate lot.

News of the purchase was kept from William Seaman until the cottage had been properly fitted out for use as temporary accommodation. He accepted the decision and liked the house well enough once he had been taken to see it and had watched Dick up a ladder, painting the stable doors. Perhaps, he said to his wife, their son's involvement in the place would serve to distract his attention from his dangerous hobby.

◆

At the end of his first academic year, a third class in French in Part 1 of the Modern and Medieval Languages tripos was not good enough to enable Dick to carry on with an honours degree; instead he settled for following the Poll or Ordinary BA course, studying Geography and Modern English. For the last term of his second year he moved his accommodation to a Trinity-owned hostel at 3 Bridge Street, next to the Hoop Hotel, another former coaching inn. From there he could cut through All Saints Passage to the college for lectures or teaching sessions. But his studies were no longer a priority. His own thoughts on his future had taken a decisive turn: the time at Cambridge would be used to prepare for a career not as a diplomat or politician but as a professional racing driver.

The Magna was in action during the Christmas holiday, with a first-class award in the London to Gloucester Trial and a repeat of the previous year's premier award in the Exeter Trial. He kept these activities from his parents, although they were puzzled when, on going to bed at Ennismore Gardens one night at about half past ten, they noticed a row of Thermos flasks and a picnic basket in the hall, and Dick taking winter clothing – tweed overcoats, caps, scarves – out of a cupboard in preparation for an adventure that he explained to them as nothing more than 'an all-night run to Exeter'.

Elsewhere in Europe, motor racing was about to open a fresh chapter in its history. That February, a few days after the National Socialist Party had seized power, Germany's new Chancellor opened the 1933 Berlin Motor Show. In a speech announcing tax benefits for car owners, a project to build an affordable family car for the masses and the inauguration of a new road-building programme, Adolf Hitler also revealed a plan for state sponsorship of a motor racing initiative. The road-building programme would lead to the network of city-to-city autobahns built by thousands of students and unemployed men working eight to ten hours a day, giving the country the world's first motorways. The affordable family car – an idea that came to Hitler in prison, while reading the autobiography of Henry Ford – would become the Volkswagen. And the motor racing initiative would lead to the creation of the Mercedes-Benz and Auto Union teams, and to six years of complete domination of international Grand Prix racing.

Like thousands of British enthusiasts, Dick would have read of these developments in the motoring magazines, and wondered if the German teams would be able to replicate the superiority they had enjoyed immediately before the Great War. Meanwhile, in March he entered the MG in the RAC Rally, a 1,000-mile event lasting five days; he finished twenty-sixth out of 108 competitors. A month later the twenty-first running of the Land's End Trial began at Heston aerodrome. The first of the 405 starters set off for Cornwall at just past eleven o'clock on the Friday night, the last competitor at a quarter past four on the Saturday morning. This time, in the Magna's final appearance after a year of service, he failed to complete the course.

◆

For his third year at Cambridge he moved to Bishop's Hostel, a house within the college precincts, just off the Great Court, used primarily to accommodate scholars but also to bring others who were having difficulty in concentrating on their work closer to the centre of their studies and away from distractions. This was a sign that he was under observation and required to work harder.

During the holidays he drove up to Pull Court at the wheel of a new 2-litre Lagonda 16-80, a fast touring car bought for him by his father. On these visits he could swim in the natural bathing pool and lunch with his parents at the Hop Pole in the centre of Tewkesbury, mentioned by Dickens in *The Pickwick Papers*. His mother told him of her legal action to prevent the use of a public right of way across their land, an effort unlikely to have enhanced her local popularity when the County Court found in her favour, overruling the County Council. And that summer he leaned on his parents once more to provide the cash for something faster: a 2-litre straight-eight Bugatti Type 35A, advertised for sale by a well-known London sports-car dealer.

The car, painted black with blue wheels, was put to early use by Dick and Tony Cliff that June on a trip to watch Tazio Nuvolari and Raymond Sommer win the 24 Hours of Le Mans for Alfa Romeo. They had made no advance arrangements for accommodation during the race and were soon to discover, like generations of British enthusiasts, that the Circuit de la Sarthe could be a cold and bleak place in the early hours of the morning, even in midsummer.

The Bugatti was a genuine thoroughbred, designed for circuit races. A gentle competition debut in Dick's hands came in the speed trials at Lewes that autumn, where he finished third in the unlimited super sports class, behind the Mercedes of Denis Conan Doyle, a son of the creator of Sherlock Holmes, busy spending his late father's royalties on motor racing. Dick's proper racing debut came in the Bugatti that October, when he finished fourth and fifth in a pair of races on a rainy day at Donington Park. This was only the fourth meeting at England's first road-racing circuit, a 2-mile layout opened earlier in the year, running through the park of a country estate between Nottingham and Derby. At last England had a proper circuit to match those on the continent, even if it was in enclosed parkland (but so was Monza). Its hazards included stretches of track bordered by trees, and at one point the narrow road ran through a tight opening between stone farm buildings. And it gave Dick his introduction to real wheel-to-wheel combat.

He would race the Type 35A only once more, taking it to Brooklands in late October for the Oxford versus Cambridge Mountain Handicap, paying the entry fee of three guineas to the organisers, the British Automobile Racing Club (BARC). This was his first race at Britain's leading circuit, where the atmosphere, when the sun shone, was that of an English garden party. Looking at the cover of the programme for the Autumn Meeting, he would have seen the venue's famously snobbish slogan: 'The right crowd and no crowding.' For spectators, the entrance fee was five shillings. Fifteen shillings bought entry to the paddock, where exotic machinery and its sometimes equally exotic owners could be examined at close quarters.

Faced with Oxford University's ban on undergraduates participating in motor races during term time, the organisers expanded the entry by inviting former students from both universities, thus giving Dick his first experience of competing against drivers ranked among Britain's best. Raymond Mays was the winner in his much-modified White Riley, with Straight second in an MG K3 Magnette. Seaman finished in a decent fifth place. The star of the meeting was to have been Nuvolari, engaged to drive Lord Howe's Bugatti in the main event. The great man arrived for practice, but was put off by his first exploratory laps of the track. According to Mays, 'He did not like the very wide corners, where each driver could more or less steer his own course. Being accustomed to road racing, the Italian found these great prairies of concrete a bit tricky and rather ill-suited to his own inimitable technique.' Announcing that he had been called to Paris on business, Nuvolari withdrew before race day.

Thinking of the uncomfortable journey to and from Le Mans, Tony Cliff remembered Seaman's Bugatti as 'a ghastly little car'. So perhaps there was no great lamentation when, in London towards the end of the year, Dick managed to collide with an omnibus outside Victoria station. No one was hurt, but the machine was written off. Something new would be required for the coming season.

◆

Whitney Straight had left Cambridge in the spring of 1933, his degree course uncompleted. Not yet twenty-one, his intention was to form his own racing team, a fully professional outfit with which to compete not just at home, among the amateurs, but eventually against the far stronger competition to be found in the Grand Prix meetings abroad. That summer he flew himself to Pescara to take the small-capacity class of the Coppa Acerbo in the MG Magnette and to win the Mont Ventoux hill-climb, setting a new record in the ex-Birkin Maserati. He ended the season at the Brighton Speed Trials, recording the fastest time of the day along the seafront in the Maserati while his fiancée, Miss Psyche Altham, a 20-year-old dancer from Cambridge better known as Peggy, beat all her male rivals in the 1100cc class at the wheel of the MG.

Neither their engagement nor Peggy Altham's racing career was destined to last, but Straight had other big plans for 1934. He ordered three brand-new Maseratis, 2.9-litre Grand Prix models costing £2,000 each, and to drive alongside him he retained the services of two men of considerable talent. The first was the Irish-born Hugh Hamilton, who had recently spent several weeks on his brother's tea plantation in Ceylon, recovering from severe chest injuries suffered in a bad crash at Brno in Czechoslovakia. The second was Rupert Edward Lee Featherstonhaugh, better known as Buddy, who had shown his prowess in Bentleys and Bugattis at Brooklands and led a parallel life as a jazz saxophonist, playing with the top London dance bands and touring the UK with Louis Armstrong.

Before taking to the track, the cars were to be modified by Reid Railton at Thomson & Taylor, at an additional cost of £1,000 each. Straight specified the installation of distinctive new heart-shaped radiator grilles and, less visibly, preselector gearboxes that, he believed, would enable the drivers to concentrate better on their cornering. He also hired Giulio Ramponi, a former Scuderia Ferrari employee, as head mechanic, working between a garage in London and – since they intended to race mostly on the continent – a rented workshop in Milan. Ramponi had also been working for Tim Birkin, who had died the previous summer from septicaemia contracted, it was thought, after burning his arm on a hot exhaust pipe during the Grand Prix in Tripoli. Several other mechanics were engaged from the same source, while Straight's company secretary – Bill Lambert, working at the team's new offices in Bush House opposite the Waldorf Hotel in central London – was another ex-Birkin man. The team's racing manager, one Jimmy Justice, was a multilingual adventurer who, at the age of twenty-five, had already been a Reuters journalist, a lumberjack, a professional ice hockey player and an amateur racing driver; later he would fight in the Spanish Civil War before reinventing himself as James Robertson Justice, a distinctively bearded character actor in dozens of post-war British films. It was Jimmy Justice who was sent to Bologna to collect the first of the Maseratis.

The announcement of Straight's plans was greeted by a letter in *The Motor* in which a reader criticised him for buying foreign cars. Straight replied immediately, pointing out that he was an American citizen but adding: 'There is no car manufactured at present in this country, and no car could be redesigned or completely designed and constructed, which would both be ready for next season's racing and compete favourably with the Maserati ... I would like to say that for purely sentimental reasons, all other things being equal, I would far rather drive a British car than a foreign one. But the lamentable fact is that all other things are very far from equal.'

Keeping a close eye on these widely publicised activities, Seaman wondered if there might be a place for him in what the newspapers were describing as 'the Straight syndicate'. The two discussed a possible arrangement. Dick wanted to buy the team's Magnette and compete in it under their umbrella, but by this time his father was unwilling to subsidise any further racing activities. His refusal was on the grounds of safety rather than cost, as Lilian recalled: 'My husband had always been very indulgent and generous to him, and had bought him many new cars, but the time came when he would not purchase any more, and positively refused to allow him to have possession of capital sums of money, with which Dick would have purchased them for himself. Whenever Dick went off racing I could see it had a very depressing effect on my husband and he would more often ask me to feel his pulse and enquire why his heart was beating like that. I knew the cause of the pulse being intermittent – anxiety as to whether Dick would return safely. Consequently I thought it wiser not to tell him when his son was away racing. I had to prevaricate and say that I believed he was away shooting in Suffolk, or with Ray Lewthwaite in Cumbria or Tony Cliff in Yorkshire.'

Refusing to give up, and still believing that the money would be forthcoming, Dick persuaded Straight to let him try the MG and the Maserati during a test day on the Mountain Circuit at Brooklands. Back at home, he drafted a letter to their owner: 'I was very glad to have the opportunity on Thursday of trying the Magnette. It quite came up to expectations and I think I shall like it very much.' His intention, he added, was to compete in the early-season meetings at Brooklands and Donington Park, and he asked Straight to have a contract drawn up. 'Can you definitely arrange to supply me with petrol, oil, plugs and tyres for these meetings? If so I should be glad if you would do so at your earliest convenience.'

He was now intent on following his friend's example and abandoning his studies for the life of a professional racing driver.

'I find that if necessary I could go down from Cambridge at the end of this term,' he wrote to Straight, 'which would enable me to participate in as many races as possible during the summer term [18 April to 9 June].' In his mind, bigger opportunities were already opening up. 'Incidentally,' he added, 'as I could be free for the whole season, I wonder whether you would consider letting me handle one of the Maseratis in a few less important events. When I tried the old one last Thursday, I found I could handle it quite easily, and as you saw I was able to take it around the Mountain fairly fast. I quite realise of course that I am rather lacking in experience, but I feel quite sure that were you to give me a trial in your Maserati team you would not regret it.'

Straight's reply, addressed to Dick at Trinity College, was terse but not without encouragement. 'Dear Seaman,' he wrote from his home address in Mayfair, 'I have been thinking over your proposal and it all seems to hinge on what you mean by "prepare". If you mean that I am to maintain your car for you throughout the season and make good any damage such as [a] broken crankshaft or anything of that sort I don't think I would be able to accept. However, the sort of thing I could do would be to prepare the car at the beginning of the season, enter it for you in races for which it is suitable, and possibly give you some assistance when it so happens that we would be racing in the same place. However, it would be best for you to tell me in greater detail what sort of thing you meant by the word prepare. And what sort of proposition you would really like to put before me.'

They had agreed a price of £650 (against a new price of £795) for the year-old Magnette, to include existing spare parts. Dick wrote back to discuss the fine print of the deal:

> I enclose fuller details of my proposition, from which you will see that you will not have to bear responsibility for anything like a broken crankshaft, and that you would only interest yourself in races of your own choosing which are likely to

show some financial return. I propose racing the car at my own expense at Donington and Brooklands regularly during the early part of the season, with no special preparation apart from carburettor tuning.

Having got to know the car pretty well, I then propose that you should enter the car for a big event like the JCC race and/or the British Empire Trophy, and such races abroad as the car is suitable for (you know about this much better than I do and I should be glad if you would let me know of the races you consider worth entering), and that before the first of these big races you would have the car thoroughly overhauled and tuned and that you would then be responsible for any further adjustment and/or repairs as should be necessary for the car's success in subsequent races for which it was entered by you. I should be prepared to supply any new parts required. I could arrange for the transport of the car, unless you could do so without inconvenience. As regards the actual racing of the car, I propose that you pay the entry where necessary, and supply fuel, oil, tyres and plugs, which I take it that you can do without extra expense. All prize money, bonus and starting money shall be divided equally between us.

On 21 December 1933, a letter from Bill Lambert was addressed to Ennismore Gardens, indicating that a draft contract was being prepared and offering to sell the Magnette's specially built trailer for the sum of £45. But Dick had spotted a similar one on offer for £5 at Thomson & Taylor and, operating on a budget defined by his allowance, he wanted to put every penny saved on such items into improving the car's performance.

A few days later Dick wrote again to Straight, making it clear how he would be coming by the cash to buy the MG. 'I shall be celebrating my 21st birthday next Sunday Feb. 4th,' he wrote, 'after which date I shall be in a position to let you have a cheque for the Magnette and to put my signature to the contract. I could come up and see you next week, on Wednesday or Thursday the 7th or 8th. Could you lunch with me at the Savoy, on either of those two days?' Straight's reply came from Bush House, offering birthday greetings and gladly accepting the invitation to lunch. By the end of the month the contract had been signed and sealed by both parties.

◆

Now Dick could get on with commissioning work on the car in preparation for its first event of the 1934 season. He entrusted it to the tuning specialist Robin Jackson, based at Brooklands, who sent an invoice for stripping and refitting all the major components of the chassis, suspension, brakes and transmission, the entire work coming to £16 10s. Bill Lambert wrote to inform him of the arrangement with various equipment suppliers: Champion plugs, Dunlop tyres, Shell-Mex petrol and Mobil oil. In a letter to Seaman, Straight told him he could paint the car any colour he liked; he left it in the original black. In January, negotiating third-party cover, he had corresponded with L. Hammond & Co., insurance brokers in the City, signing himself 'R. J. Beattie-Seaman', probably the effort of a 20-year-old to give an impression of authority and the only recorded instance of his use of the hyphenation. Now he was ready to go.

His cheque for £650 was acknowledged by Straight in a letter from his new home address on Norfolk Street, off Park Lane, a house he was renting from P. G. Wodehouse and that he had ordered his younger brother Michael, who had followed him to Trinity College, to fill with paintings by the English modernist Ben Nicholson in time for a house-warming party. It was dated 4 March, the day after Dick had raced the car for the first time at Brooklands, finishing out of the places in two Mountain handicap races and one sprint handicap. Straight wished him good luck for 'an exceptionally successful season' and offered consolation for the disappointing performance first time out, which he had been at the track to observe: 'I am sorry that you didn't win anything, but I am sure that this was really all for the good because you will win something later on. I thought you took the Fork Corner' – the tricky double-apex hairpin on the Mountain circuit – 'very well.' The letter closed with a thought that struck home. 'Certainly if you were going in for racing seriously it would be advisable to leave Cambridge,' Straight told his friend. 'But of course that is a personal matter for you to decide.'

◆

It was all the urging Dick needed, and within a couple of weeks the decision had been made. When Lent term ended in the middle of March, his possessions were cleared from the rooms in Bishop's Hostel and his time at Cambridge was over. His parents were aghast when he arrived at Ennismore Gardens and told them he would be spending the summer racing in Europe. They begged him to reconsider, but for the first time he flatly defied them. 'We realised that very overpowering influences had been brought to bear on him,' Lilian concluded. In the ensuing silence, it was William who spoke first, reminding Dick of their hopes for him. 'Motor racing is neither here nor there,' he said. 'It is just a little sport and amusement, and leads to nothing.' But Dick refused to yield. 'It's because you're both so colossally ignorant on the subject, or you'd realise that men have been known to take up motor racing as a career, and to have made a great success of it,' he said. 'There's a great deal more knowledge and skill in it than you would think or believe.'

His defiance was not the expression of rebellious youth. Over a period of two and a half years he had examined the prospects ahead of him and reached a firm conclusion, which he explained to his mother when she asked him to come to her study for a talk the next morning. She began by repeating the things they had said to him the night before, and in particular the hopes they had vested in him. Again he held firm. He was completely unsuited, he told her, to life in an office or legal chambers: 'I'd be bored to death and I'd never make a success of it.' He preferred an outdoor life, he said, with travel to foreign places and new experiences, unlike his English friends, who were good fellows but mostly insular and narrow in their outlook. Travelling through Europe, he said, he met people who opened his eyes to what was going on in the world. 'Every time I return to England I wonder when we're going to wake up and do something about it here.'

From his perspective, life as a racing driver was not even a particularly unorthodox choice. He had grown up reading about heroes and their deeds, and now he had manoeuvred himself onto the fringe of their world. He believed himself capable of joining them; what it would take from this point was hard work and adequate resources. He was in no doubt of his own ability to make the necessary commitment. Nor, if the resources were available, did he feel any compunction about persuading those who held the purse to untie its strings. This was not, to him, a frivolous business. The ambition to join the ranks of Segrave, Campbell, Mays and Straight was a wholly serious affair. He would share the risks they ran, of course, but this was a world in which the taking of a risk – whether while breaking a speed record, making a solo flight across a continent or conquering a Himalayan peak – seemed an essential part of any worthwhile challenge. And, beyond a certain point, there was no way to break it gently to those who would rather he had made a very different choice.

Contemplating the reality of a strong, self-willed and determined son, Lilian pointed out the damage his decision was likely to inflict on his father's health. 'Nonsense,' he replied. 'Father will live for years yet, with your care and companionship.' In the end, keen above all to avoid the possibility of a serious rupture in their relationship, she backed away from the confrontation. For a moment she thought about stopping his allowance, a sanction now within her legal power. 'But looking across at him,' she wrote, 'wearing a new grey–blue suit which had just arrived from Savile Row, and one of the blue striped ties I had bought him to go with it, he looked so young and handsome and charming, and with all the keenness and enthusiasm of twenty-one years of age, that I had not the heart or inclination to deliver this dire threat.'

Dick seemed to take her silence for capitulation. 'Right,' he said. 'I've got several appointments this morning. See you both at Claridge's for lunch at 1.15.' Then he left the room. And the moment when she might have altered his destiny, she thought later, had gone with him.

8

The price of happiness

On 14 February 1934, ten days after his son's twenty-first birthday, and with his health slowly failing, William John Beattie Seaman sat down to make a will. Upon his death, he had decided, his estate would be divided evenly between his wife and his son (who would also receive 'any personal jewellery, watches, trinkets and personal ornaments and all my old family silver'). His wife was to be given the sum of £2,000 immediately upon his death, as was her daughter, Vahlia. A sufficient sum would be set aside by his trustees (his wife, his son and his solicitor) to produce an annual income of £100 after income tax for his sister, Florence. Two funds – one of £7,000 and the other of £3,000 – would be set up, the income from the larger to go to his daughter, Dorothy, and that from the smaller to her three daughters when they reached the age of twenty-one or married, whichever came first.

In the case of Dick's inheritance, a significant provision stated that he would not come into his half of the estate until he had reached the age of twenty-seven. By showing little interest in his Cambridge studies, and thereby in the sort of career his father had in mind for him, and by frequently persuading his parents to pay for new racing machinery, and by attempting to keep them in a state of semi-ignorance of his activities on the track, Dick had convinced his father that he was not yet mature enough to be trusted to handle such a fortune. This was a common enough practice among the wealthy of the era when they came to consider the fitness of young heirs to cope with an unearned legacy.

Then came two paragraphs indicating what should happen were Dick to die before reaching the age of twenty-seven. Were he to have had children by then, his half of the estate would be shared between them. In the absence of children, it would revert to his mother. And if she, too, were dead, the entirety of the estate would be shared between William Seaman's daughter, Dorothy, and Lilian's daughter, Vahlia, or by their children if they, too, were not alive to receive it.

Eleven months later William returned to Lincoln's Inn to add a brief but brutal codicil: 'Whereas by clause 3 (b) I have bequeathed to my Wife's daughter Vahlia Graham Pearce the sum of two thousand pounds I hereby revoke the said legacy to the said Vahlia Graham Pearce and I declare that I do so because the said Vahlia Graham Pearce has been given many sums of money by myself and by my Wife and the said Vahlia Graham Pearce has shown that she is not capable of making reasonable and proper use of money given to her.' There were limits, then, to his generosity.

◆

After its undistinguished debut in his hands at Brooklands at the beginning of March, the Magnette – still painted black with silver wheels, as it had been when Straight drove it the previous season – carried Dick to the fastest time of the day in the 1100cc class at the Inter-Varsity Speed Trials on the Eynsham bypass, an event whose relaxed atmosphere could be judged from a sentence in *Motor Sport*'s report: 'Everyone by this time was feeling hungry, so an hour's luncheon interval was declared.' Dick asked the MG company about updating his car to the 1934 specification, but their estimate – about £220 for modifications to the brakes and bodywork – was beyond the limit to which his allowance would stretch.

He raced without further success through the spring and early summer at Donington Park and Brooklands, including a retirement in the important British Empire Trophy, run as a handicap over a new Brooklands layout intended to mimic the features of a road circuit. 'Instead of sandbanks, hurdles or strings of flags,' *Motor Sport* reported, 'trusses of straw were used in true continental style.' The thirty-nine starters included another novelty: a new racing car called the ERA, produced by the boldly named English Racing Automobiles Ltd. With a chassis drawn up by Reid Railton and built at Thomson & Taylor, a 1.5-litre engine designed by Peter Berthon, and a supercharger conceived by Tom Murray Jamieson, the project was presided over by Raymond Mays. The basic funding was provided by Humphrey Cook, a wealthy amateur driver who had begun his motor sport career at Brooklands before the war and whose fortune, inherited at the age of twelve after his father's death, had come from a wholesale drapery business in London. The cars were being built at the premises of the Mays family's wool and leather business in Bourne, Lincolnshire; thanks to Cook's backing, which eventually amounted to £75,000, the workshops were well equipped. A factory team was planned, and Mays also hoped to sell cars – also available in 1100cc and 2000cc form – to private owners.

Painted in a distinctive pale shade of the national racing colour called Liberty green, the first ERA missed the start of the British Empire Trophy while a broken oil pipe was being fixed. When it set off, five minutes late, Cook was at the wheel, with Mays hopping in to take over at the mid-race pit stop. There was a fatality – the first in a race in which Seaman had taken part – when John Houldsworth, a 22-year-old Cambridge garage owner, lost control of his Bugatti while moving out of the way of Straight's Maserati. His car veered up the banking, somersaulted three times and ejected its driver, who succumbed to severe head injuries in hospital that evening. Straight, his car painted in the white and blue racing colours of the United

States, looked certain to win until fuel-feed problems dropped him to second behind George Eyston's MG.

It was the ERA that captured Dick's attention. Despite a bad start, its potential in the voiturette class – for cars of up to 1500cc – was clear. No British manufacturer was in a position to challenge the Mercedes-Benz and Auto Union teams that, with the aid of state funding, had just made their debut in the full Grand Prix category for cars of unlimited capacity. 'British constructors, completely lacking financial backing or support from the powers that be, had to rely on private enterprise and enthusiasm in such endeavours as they might make to uphold the country's prestige in this constructive and healthy sport,' Mays would write many years later. He and his partners had produced a car built specifically to challenge the top continental teams – Alfa Romeo, Bugatti and Maserati – in the voiturette events at Grand Prix meetings. As Dick looked to the next season, he began to wonder whether the ERA might be the car to take him a step further, into full-scale continental racing.

◆

A first trip to the continent with the Straight team in July saw him fail to make a mark in a voiturette race on the street course at Albi in south-west France. He was fined 100 francs for receiving a push start after stalling the MG on the grid and retired after six of the eighteen laps, Pierre Veyron heading a Bugatti one-two-three. That same day, however, there was an important achievement for the team when Buddy Featherstonhaugh won the Grand Prix d'Albigeois, driving the ex-Birkin Maserati. Hugh Hamilton, in one of the team's new cars, had taken an early lead in a race whose quality was somewhat reduced by the running of the Coppa Ciano in Livorno and the Dieppe Grand Prix on the same day. But an unscheduled pit stop put him behind his teammate, allowing Featherstonhaugh to become the first British driver to win a continental Grand Prix – albeit not one of the classics – since Segrave's victory at Tours in 1923, and inducing Dennis May of *The Motor* to observe that he had 'imperilled our national let's-be-good-losers tradition'. This, May wrote, was despite the winner being 'better known outside these pages as the head man of the Buddy Featherstonhaugh Sextet than as a racing driver'.

Three weeks later Seaman and Hamilton were the passengers in Straight's plane as they flew to the Klausen hill-climb in Switzerland, where Dick looked on as his teammates drove a Maserati and the MG. Their next racing appointment was in Pescara, halfway down Italy's Adriatic coast; the journey included a stop in Milan, where Ramponi and his mechanics refettled the cars. This was the setting for the Coppa Acerbo races, founded by the Fascist politician Baron Giacomo Acerbo, a member of an old Abruzzo family, and named in memory of his brother Tito, an infantry captain killed in battle near Venice in 1918. In Pescara the Straight team were confronted not just by their rival competitors but by a fast and hazardous 15-mile circuit running from the seafront up into the villages in the foothills of the Abruzzi mountains and back again, with two long flat-out straights. Coinciding with the public holiday of Ferragosto, the week of competitions began with a twenty-four-hour sports-car race and continued with a four-lap contest for the voiturettes – the Coppa Acerbo Junior – on the Wednesday before concluding with the race for Grand Prix machines on the Saturday.

A year earlier Straight had driven the Magnette to victory in the junior race. Now, with a new supercharger fitted by Robin Jackson, Dick finished a respectable third behind the MGs of Hamilton – who had stalled on the grid, requiring a push start before driving through the field – and Raffaele Cecchini, a well-known amateur from Rome. Writing home to his mother, Dick declared himself 'quite pleased' by the result. Cecchini's K3, he said, was 'a very special one, much faster than mine', while Hamilton was 'much too good a driver for me to compete with as yet'. He wrote to Robin Jackson, however, to complain that the supercharger seemed to have lost some of its efficiency, and suggested raising the compression; as ever, he was concerned not to neglect the small mechanical details that might make an important difference. The race was witnessed by the British journalist Barré Lyndon (the pen name of Alfred Edgar, later to make a career as a Hollywood screenwriter), who noted his impressions: 'R. J. B. Seaman ... although virtually a newcomer to the racing world, drove with considerable zest' and was 'rapidly securing recognition as a man who might eventually be very widely known'.

For the main event, the country's second most important race of the season, the two new government-sponsored teams from Germany turned up to challenge their rivals on the Italians' home ground for the first time. On a track made slippery by intermittent showers, Rudolf Caracciola established an initial lead in his Mercedes-Benz before crashing on the slick surface. So many cars were delayed by mechanical problems – including the Maseratis of Straight and Hamilton, who both retired – that Guy Moll, the brilliant young Algerian driver, was challenging for the lead at half-distance in his Scuderia Ferrari-entered Alfa despite having made two stops to change plugs and cure a misfire. As the roads dried and the temperature rose in the closing stages, Moll put a wheel into a ditch on a narrow section of the 170mph downhill stretch back to the seafront while lapping the Mercedes of the former German motorcycle champion Ernst Henne, who was driving in his first four-wheeled Grand Prix. The Alfa smashed into the stone parapet of a bridge, hurling Moll out of the cockpit and into a concrete post, killing him instantly.

The next meeting on the Straight team's schedule took them to Switzerland for the Prix de Berne at Bremgarten, a 5-mile road circuit with deceptively fast, tree-lined bends. Dick and Hamilton were entered for the 100km voiturette race in the two Magnettes, Seaman's familiar black car and a silver one for his teammate. The rest of the field of twenty-three cars included the Bugattis of Veyron and Ernst Burggaller (a member of Manfred von Richthofen's squadron during the war), Lord Howe's Delage, the Maseratis of the Italian aristocrat Luigi Castelbarco and the Swiss driver Hans Ruesch, and two women, Anne-Cécile Rose-Itier, a 44-year-old French divorcée, and Marie-Louise von Kozmian, a Polish countess, both in Bugattis. Hamilton made the fastest lap in practice, with Dick third, but the system of balloting used to determine grid positions saw them starting together at the very back of the grid. The race was held in pouring rain, but after seven of the fourteen laps Seaman was up to sixth place, while Hamilton had retired with engine problems. Dick continued to work his way through the field and took the lead on the eleventh lap, having passed Veyron into second place before profiting from the retirement of Romano Malaguti's Maserati, thus conquering the 1500cc cars in his 1100cc machine. This was the first win of his career, three years after his debut at Shelsley Walsh, and it had come in an international race against decent opposition on a difficult continental circuit after a remarkable drive from the back of the grid at an average of 74.9mph in unpleasant conditions. He was twenty-one years old.

Still glowing from his win, having accepted the congratulations of the president of Switzerland and the British ambassador, he watched Hamilton step into one of the Maseratis for the full-scale Grand Prix. Three hours later, Hans Stuck's Auto Union had already taken the chequered flag when Hamilton, in seventh place, slid wide on a fast bend between Wohlenstrasse and Forsthaus, barely a mile from the finish, the car spinning back across the track and hitting a tree. Some observers insisted he had lost control when a front tyre deflated. The 29-year-old Irishman was thrown out, suffering injuries from which he died instantly.

To Dick fell the task of helping the British consul with the arrangements for the funeral, held in Berne on the Wednesday, as well as dealing with requests to buy wreaths and comforting

Hamilton's mother when she arrived. Two days after the race, on 28 August, he sat down in his room in the Bellevue Palace Hotel and wrote a letter to Straight, who had been competing at Comminges that weekend. 'Everyone here has been marvellous,' he wrote. 'The automobile club have arranged all the details about Hammy's funeral. He lay in the chapel of the hospital yesterday, surrounded by flowers from all the other drivers, the automobile club and the French and English legations. His head was not badly hurt, but his face was bruised and cut, and I am certain it is better that his mother should not have seen him. Chiron tells me that he was fairly close behind Hammy when it happened. It was a left-hand bend through a wood, which was rather lumpy and could be taken at about 110mph. Apparently Hammy got a wheel into the loose stuff on the right-hand side of the road, the car skidded and hit the trees on the other side of the road. Chiron said he nearly did the same thing several times on that bend. It is such a pity, as Hammy had been very pleased with the way the car had been going during practice and up to the pit stop. He would have finished seventh if he had completed the lap. It was of course a terrible blow for Mrs Jeffries [Hamilton's mother], but she has borne up wonderfully considering . . .'

His own parents had been spending that weekend at the Grand Hotel in Folkestone, hoping that the sea air would benefit his father's health. When Bill Lambert called from London to give them the news of Dick's win, Lilian picked up the phone. Thanks to an unclear line, she thought at first that Lambert was telling her that Hamilton had won the Grand Prix and Dick had been killed. Although the misunderstanding was quickly corrected, a hotel page had to help her from the phone booth to a chair, before she went up to her suite, where she found her husband asleep. She sat on the balcony, looking over the sea and thinking of Dick's most recent letter, which contained a warm mention of the teammate he had now lost. Perhaps, she thought to herself, this might change his mind about racing as a career.

The next day she was due to attend a directors' meeting in London. Saying nothing to her husband, she left strict instructions with the hotel manager and the floor waiter that he should not be shown newspapers containing reports and photographs of the race lest he be alarmed by the news of the fatality. On her return to Folkestone in the early evening, however, she discovered that her request had been ignored. In the sitting room of their suite, her husband was surrounded by newspapers containing reports of the race and of Hamilton's death, confused and seemingly incapable – even when she read the stories to him, carefully emphasising the facts – of understanding that it was not their son who had died. He talked about needing to go to Switzerland to bring the body back, and blamed her for allowing Dick to continue in the sport. 'You could have prevented it,' he told her.

Eventually she calmed him and, with the help of a valet, put him to bed. She was in her room, changing for dinner, when she heard a crash and a heavy thud. She rushed into his bedroom and found him lying unconscious on the floor. The hotel called a doctor, who found that he had suffered a stroke and called for an ambulance to take him to a nursing home. He was there for some days, his wife waiting for him to return to consciousness but deciding against sending Dick a letter or a telegram to let him know of his father's condition while he was occupied with organising his teammate's funeral.

◆

Dick drove Hamilton's Bentley back to England, towing the silver MG on a trailer. His mechanic, Jim Burge, towed Dick's black Magnette behind the Lagonda. A couple of days later Dick made his way down to Folkestone. He met his mother at the hotel, where she asked about Hamilton's fatal injuries. He chose to soothe her with the same evasions. 'He looked wonderful in death,' she was told, 'and there was only a mark on his forehead.' Matching Dick's comforting falsehood with one of her own, she told him that his father had been thrilled by his success, adding that he was in a nearby nursing home 'for a little treatment and rest'. 'Didn't I tell you,' Dick replied, 'how interested and pleased he'd be, once he got used to the idea of my racing?' They went to see him, and she allowed her son to assume that her husband was simply asleep throughout their visit.

Reassured, Dick set off for North Yorkshire, to stay with Tony Cliff and shoot partridges. Looking ahead to the imminent Mont Ventoux hill-climb, he wrote another letter to Straight, asking if he could borrow a set of wheels from one of the Maseratis to use on the back of the MG. 'It gives a bigger tyre section and improves roadholding,' he said. It must have worked. On 16 September he achieved his second success in a significant continental competition, taking a class win in the Course de Côte on the long climb up the mountain rising out of the vineyards of the Vaucluse, On a day when early sunshine gave way to showers and mist, Stuck's Auto Union took the victory in the unlimited class with a time of thirteen and a half minutes, a minute faster than the record Straight had set in the Maserati a year earlier. Straight improved his time of the previous year but still finished twenty seconds down on the winner. Dick's time in the little MG, 16 minutes 5.8 seconds, was faster than the winners of the 1500cc and 2000cc classes.

With the team were the mechanics Giulio Ramponi, Jock Finlayson and Bill Rockell. Dick had driven there in the Lagonda, but the car was badly damaged when Rockell, who was driving it to their hotel, could not avoid running into the back of the team's truck when Finlayson misjudged a bend in the dark and stopped suddenly.

◆

Once William Seaman had recovered consciousness and was well enough to be taken back to London, it became evident that a partial memory loss caused by the stroke had erased all knowledge of the events in Berne. His wife told him of Dick's

success but chose not to speak of Hamilton's death. During a
fine spell of autumn weather she took him up to Pull Court,
where he was soon well enough to offer opinions on hanging
pictures throughout the house and filling the shelves of their
library, and to admire the variety of trees in the grounds.

Their son was now regularly opting out of meetings at
Brooklands and Donington in favour of European competition.
Accepting an invitation from George Eyston, he drove a works
MG in the voiturette category of the Masaryk Grand Prix on
the Brno circuit, a demanding 20-mile layout using poorly surfaced public roads. With the Lagonda out of action, he towed
the Magnette to Czechoslovakia behind a Fiat borrowed from
Straight. The 272-mile race for voiturettes was run together
with the Grand Prix cars, starting two minutes later and finishing two laps earlier. After four hours of racing, the class
winner, in a Maserati, was Nino Farina, the future first world
champion of post-war Formula One, while Eyston finished
fourth in a Magnette, one place and ten seconds ahead of Dick.
The meeting not only gave Seaman another taste of real long-
distance road racing but also the chance of a closer look at the
German teams: the GP was another triumph for Auto Union,
Stuck winning ahead of Luigi Fagioli's Mercedes.

A week later Seaman was back in England and in the cockpit
of his own MG for the Nuffield Trophy at Donington Park,
a 100-mile handicap for cars of up to 1500cc. In a persistent
drizzle, he finished a distant second to Mays' ERA, which was
winning its first long-distance race – 'A wonderful stimulus to
us all,' Mays wrote. Dick's season with the Magnette finished
at Brooklands, where he was unplaced in two handicaps at the
Autumn Meeting but left a mark by setting a new lap record for
his class. Having done its work, the now well-used MG was sold
in October for £400 through the Bellevue Garage to Reggie
Tongue, a wealthy young man from Lancashire.

To replace the Lagonda as his road car, Dick acquired a powerful and sturdy Ford V8, modified by the south London garage

owner Leslie Ballamy, who added his own patented design of independent front suspension, a two-speed rear axle, a new steering box and special shock absorbers for a premium over the list price of £280. After seeing the example Ballamy had built for Malcolm Campbell, Straight ordered four of them for his team. One went to Seaman, who found it ideal for the long drives to and from continental meetings, sometimes towing his racing car; he would keep it for the rest of his life. But when Ballamy approached Dick to ask for financial backing for a company to market his modifications, he was turned down. 'My trustees are interested only in gilt-edged securities,' Seaman wrote back.

Soon after Mont Ventoux, Straight surprised Dick by announcing that he was disbanding his racing stable and would be selling the Maseratis. He had been offered a contract to drive with the Auto Union team, but had declined. It was the end of what might have become one of the great Grand Prix careers; a judge as shrewd as Ramponi believed Whitney was good enough to challenge the likes of Nuvolari and Caracciola. The blow of Hamilton's death at the wheel of one of his cars might have been a factor, but Straight was a businessman first and foremost and the team had not fulfilled his ambition of becoming a self-funding operation: its income for 1934 had totalled £10,325 against outgoings of £13,100.

Now he was keen to concentrate on new commercial enterprises, principally a chain of aerodromes in southern England, in which he hoped to involve Seaman. He was also engaged to be married to Lady Daphne Finch-Hatton, the 21-year-old daughter of the Earl of Winchilsea and Nottingham and the niece of Denys Finch-Hatton, the big-game hunter and lover of the Danish aristocrat and writer Karen Blixen, who had been killed when his Gipsy Moth crashed near his home in Kenya in 1931. As beautiful as she was well connected, Daphne was frequently photographed at fashionable events, her clothes and hairstyles the focus of constant attention; as a couple, she and

Whitney were a glamorous adornment to London's night clubs and garden parties. Her father, however, had insisted that his daughter's future husband must stop racing, and it was time to move on.

◆

As winter approached, Dick confronted his mother with another request: he needed £2,000 to buy an ERA. He had been impressed, he told her, by Raymond Mays' performances in the car, and had written to Mays in October asking if he could be included in the works team for 1935. The reply explained that, for financial reasons, their plans involved selling cars to selected customers who would then be entered and run by the team, the owners contributing to the costs. 'If you are interested in coming in with us on these lines,' Mays wrote, 'we should be glad to have a talk with you.'

Dick had been in contact with Gerard Strina, a retired British Army officer who was working as a Milan correspondent for Reuters and the *Daily Express* and had an interest in racing. Knowing that Dick was looking for the right car, Strina spoke to the Maserati brothers in Bologna, who offered their new six-cylinder car for 100,000 lire (about £1,700), or an engine alone, to be fitted to a British-built chassis, for 45,000 lire. But in November Mays offered to sell Dick a new 1.5-litre ERA for £1,700, and that was that.

Lilian was horrified by her son's proposal, outlined over the breakfast table. 'No,' she told him. 'Certainly not.' As she retreated into her study, he followed her and demanded that she explain her refusal. Her reply was straightforward. She had promised his father that she would not advance him the money with which to buy any more racing cars, because it caused him so much anguish. 'Then why tell him?' Dick replied. When she refused to give way, he paced the floor before expressing further astonishment that she would refuse him something on which he had set his heart. Then he announced that he had already ordered the car, and he expected her to advance him the money out of the legacy that would not become available to him until his twenty-seventh birthday, in five years' time. He tried to reassure her that this way of doing things would not be for ever; one day he would be in a team that would pay him to drive their cars.

She began to consider the possibility that if she continued to reject his demands, he might try to borrow against the trust fund in order to pay for the car and thus begin a process of frittering away his inheritance. Reluctantly she unlocked her desk drawer, took out a cheque book, and wrote him a cheque for £2,000, fearing the consequences but consoling herself with the thought of the happiness it would bring him, whereas the money would otherwise disappear in tax on the family's investments. Why, then, be churlish? He would only be young once.

Knowing that she was defying her husband's instructions, she and her son decided to keep the news from him. On Dick's visits to Pull Court he would take part in discussions about furniture and decoration, but before long he would be telling his mother that he had to go, sometimes for a meeting in London with Whitney Straight about aerodromes, sometimes to visit Bourne in order to monitor the progress of his new car, leaving her to concoct a cover story.

In the second week of December, William Seaman was sitting one morning in front of a log fire at Pull Court, with a tartan shawl around his shoulders to keep out the cold, when a housemaid came in. 'If you please, sir,' she said, 'news has just been brought up from the village that Mr Richard left with Mr Whitney Straight in an aeroplane at six o'clock this morning, bound for South Africa.'

Turning to his wife, William Seaman demanded to be told if she knew about this. She did not, she said. She had heard nothing of it. He did not speak again for the rest of the day. His pulse weakened and the next morning he was taken back to London and installed in a nursing home in Earls Court, a

mile from Ennismore Gardens. When he was given a cable sent
by Dick from Cairo, en route to his destination, he would not
allow it to be prised from his hand.

◆

The trip represented Whitney Straight's last adventure as
a professional racing driver. He took his black Maserati to
South Africa, while Seaman negotiated the loan of a works K3
Magnette from MG. Under the deal, the outward transportation costs would be paid by MG and Seaman would attempt
to sell the car for £500 in South Africa after the race; if no
buyer was found, he would be liable for the costs of its return
to England.

A third member was added to the party. Michael Straight,
Whitney's 18-year-old brother, had just completed his first year
at Cambridge, studying economics at Trinity. He had become
an Apostle and that summer, having also joined the Communist
Party, he had visited the Soviet Union, taking a Russian ship
to Leningrad in a party that included Anthony Blunt. Now the
younger Straight had also bought himself a Railton Terraplane,
an open sports tourer built by Reid Railton on the basis of a
Hudson Terraplane, an American car with a powerful 4-litre
straight-eight engine. With no experience of racing whatso-
ever, the younger Straight would be driving the car in the race.

Ramponi had embarked well in advance, accompanying
the cars on the 7,000-mile sea journey. Seaman and the two
Straights travelled down in a six-seater, twin-engined De
Havilland Dragon biplane, with Whitney at the controls. The
party was completed by Dewdney, the elder Straight's valet –
'the worthy Dewdney', as Whitney habitually referred to him.

Almost half a century later, Michael would describe the trip
in his autobiography: 'The Dragon, capable of 110mph, was
equipped with very few instruments: an altimeter, a tachometer,
a compass that was none too accurate, and an airspeed indicator
that failed when we first took off and never worked again. We

had no radio, but that did not matter much as there were no radio aids in those days.' Leaving from Heston, they flew against a strong wind but completed the first leg to Marseille in a day, averaging 60mph. On the second day they made it to Cairo, from where Dick sent a cable to his parents, and on the third they touched down in Khartoum. On the fourth day, as they headed for Salisbury, the capital of Rhodesia, they descended to 500ft in order to watch elephants and a hippopotamus. On the fifth morning, however, the thin air at Salisbury's altitude, 1,500 metres up in the high veld, defeated the Dragon's attempt to take off. As the runway ran out, the plane leaped over an irrigation ditch, ripped through a barbed-wire fence, and scattered a herd of gnu before coming to a halt. Two days were spent repairing the damage to the lower wing and a strut before, using every yard of the runway, another take-off was successfully attempted. When they eventually touched down in East London, on the Indian Ocean, a large crowd was waiting at the airport to give them an enthusiastic welcome.

The East London Border Hundred would be South Africa's first international motor race, held over the 15-mile Marine Drive circuit, including a 2-mile stretch along cliffs above the ocean. Some of the road was asphalted; much of it was gravel and earth. The delay at Salisbury meant they had only two days to practise on the course for a handicap race featuring eighteen entries, among which the Straight team – even Michael in his Railton – assumed the status of favourites, being the only truly international entries.

There was time for a shark-fishing expedition – Whitney posing with his rod and a hammerhead – and for press interviews. A writer for the *Cape Argus* took the opportunity to profile the team's leader. 'He is about five feet nine inches in height and slightly built,' he wrote. 'He is rich. He has brought a valet with him to South Africa and has taken a luxury suite at one of the leading hotels. I do not suppose the 250-guinea prize matters to him in the least.' The *South African Lady's Pictorial* had sent a writer among the fashionable crowd in the paddock, with a brief to find the female angle. 'The race track,' she concluded, 'is no place for women. These fiends of the speed world become completely blind to the presence of the fair sex, and can talk of nothing but mysterious details of the insides of their various machines.'

A crowd estimated at 40,000, kept in order by 500 marshals, watched the cars set off at timed intervals, determined by the handicappers. The Railton started in sixteenth place, Dick's MG in seventeenth and the Maserati eighteenth and last of all. They were preceded by local drivers in a variety of familiar British marques – MG, Frazer Nash, Austin, Singer and Riley plus a Talbot, a Ford and two German cars, an Adler and a two-stroke DKW, for whom the new German national flag, incorporating the Nazi swastika, was flown alongside the Union Jack on poles above the leaderboard.

Michael Straight remembered seeing one car smashed into a rock face on the opening lap, and a clump of fallen pines where another had torn a path before going over a 100-foot drop. He started to pass the cars that had set off ahead of him, but on the fourth lap he himself was passed by Seaman. 'A glorious scrap went on between the two past the Grange Grove Hotel,' the *Daily Dispatch* representative wrote, 'Seaman taking the lead after a hectic few moments.' A lap later Michael saw Dick's car stationary by the side of the road while its driver struggled with a failing fuel pump. Whitney passed his brother on the sixth and final lap, on his way to taking the victory at an average speed of 95mph, receiving a large gold cup from the country's Minister of Railways and Defence, Oswald Pirow, a man who had met Adolf Hitler during a visit to Germany in 1933, admired his policies, and would eventually campaign for the division of South Africa into black and white areas. The Ford V8 of a local man, J. H. Case of Queenstown, came second, ahead of Michael's Terraplane in third. Seaman had restarted and worked his way up to second place but was then delayed by further problems with the pump, eventually finishing fifth.

'Great Day for East London,' the *Daily Dispatch* proclaimed over a double-page spread on the race. Afterwards the Maserati and the Ford were taken on trailers to Johannesburg, where they were displayed in the showroom of the local Ford agent. On the first day alone, three thousand turned up to admire the exotic machinery at close quarters. The Maserati was for sale, its owner announced.

The three drivers of the Straight team flew the next day to the capital, where they watched the horse racing at Turffontein and attended a private party before starting the return journey. On the way to Victoria Falls they flew through thunderstorms and a swarm of locusts that damaged the propellers. During a stop at Epika in South West Africa they went on safari with the intention of shooting a lion, but were out of luck. At one point they were forced down onto an emergency strip in the middle of nowhere; when they tried to take off, the wheels got stuck. To lighten the load, they left Michael behind, with the pledge that he would be picked up after Whitney had dropped Dick and Dewdney at the next stop. The elder brother kept his promise, but not before Michael had been surrounded by tribesmen who gave him food and drink: a slice of meat that he suspected might have been human, and a concoction that he was later told had been mixed from cow's blood and urine.

9

All the hard things

A news agency photographer was waiting for them when the party landed back at Heston on the afternoon of Sunday 13 January, a couple of hours later than anticipated. His picture of the Straight brothers in their leather coats, standing against the Dragon, was published in the *Daily Sketch* under the heading: 'Motorists arrive by air'. It would not be long before the news broke: after this last victory, Whitney Straight was giving up motor racing to pursue other interests.

Lilian Seaman was also at the aerodrome to greet them, at the invitation of Straight's mother, Dorothy Elmhirst, by whom she was much impressed ('one of the most cultured and beautiful American women I have ever met'). William Seaman had to be dissuaded from joining the party, accepting the decision on the promise that his son would be taken to him as soon as he arrived. Dick was surprised to see his mother when he stepped out of the Dragon. He had never asked her to see him off on any of his expeditions or to greet him on arrival. But the whole group enjoyed a late lunch in the aerodrome's dining room, with champagne to celebrate their safe return. As the young men described their experiences, Lilian looked at her watch and was surprised to discover that it was four o'clock, and getting dark.

They hurried back to London and were astonished, as they drove along Princes Gate towards Ennismore Gardens, to see the figure of Dick's father illuminated by the street lights as he stood on the pavement, looking towards Knightsbridge, agitated by their late arrival. He had been out there, the housekeeper said, since noon, refusing to come back in and eat the lunch prepared for him. As the three of them went inside, there were no recriminations. 'He well knew,' Lilian wrote, 'that Dick hated anything in the shape of emotion.' Listening to his son's stories of the trip, William began to relax.

◆

After his parents had returned to Pull Court, Dick wrote a letter to his mother in which he talked about ordering the ERA and outlined his ambitions for the season. This was a subject, like the purchase of Pull Court, that she had kept from her husband. She was reading the letter when she was called outside to speak to a workman, and left it on her writing desk. Having risen a little earlier than usual, William came down to see her in her study and spotted the letter. Since they always read each other's letters from their son, he picked it up.

The shock was severe. When his wife came back indoors, he confronted her with his discovery that she had given Dick the money to buy a new racing car, against his very explicit wishes. They argued, and she told him that had she not done so, Dick would have borrowed against his inheritance. That, William told her, is a pistol for him to hold at your head whenever he wants something. Furious at what he saw as a betrayal, and disturbed by the fear of what Dick's further pursuit of his career as a racing driver might mean, he sank into a silence that persisted for the rest of the day, even when his wife took him out for a drive. After tea in the Great Hall, during which he did little other than gaze into the blazing log fire, he announced that he was going to bed early. His wife handed him some magazines, suggesting that he take them upstairs with him and read them

until she came up to see him. While he did so, she went off
to the chapel, where she had to choose suitable oil paintings
on religious themes before the arrival of a picture-hanger the
following morning.

She was still in the chapel when the sound of running footsteps preceded the arrival of the housekeeper, who told her that
Mr Seaman had fallen down the stairs. She hurried to him and,
despite hearing his reassurance that nothing was broken, saw
that he seemed weak and badly shaken. He resisted the idea of
summoning the local doctor, but agreed that they should travel
back the next morning to London, where he could see his own
physician. But the real point of the trip, he stressed, would be
to see Dick and to give him a simple message: if he insisted on
racing the ERA, he would be disinherited.

◆

When William rose and dressed the next morning, nothing
Lilian said could dissuade him from making the journey.
Reaching Ennismore Gardens in the late afternoon, they found
a letter from Dick, announcing that he had gone to stay with
friends for a couple of nights. There would be no ultimatum
that day, or the next.

William's physician, Nestor Tirard of 83 Sloane Street, examined him but could find nothing seriously wrong and simply
advised rest. Without the stamina for eating out in the evenings,
William went out to lunch during the following days with his
wife and his friends at some of his favourite restaurants. But he
ate little, and Lilian could see that the prospect of confronting
Dick was weighing heavily on his mind.

Their son was due to return during the evening of Thursday
31 January, but in the afternoon a telegram announced that his
arrival would be delayed until the middle of the following day,
adding that he would then be going to Suffolk to spend the
weekend shooting with Tony Cliff. Once again, Lilian kept
the news from her husband, who went to bed early, believing

that he would see Dick at breakfast. But when his wife went into his bedroom at half past seven the next morning, intending to give him his usual cup of tea, she found him lying on the floor next to the bed. He was immobile, but conscious enough to ask: 'Where have you been? I've been calling out for you.' He had got up, he said, to see if Dick had returned, but had fallen and lain helplessly on the floor all night. She and the housekeeper helped him back into bed and awaited the doctor.

While Dr Tirard was examining him, William began to cough blood into his handkerchief. The doctor announced that he would have to return to the nursing home, and called for an ambulance. The patient objected, to no avail. He shouted with pain as he was carried out by the ambulance men, and again at the end of the short journey while being transferred on a stretcher to Collingham Gardens, a red-brick building in Earls Court. His wife travelled with him and saw him settled before going home to await her son's arrival. When Dick walked through the door, she simply told him that his father was back in the nursing home. She said nothing about the argument over the purchase of the ERA or the threat to his inheritance. She declined Dick's invitation to lunch at the Royal Automobile Club in Pall Mall, where he was meeting friends, saying she wanted to stay at home before going back to the nursing home. Dick asked her if he should stick to his plan of travelling to Suffolk that afternoon, or whether she wanted him to stay with her and visit his father. Fearing a confrontation that might have serious consequences, she reassured him that everything would be fine. So off he went, after leaving the phone number of the house where he would be staying and making her promise to let him know if she needed him to return.

At the nursing home that afternoon she was told that her husband's temperature had risen to 104 degrees, while his pulse had weakened considerably. At his bedside, she heard him ask in a feeble voice if Dick had returned. Yes, she said, she had seen him but the doctor had said he should have no visitors other than her on his first day. The lie covered up her attempt to avert potential disaster. 'Perhaps tomorrow,' he whispered, and went back to sleep. She sat with him that evening before going home, and returned at eight o'clock the following morning. He had weakened further, failing to recognise her or respond to her words. In her memoir she recalled bending close and hearing him say, 'It's all over now, Dick. All the hard things are said and done with.'

He slept again, waking at four o'clock in a slightly better state. She asked the doctor if they could have a second opinion, nominating Lord Horder, an eminent diagnostician whose patients had included King Edward VII and two prime ministers, Bonar Law and Ramsay MacDonald. An appointment was made for the next morning and she stayed with her husband, listening to him whisper to himself, until eleven o'clock that night, when she went home to bed. She left instructions with the nurse – who was sitting in a chair behind his bed, sewing to pass the time – to use his special cough mixture, and to telephone her if necessary.

She had a bath and brushed her hair before going to bed, and had just gone to sleep when the phone rang. It was the night nurse, reporting that there had been a change in his condition. Full of alarm, she dressed and prepared to return to the nursing home. It was half past one in the morning, and the family's chauffeur had long since locked up the mews garage and gone home. Phone calls to the nearby taxi ranks went unanswered. She put on her coat, went out of the house, and began walking towards Knightsbridge. A Daimler approached, driven – in her almost hallucinatory recollection – by a woman in a pink evening gown and a diamond tiara, with a man wearing a ceremonial sash in the back. As she stood in the road and waved her umbrella, the car stopped. She told the occupants of the urgency of her journey, and asked for a lift. Her request was readily granted. A few minutes later she got out of the car and walked into the nursing home. Dr Tirard was standing in the hall. He walked towards her. 'I'm so sorry,' he said. 'He has just died.'

She asked to see her husband. Resisting suggestions that she should wait until morning, she made her way to his room, where she saw his body lying in a contorted position on the bed, with an oxygen cylinder still standing nearby. What, she asked, had happened for him to die so suddenly? A nurse replied that he had suffered a bad coughing fit, and she had given him some of the cough mixture. 'Where is it?' she asked, and the nurse pointed to the mantelpiece. There she saw two bottles, almost identical in size, shape, labelling and the dark-brown colour of the liquid they contained: one the cough medicine, the other a liniment. She took the thought no further. Her husband had died in a strange room, at the age of seventy-six, without her. They had met almost a quarter of a century earlier, in a very different world, and had answered each other's needs. Over the years they had enjoyed travelling together on land and sea, lived in several fine homes, and brought up a beloved son who had given them both joy and pain. Dick was now fatherless, and she would have to break the news to him.

Dr Tirard drove her home to Ennismore Gardens, trying to take the edge off her grief by telling her how well she had cared for her husband in his final years. When he had gone she walked into William's bedroom, looking at his possessions, each in its proper place; she would leave them undisturbed for the next four years, until another loss brought even greater devastation to her life. Unable to sleep, she got up early and telephoned the house in Suffolk, where Dick was brought from his bed to speak to her. His response to the news suggested that his emotions had long ago detached themselves from a father whose failing health had rendered him an increasingly remote and disapproving figure. You must be philosophical about it, he told his mother. Be calm and brave. The long years of a gruelling experience are over.

After he added that he would be driving back to London

immediately, she returned to the nursing home. As the eight o'clock communion bell rang from a church across the road, she went in for a last vigil at her husband's side. She was back at home and on the phone to Pull Court, informing the staff of their master's death, when her son arrived. After they had embraced, Dick asked why she had let him go to Suffolk. Had his father asked for him before he died? 'He mentioned your name right up to the very end,' she replied, 'but I didn't know he was going to die when I left him for the night.'

It was Dick's idea to go for a drive around Hyde Park. After three circuits of the park on a grey February morning, they went to her club on Dover Street in Mayfair for black coffee and a cigarette and a discussion about where William should be buried. Dick had to be persuaded to accompany his mother back to the nursing home and to view his father's body. At first he showed no emotion. But as she knelt by the bedside, he slipped away to the back of the room, behind a screen. When she got up to see him, she found that he was sobbing. Later that afternoon they drove through Chelsea and across the Thames to Putney Vale cemetery, looking around the 47-acre site and deciding that a position on the far side, bordered by the trees of Wimbledon Common, would be ideal. As non-parishioners, the plot would cost them £150.

That evening they watched as the body was taken from the nursing home on its short journey to Ennismore Gardens, where the coffin was placed in the drawing room. Dick again told his mother how much he regretted going up to Suffolk. But thank goodness, he added, that his father had not known about the purchase of the ERA. His mother said nothing.

Following the funeral service at All Saints Church in Ennismore Gardens, the family travelled behind the hearse to Putney Vale and stood by as the coffin was lowered into the grave. They were taken home in silence. The next day Dick announced that he was driving his mother down to Torquay, where they spent several days touring the Devon countryside, stopping at fishing villages and abbeys. He took her to Dartington Hall, where she could see for herself the work Whitney Straight's mother and stepfather had done to create a community based on enlightened education and rural crafts. She bought wicker baskets and pottery, wooden fruit bowls and cheese boards, scarves and rugs. They visited the theatre and ballet schools, and had lunch with the estate's managers. 'The day spent at Dartington had taken me completely out of myself, and made me forget my sorrow for some hours,' Lilian concluded.

The night before their return to Ennismore Gardens, Dick made a suggestion. Instead of going back to Pull Court, where she would be virtually alone in her mourning, she should stay in London and keep herself busy. There was, for instance, an imminent board meeting of the Ranelagh Club, a fashionable country club in Barnes, where the Seamans had spent much time during Dick's childhood and of which she had recently become the first woman director. And, he added, he would be around to take her out between his own various commitments. She accepted his advice.

◆

Soon after his return from South Africa, Dick had received a letter from Cowley in which the MG sales department expressed anxiety over the fate of the Magnette; it appeared to be still in South Africa, without a buyer. During the next few days the car was located and arrangements were made for its return to Southampton via the SS *Arundel Castle*. In mid-March he received an invoice for £40 12s. 3d. – the cost of freight, wharfage, shipping, landing, customs attendance, dock and marine insurance charges.

Dick turned down Straight's offer to sell him the old ex-Birkin Maserati, together with its spares and a transporter, for £400. His mind was set on the ERA. In an article for *Speed* magazine at the end of the season, he would reflect on the strategy behind the decision he made after learning of Whitney's decision to fold the team. 'I was anxious to continue racing on the continent, as I much preferred this to racing in England,' he wrote. 'On the choice of car, I had two alternatives. Either I could get a big car such as an Alfa or a Bugatti and be able to compete with it in the big Grand Prix races, at the risk of almost certainly being outclassed by the German cars; or I could stick to the 1.5-litre class with a small English car, such as an ERA, and probably stand a fair chance of winning something. I decided on the latter course.'

Under the terms of the deal agreed with Mays, ERA would provide a lorry and the services of a mechanic. Dick also had a Dodge truck of his own, bought from Straight for £230. If Dick's car was the only ERA entered in a race, he would pay all expenses and keep all the prize money. If there were others, everything would be shared. Spare parts and work on the car at Bourne would be charged at cost price. He would pay for tyres and transport. He would receive bonuses for using Shell–Mex fuel and oil, like the works cars, although there would be no retainer; he wrote to Cleveland, one of their rivals, to see if he could get a better deal, without success.

As soon as he was back, he began contacting the organisers of continental races. He accepted an offer of 4,000 French francs in starting money from the organiser of the Picardie Grand Prix and 1,400 Belgian francs from Chimay, while the Swiss upped the previous year's money from 500 Swiss francs to 800 in recognition both of his win with the Straight team and of his new status as an independent entrant. A hitch arose over the Picardie race when the organisers advised him that he would need a 2-litre car in order to satisfy their regulations, based on the very fast nature of their circuit. 'I assure you,' he wrote back in excellent French, 'that the 1.5-litre car has stunning speed,' but their offer was withdrawn. An application to enter the Avusrennen, on a new high-speed track laid out on the parallel carriageways of an autobahn on the outskirts of Berlin, was turned down on similar grounds.

The car, however, would not be ready in time for the early-season meetings in which he was hoping to compete. In a letter to Raymond Mays on 22 March he requested a delivery date in time to race at Donington Park on 13 April, but his hope was not fulfilled. Determined not to allow his start to the season to be postponed, he was at Brooklands to see Mays driving the first ERA, known as R1A, and made an agreement to use the car at the Donington meeting. He had entered a 25-mile handicap, divided into two heats, for cars of up to 3500cc, with the handicaps awarded according to engine size. In the second race he was pipped for the win practically on the finishing line by the 2.3-litre Bugatti of Charlie Martin, whose car – like Martin's education at Eton, where he, too, illicitly kept a motorcycle – had been paid for by his Welsh family's steel fortune. He and Dick would become good friends. When the times of the two heats were put together, the winner was shown to be Martin, with Seaman third – an encouraging overture to his season with ERA, although he was irritated by the continuing wait for his own car.

◆

At the Donington meeting, Dick met a man who was to be one of his closest friends for the remainder of his life. With George Cosmo Monkhouse, then aged twenty-seven, he shared two great interests, the first being motor racing. Monkhouse was an enthusiast, although he neither owned nor drove racing cars; instead he photographed them. Another Cambridge man, he had studied engineering at Jesus College from 1926 to 1930 before taking a job as a graduate trainee with Kodak, where he had risen to the position of assistant works manager at their factory in Harrow. Recently he had begun taking pictures at race meetings, at first using a small Graflex camera and then a Speed Graphic provided, along with all its necessary paraphernalia, by his employers. The first time he used the new equipment had been during a visit to the Dieppe Grand Prix in 1934.

Monkhouse's companion on that cross-Channel excursion was Richard Bickford, a contemporary at Cambridge. Bickford had introduced him to motor racing with a first visit to Brooklands, where Monkhouse watched the Double-12 race and was impressed by the way the red Alfa Romeos were able to beat the thunderous and much larger green Bentleys. But the racing at Dieppe, over public roads closed off for the Grand Prix, was a different experience: the spectacle of Louis Chiron's Alfa, entered by the renowned Scuderia Ferrari, beating the Maseratis of Philippe Étancelin and Whitney Straight stirred his blood. When he got home, Monkhouse printed up his best shots and showed them to John Dugdale, who was reporting on the race for *The Autocar*. Dugdale – praised at Rugby for his paintings of motorcyclists, racing cars and seaplanes – had joined the magazine's staff as a reporter in 1933; he liked Monkhouse's photographs, and they were used to accompany his piece. Encouraged by that acceptance, and by the fee that arrived as a result, Monkhouse took to spending his weekends at one racing venue or another.

It was Bickford who brought Dick and George Monkhouse together at Donington. Bickford and Seaman, already friends from their Cambridge days, were preparing to set off the following weekend in Seaman's new plane to see the Monaco Grand Prix. A month earlier, after gaining his pilot's licence, Dick had bought a second-hand De Havilland Gipsy III Moth – a single-engined, two-seater biplane, registered G-ABYV – for £550 plus five guineas for a renewal of the certificate of airworthiness. Bickford had already attended the Monaco race twice, travelling on both occasions by car. He accepted Seaman's invitation to join him in the Gipsy Moth because he was not keen to repeat what he considered to be a monotonous four-day round trip by road.

Later he wrote an entertaining account of the trip for *The Sports Car*, a monthly magazine for MG enthusiasts. They had set off at dawn on Good Friday from London in an aeroplane capable of a maximum speed of 90mph and flew straight into increasingly thick cloud. After barely clearing the South Downs, they found conditions over the Channel so bad that they turned back and landed at Lympne. By mid-morning the visibility had improved enough to have another go, but a strong headwind meant that they barely seemed to be moving as they approached Berck, on the French side of the English Channel, where they landed in order to complete customs formalities. While they waited, they watched the arrival of a specially chartered Imperial Airways flight carrying the bandleader and impresario Jack Hylton, setting off on a European tour with his musicians.

On their next stop, at Le Bourget, just north of Paris, an airport official rode out to meet them on a bicycle. The wind had dropped by the time they resumed their journey, and they landed in the early evening at Lyon, where they spent the night. With the final 300 miles to cover, they rose late and attempted to set off at eleven o'clock, only to discover that the Gipsy Moth's engine was running on three of its four cylinders. 'After some delay, a shorting plug terminal was spotted,' Bickford wrote, 'and by then a powerful wind had sprung up – again right in our faces – but we were informed by the local weather experts that at 4,500ft this would dwindle to a mere breeze.' Discovering that it did no such thing, Seaman was forced to drop back down to 1,000ft, following the Rhône Valley to Marseille at an average of about 50mph; an emerald-green coupé on the road below was about to overtake them until it was slowed by the entrance to a town. But they persisted, enjoying a meal in Marseille before continuing to Nice and thence to Monaco, where they were in time to watch the Mercedes team practise on Easter Sunday morning, the day before the race, with Caracciola, Fagioli and Manfred von Brauchitsch in the new silver W25 machines. The young Englishmen were impressed by the organisation of the German personnel, a platoon of uniformed mechanics supervised by Alfred Neubauer, the portly, trilby-hatted team manager.

'The three cars arrived together with plenty of time to spare, and were placed with their backs to the pits at exactly the same angle and the same distance apart,' Bickford wrote. 'Each car had two mechanics who arranged the pit about a quarter of an hour before the start; then they marched up to the cars, took off the bonnets as one man, parked them, perfectly spaced again, in front and to the right of each car, and started the engines. Then one mechanic sat in each with his foot on the throttle, while the other stood at ease until the motors were warm, when they were switched off together and all the plugs changed. After a final trial of the engines, the bonnets were replaced, and the cars wheeled out to the start in line ahead. The whole performance was like a P.T. squad at the Royal Tournament.'

The next day, still talking about Fagioli's victory, they left for home, only to return to Cannes when thick cloud near Fréjus prevented their progress. After lunch and a walk along the Croisette they tried again at 5 p.m., flying through dense rain that forced them to follow the railway line as far as Montélimar, where they spent the night. Wednesday began with a wait until they were assured that cloud in the Lyon area had cleared. Having refuelled there, they set off again via Dijon, pushing on through strong headwinds, again following the railway to Paris. There they ate, refuelled and cleared customs before taking off for Lympne, where they landed just before eight o'clock in the evening. The Gipsy Moth's lack of lights meant they had to stay there overnight before undertaking the final leg home the following morning.

Bickford could not help noting that they arrived in London at just about the time they would have returned had they made the trip by car. Nevertheless he was full of admiration for his friend's navigational ability: 'In the whole trip, over ground he had never flown over before, we were never a mile off our course, in spite of the adversities which we encountered.'

◆

Dick's dealings with Straight were now taking a different form. He accepted an invitation to become a partner in Air Commerce Ltd, a fledgling airline based at Heston aerodrome, and in Ramsgate Airport Ltd, the first stage in a proposed network of aerodromes in southern England. Dick was soon negotiating with Ramsgate town council over a lease, at a starting rent of £250 a year, on buildings from which to operate a flying club, air taxis, an airline running a summer shuttle service to London, and a restaurant. He had invested £500 in £1 shares in the company.

Shortly after his return from the Monaco trip, however, Dick's exploits as an aviator got him into trouble with the Air Ministry. A letter arrived at Ennismore Gardens, signed by the Deputy Director of Civil Aviation, informing Dick of a complaint lodged by a Mr R. Gibbings of The Orchard, Waltham St Lawrence, near Reading in Berkshire, alleging that an aircraft had disturbed his peace by flying low over his house and grounds – low enough, in fact, for him to have noted its registration, which identified it as Dick's Gipsy Moth. 'The Air Ministry strongly deprecates flying over residential districts at such an altitude as to cause, apart from danger, annoyance and unnecessary disturbance,' the Deputy Director wrote. 'I am accordingly to request you to furnish this Department with a statement by the pilot concerned and to ensure that care is taken to obviate further cause for concern.'

In his reply, Dick declared himself 'most astonished' at the nature of the complaint: 'On the date in question I was flying from Reading to Heston and on the way practised a forced-landing approach over an obviously rural neighbourhood. I glided down towards a field with my engine throttled back, and then opened up my engine again and flew away. I did not circle round in a manner that could cause annoyance. I am sure you will agree that in these circumstances there was no cause for just complaint.' The Deputy Director responded that he had 'noted the circumstances you mention but in order that similar complaints may be avoided would be glad if care could be exercised when practising forced landings in future to select a place as remote as possible from private residences or dwellings'.

◆

The presence of Bickford at their initial meeting also opened up the second dimension of the friendship between Dick and George Monkhouse: a shared enthusiasm for jazz. During his Cambridge days Monkhouse had taken up the guitar and the banjo, becoming adept enough to join the ensemble led by the pianist Federico 'Fred' Elizalde, a Spanish Filipino, born in Manila and brought up in Madrid, where he had been a child prodigy. On arriving in England to study law at Cambridge, Elizalde assembled the ten-piece Varsity Band, which recorded 'Ain't She Sweet' for the Brunswick label in March 1927. Three months later, renamed the Cambridge Undergraduates, they cut 'Stomp Your Feet' for HMV. Monkhouse's banjo could be heard on these recordings, strumming four chords to the bar in a limited but effective way. Soon he would be leading a session for the Parlophone label, recording tracks under the name of George Monkhouse and his Cambridge University Quinquaginta Ramblers.

Bickford was a trumpeter and an occasional reviewer of jazz records for *Rhythm* magazine. He, too, had played with Elizalde – in the style of Bix Beiderbecke, according to Monkhouse – and was present on George's recordings. One of a group of modern-minded young men who responded equally to the sound of jazz and the roar of highly tuned engines, Bickford had competed in an Alvis and a borrowed Bugatti at various speed events. Others who shared his twin enthusiasms included the popular bandleader Billy Cotton, who raced at Brooklands for the first time that year in a Riley, and Buddy Featherstonhaugh, now, after the demise of the Straight team, busily burning his way through a £200,000 inheritance at the wheel of various Alfas and Maseratis as well as playing the saxophone in top-name bands.

Dick became a regular visitor to Monkhouse's flat at 197 Elgin Terrace, Maida Vale. They both collected 78s and shared their enthusiasm for the latest recordings from America. Dugdale occasionally joined them at the flat, where Monkhouse would turn up the volume of his gramophone to rafter-rattling levels. 'He liked the feeling of being right there in the band and the music,' Dugdale wrote. 'It didn't help conversation much, but we usually adjourned there late, after dining in Soho, where these two enthusiastic trenchermen loved the jellied eel at a German restaurant.'

10

Perfidious Albion

Spring had almost gone, and there was still no sign of Dick's ERA. He filled in some of the time, and pleased his mother, by organising a motor gymkhana at the Ranelagh Club, to be held in May, before his programme of continental races got under way. The event included a coachwork competition divided into three classes – for cars costing new not more than £500; not more than £1,000; and unlimited – each subdivided into open and closed bodywork. The gymkhana competitions were to be run under RAC rules – 'with the exception', Dick wrote to the club, 'of the reversing race, which might be rather dangerous, and I think ought to be eliminated for that reason'. He had been keen enough on ensuring its success to write to his contacts on the motoring magazines in order to drum up interest.

Playing for time, Raymond Mays wrote to him to ask for a schedule of his proposed races. The company's manufacturing capacity was being stretched to its limit and beyond by the need to prepare three cars for the works team and finish a first customer machine. That one was destined for Pat Fairfield, a Liverpool-born driver who had grown up in South Africa and returned to study land management at Trinity, where he was three years ahead of Dick and likewise did not complete his degree. Having driven Rileys with some success, and shaken off the early nickname of 'Skidder' Fairfield, he had ordered the 1100cc version of the ERA, with his eye on its potential in handicap races. Peter Berthon wrote to say that they would try to get Dick's car finished in time for the Mannin Moar race at Douglas, Isle of Man, on 31 May but that deadline was also missed.

Straight still owned his Maseratis, and was willing for Seaman to drive one of the 3-litre cars in the Mannin Moar. But when Dick heard that the driver would have to be responsible for all transportation and travel costs and mechanics' expenses, in return for a mere 30 per cent of any winnings, he lost interest. Instead he was counting the days until the ERA would arrive. The next deadline would be set by the Grand Prix des Frontières at Chimay in Belgium on 9 June, to which he travelled with Bickford. To his great relief the car, designated R1B, finally turned up. He had asked for it to be painted black, like his Magnette, with black wheels to match, and its owner adopted black overalls and a black linen helmet.

Faced with a flotilla of Bugattis and a couple of Maseratis, he took the lead on the first lap, set a new class lap record on the second, and appeared to be sailing to the first victory abroad for an ERA when a piston failed on the back leg of the circuit during the third lap, putting him out. He was forced to watch in frustration as victory went to Rudolf Steinweg of Germany in a Bugatti. Dick was gratified to receive a letter from the organisers, congratulating him on setting a new outright lap record. 'Your first lap (10km 870m) from a standing start was completed in 4 minutes 48 seconds, an average speed of 135.87km per hour,' they wrote. 'You are authorised to use this fact in any publicity on the subject of your performance.'

At the Nürburgring for the Eifelrennen meeting a week later, he was clearly functioning as a semi-works entry. His car's all-black livery made a sharp contrast with the cheerful light green of the factory machines, but at the races it was looked after by the same mechanics, under Berthon's supervision. The team's race entries, travel, accommodation and so on were now in the hands of a man named Tony Birch, the son of a Bournemouth car dealer. Birch had been MG's representative in Germany as well as Hamilton's manager; he was twenty-six years old and knew his way around continental motor sport.

The team arrived early and Mays spent a couple of days driving round the 14-mile circuit in his black 3.5-litre Bentley sports saloon, trying to familiarise himself with the layout and its 174 corners. The dark forests and the narrow strip of road winding through the Eifel mountains led him to describe the circuit as 'sinister'. But when the three days of practice began, it became apparent that the only serious rivals to the ERAs in the voiturette race were the Maseratis of Hans Ruesch and Count Luigi Della Chiesa. Seaman's car, fitted with new pistons, needed to be run in, which meant that he was only able to put in serious laps on the third and final practice day. Nevertheless, he made the fastest time, and was perturbed when *The Autocar* gave that honour to Mays – who, according to the magazine's reporter, had called to announce that there had been a mix-up and the fastest time had been his.

Morning rain had cleared away and a huge crowd had emerged from their hotels, hostels and tents when the grid for the eight-lap race lined up, the field of a dozen voiturettes swollen to thirty-five by the inclusion of the classes for sports cars and 800cc single-seaters. The 'Horst Wessel Song' – the National Socialist Party anthem, written by a Brownshirt leader who had died after being shot by communists in 1930 – was played over the loudspeakers while the spectators stood to respond with the Nazi salute. T. P. Cholmondeley-Tapper, a New Zealand-born amateur competing in a Bugatti, recorded that he did not join in: 'Standing to attention with my hands by my sides, I felt very conspicuous and thought I might possibly be strung up when the playing stopped.'

The race began with an innovation: a system of starting lights, showing amber for thirty seconds before turning green. Seaman, starting from the fourth row of the grid, had moved up to third place by the end of the opening lap, behind the works ERAs of Mays and Tim Rose-Richards, a young stockbroker who had gained a place in the team. Seaman got past both of his colleagues on the second lap, helped by Mays' problems with his car's fuel pressure. After five laps Seaman was leading by twenty seconds, but his engine started to lose oil and at the end of the sixth lap he was forced to stop to fill the empty dry-sump tank, dropping him to fourth place, which he held to the finish.

At the front, Mays battled to hold off Ruesch's Maserati and hang on to ERA's first continental success. His tactics were not much to the liking of the Swiss driver or the correspondent of Switzerland's *Automobile-Revue*: '[Ruesch] attempted several times to come alongside, but was pressed to the left and once dangerously made contact with the roadside embankment. The fact that the ERA people were reluctant to give way was confirmed by different drivers.' This criticism seems to have been directed specifically at Mays, who finished ahead of Ruesch, with Rose-Richards third, Seaman fourth and Cook fifth: overall, a magnificent result for the team, greeted with the playing of 'God Save the King' over the loudspeakers: 'A pleasant relief from the German military music that had been ringing in our ears,' wrote Cholmondeley-Tapper, who had retired with low oil pressure.

'What a thrill,' *The Motor*'s correspondent wrote, 'to see the green of England leading the red of Italy, the blue of France and the white of Germany. It seems a pity that one of our principal champions, Dick Seaman, had a black car in this truly international race.' In the afternoon Dick was given another glimpse of the might of the German teams, Caracciola winning the big race after an electrifying duel amid heavy showers with Bernd Rosemeyer, a former motorcycle champion and Auto Union's new star. Spending the meeting in close proximity to the Grand Prix teams, he could appreciate the professional approach shown by the Mercedes team in particular, down to the way the mechanics wore brown overalls during the practice sessions before switching to white for race day. This, he could see, was the way a top team should be run.

Further down the scale, a problem presented itself to those foreign entrants due prize or starting money. German currency restrictions stipulated that no more than ten Reichsmarks – less than £1 – could be taken out of the country, and any sum deposited in a bank account would be exchanged at less than half the rate available in Britain. Some recipients, including Cholmondeley-Tapper, took the risk of stuffing banknotes up various bits of piping inside their cars, giving themselves a few nervous minutes during inspections at the frontier customs posts.

◆

For the second race in a row, Dick had found himself frustrated by problems beyond his control. Despite writing to Berthon with suggested modifications, the disappointments were to continue. For the next meeting, the Kesselberg hill-climb in Bavaria, he had told Berthon that he would be arriving several days ahead of the event. The ERA was to be brought down from the Nürburgring by the team's mechanics, Percy Pugh and the usefully multilingual Vic Evans. They had stayed in Adenau after the Eifelrennen, and their early arrival at Kesselberg would give him time for a couple of days' extra preparation. Without telling Seaman, however, Berthon extended the mechanics' stay in Adenau; the car would not arrive at Kesselberg until two days before the competition, instead of four. Tony Birch – who, after a series of disagreements with Berthon, was on the brink of terminating his brief employment with the company – endeared himself to Dick by taking a hand. Having pointed out the problem to Berthon and being told 'to bloody well mind my own business', he drove the truck containing the car to Kesselberg himself in time to meet Dick.

A reconnaissance run up to the mountain pass persuaded Dick that this was nothing short of 'the most beautiful venue for a racing event that I know'. But as he took the car out for a warm-up on the morning of the event, the front brakes locked without warning, bending the front axle. He spent fifteen minutes disconnecting the front brakes altogether before making a gentle ascent with only the rear set functioning. Unsurprisingly he could finish no better than sixth in his class, with the overall victory going to Stuck's Auto Union.

Now thoroughly fed up, he wrote a formal letter to ERA with a list of eight demands to be carried out in time for the Nuffield Trophy at Donington Park. These included the fitting of a new engine with the latest modifications, repair of the front brakes and a gearbox overhaul. The work was done in time, but there was more frustration at Donington as R1B's engine suffered damage when an oil cap was not closed properly. He was forced to scratch from the race, which was won by Fairfield's 1100cc ERA, and headed back to London. There Whitney Straight was to marry Lady Daphne at St Margaret's Church in Westminster, with Dick among the ushers and his mother among a congregation of more than 200, also including one of Daphne's former boyfriends, a young stockbroker named Ian Fleming. The bride and groom posed for the cover of *Country Life* before a reception at Dudley House on Park Lane, one of London's grandest residences.

Back at Bourne, the mechanics had a week to make further repairs. Seaman left the wedding reception to fly himself from Heston to Dieppe, where he, Mays, Cook and Fairfield were among the entries for the Grand Prix des Voiturettes that Sunday, 20 July. They were joined by a fifth ERA: a 1500cc machine newly acquired by Prince Birabongse Bhanudej of Siam, a Cambridge student who had begun racing earlier that season with a Riley and a Magnette. The ERA had been bought for him by his cousin and informal guardian, Prince Chula Chakrabongse, as a present for his twenty-first birthday, which had fallen a few days before their arrival in France. The highlight of the birthday party, held at the Chelsea studio of

Prince Birabongse's art teacher, had come when the car, finished in Bourne earlier that day, was wheeled into the studio shortly before midnight and unveiled before the party guests, each of whom was invited to sit in it (one, the wife of the choreographer Léonide Massine, had to be extricated with some difficulty, having wedged herself in). In Dieppe the Prince was entered as 'B. Bira', a choice of pseudonym that would make life much easier for race organisers and journalists alike over the next twenty years. The car was painted a bright peacock blue, its hue selected by Chula to match a piece of fabric cut one night from the gown of a girl with whom he was dining at the Savoy.

Even in the exotic world of motor racing, populated by its fair share of aristocrats and eccentrics, Bira and Chula were rare creatures. As members of the Siamese royal family, their material resources appeared infinite. Both were aesthetes, but their temperaments and interests were contrasting. Chula seldom rose before noon and was famously regal in his manner. After Harrow and Trinity he had become an author, writing books about travel, motor racing and his country's history, while supervising the activities of the team he set up for his cousin, which they named White Mouse Racing. Bira, the grandson of King Mongkut (the model for the Yul Brynner character in *The King and I*), was more unassuming. He had left Eton for private studies with Charles Wheeler RA, who helped him develop a genuine talent for sculpture. But it was on the circuits that Bira made his reputation as an excellent driver capable of winning second-rank races.

Dick had known the family since Prince Abhas, Bira's older brother, had coxed his Trinity eight at Henley in 1932. In Dieppe they were all staying at the Hôtel Royal, a huge belle époque palace on the fashionable seafront, separated from the beach by a lawn, and a favourite subject of the English painter Walter Sickert. The town had hosted the French Grand Prix in 1907 and 1908, over a 48-mile circuit. Since 1929, however, the racing had taken place over a much shorter layout between villages south of the town, with long straights and tricky corners, and hillsides providing vantage points for spectators. Seaman was unhappy after the first two days of practice, in which he could do no better than set the sixth fastest time. Blaming the car's uneven running on an incorrect fuel mixture supplied by the organisers, he wired Shell-Mex in London to send a batch of the correct fuel on the night ferry from Newhaven in time for the final practice. His diagnosis was correct: at the end of the session he and Fairfield were the only drivers to record times below 3 minutes 50 seconds, with Seaman nine seconds faster than his teammate.

Nineteen cars started the race in blustery conditions beneath dark clouds, the threat of rain thinning the ranks of spectators. Unusually for a Grand Prix, the race was defined by duration rather than distance, lasting two hours. Mays took the lead ahead of Seaman, the pair roaring away down the poplar-lined road to the first corner and completing the opening lap with such a gap to the rest of the field that the ambulances were alerted on the assumption that a multiple accident had taken place. On the third lap, the novice Bira created a minor sensation by passing Lord Howe's Delage for third place. On the fifth lap the two leading ERAs were still racing together when Seaman's supercharger drive sheared, stranding him in the village of Saint-Aubin.

Mays and Bira were now first and second, until Bira came in to change a plug and dropped to fifth. Mays continued to lead until he came in for a complete change of plugs, sipping tea while the mechanics did their work, before jumping back in to discover that a piston had been damaged, ending his race. Fairfield led to the chequered flag, with Bira overtaking Veyron's Bugatti on the penultimate lap to take an astonishing second place and – although a supreme irrelevance to a young man of his means – the 10,000 francs offered to the runner-up.

That evening Dick interrupted the Bourne mechanics' supper by 'tearing strips off them', in the words of John Lea, the engine specialist and therefore the principal victim of his anger. Lea subsequently expressed the view that Seaman was 'a marvellous driver, but determined always to get his own way, to the point of bullying if necessary'. Seaman and the Siamese princes were among those at the victory party later that night, where an impromptu cabaret was performed by members of the Ballet Russe de Monte Carlo.

By now Dick had discovered through conversations with an ERA mechanic – probably Lofty England, who had grown equally critical of the team's standards – that Mays and Berthon had sold him not the brand-new car he had ordered and paid for but a new chassis with a rebuilt engine from R1A, the very first ERA. That, he believed, was the primary source of his problems. There were testy exchanges, and before long the two sides had reached a position of intense mutual dislike. After railing long and loud against what he described as ERA's 'perfidy', Dick could not wait to cut his ties with Bourne.

◆

'I have definitely finished with ERAs, they are quite hopeless,' he wrote to the honeymooning Straight. 'Giulio [Ramponi] is at the moment busily engaged in making the car in the right way, and I hope it will now go properly.' But the real purpose of his letter was to give a business update to Straight, who was heading for the Mediterranean with Lady Daphne on board the SS *Rex*, a luxurious Italian liner known, thanks to its parasol-shaded swimming pools and stylish furnishings, as 'the Riviera afloat'.

Dick mentioned that he had helped inaugurate their air shuttle service from Ramsgate to Ostend; they were met by the mayor in full uniform, who took them to a lunch at which Seaman was among the speakers before they flew on to another civic reception at Le Zoute, with 'tea, ice cream, champagne and more speeches'. He gave news of the receipts from joy-riding, of difficulties with customs officials at Dover, and other

problems. 'I am afraid the recent air crashes, especially the one at
Heston, have had a very bad effect on Air Commerce's business,'
he continued. 'However, this applies to all the companies, and
we are not the only one that has suffered by any means.' Two
people had been killed and five injured earlier that month when
a Dragon of Blackpool and West Coast Air Services stalled,
crashed and caught fire soon after take-off, damaging public
confidence in an industry that was still in its fledgling stage.

Straight had not yet received Seaman's letter when, with the
Rex approaching Gibraltar, he set down his thoughts about
creating a network of airports offering routes to continental
Europe, mentioning Ramsgate, Bournemouth, Eastbourne and
Torquay. He concluded by giving his opinion on the choice of
colour scheme for a new Air Commerce aeroplane. Seaman
had wanted red and white, but Straight preferred dark blue and
white: 'more dignified colours, more restful and confidence
inspiring than red and white,' he thought, before finishing with
a handwritten postscript: 'Daphne sends her love.'

◆

John Dugdale had listened to Dick talking about his ambitions
and frustrations: 'He was a very strong-willed and determined
fellow, and his natural desire to beat the official ERAs was
undoubtedly stimulated by his scorn at what he considered were
shortcomings in the preparation of his own car. They had nur-
tured a formidable rival.' Seaman was demanding, not always
diplomatic, and sharply aware of when he was being taken for
a ride. The decision to put the preparation of his car into the
expert and trusted hands of Ramponi would unlock a change
of fortune.

The Seaman family's double-fronted garage in Ennismore
Gardens Mews was being transformed into a racing team's
workshop, with Dick settling into an office in the upstairs
rooms – once the coachmen's quarters – while Ramponi
worked downstairs with Jock Finlayson, another recruit from

the defunct Straight outfit. Soon Lofty England would also join them, finally leaving ERA after one last row. According to Dugdale, Seaman and England were particularly well matched: 'They were two of a kind – men of great directness and determination.' Tony Birch was engaged as the team manager, on a percentage of their winnings, with the expectation that he would put his knowledge of the European scene to good use in Seaman's cause.

New priorities were being established. Owning the Gipsy Moth had been fun, but now Dick sold it to a man with a soap factory in Manchester, having convinced himself that his skills at the wheel would be sharpened by the long drives to continental races. The Dodge lorry was painted black, to match the livery of the racing car it would carry. He had his own team at last.

11

Boot polish and tear gas

The key to the new enterprise was Giulio Ramponi, a motor racing man through and through. Born in Milan in 1902, he had acted as riding mechanic to several well-known Alfa Romeo drivers, including his uncle, the part-time opera singer Giuseppe Campari. He accompanied Enzo Ferrari to victory in the 1923 Circuito del Savio and was alongside Antonio Ascari when they won the following year's French Grand Prix. In 1927 he became Alfa's chief test driver, but returned to the mechanic's seat to win the Mille Miglia twice as Campari's riding mechanic, in 1928 and 1929. Given a chance to take the wheel himself, he travelled to England to win two big handicap races at Brooklands, the 1928 Six-Hours and the 1929 Double-12, a twenty-four-hour race run in two daylight chunks on consecutive days to avoid night-time noise restrictions. The sight of his 1500cc Alfa beating the mighty Bentley Speed Six was the vision that had inflamed Monkhouse's imagination on his first visit to a motor race. Developing racing cars rather than driving them, however, was Ramponi's destiny. At Alfa Romeo he had soaked up information from two great engineer-designers, Vittorio Jano and Luigi Bazzi, before joining Straight's new outfit at its Milan base.

Now respected in British racing circles for his practical

knowledge of racing-car construction and preparation at the highest level, he returned to London after Straight disbanded the outfit. When one of the Maseratis was sold to Harry Rose, the son of a Manchester mail-order magnate, Ramponi's services were included as part of the deal, on the insistence of the new owner. Once Dick had made the decision to cut his ties with ERA, it was necessary to receive Rose's permission to hire the Italian. Ramponi promptly set to work on R1B, modifying what he considered to be Reid Railton's inadequate front suspension design and Tom Murray Jamieson's supercharger, and getting to the bottom of the problems with Berthon's engine. The refettled car had to be ready for the Grossglockner hill-climb on Saturday 4 August. By dint of hard work in the mews followed by a marathon drive across half of Europe, Seaman and Finlayson reached the pass, on Austria's border with Italy, by the Thursday evening, having stopped en route to change a broken spring on the Dodge.

The Hochalpen pass was a brand-new road, opened the day before the competition by the Austrian president. The hill-climb was run over a 12-mile section, with a gravel surface; the German teams had taken a look and decided to stay at home. On a rainy weekend, the event was won by Mario Tadini in one of the Scuderia Ferrari's Alfa P3s, in 14 minutes 42 seconds. Second overall – and the winner of the voiturette class – came Seaman, a mere twelve seconds slower than the Italian team's full Grand Prix machine. 'It was a climb which put all others in the shade and sent the crowd into an excited state of appreciation,' *Motor Sport* reported, and published a photograph of the black ERA taking a right-hander at speed, straw bales marking the apex but nothing guarding the sheer drop on the outside of the bend. The German ambassador to Austria, Franz von Papen, had attended the race; after the prize-giving he returned to his official car to discover that someone had let the air out of all four tyres.

◆

In considerably better heart, Seaman and his team headed to Pescara for the Coppa Acerbo, stopping on the way in Milan, where they used the old Straight team garage to work on the ERA before heading south. Accompanied by Birch, Dick drove down in the Ford V8. Meeting them at the resort on the Adriatic coast was the tall, gangling, bespectacled figure of Robert Fellowes, another former Cambridge undergraduate whose obsession with motor racing had got in the way of his academic progress. The son of a colonel in the Indian police, two years older than Dick, Fellowes had obtained a mediocre degree before going to France to broadcast jazz records to a UK audience on Radio Normandie, an English-language commercial station broadcasting from a transmitter in Fécamp, before transferring to Radio Côte d'Azur, based in Juan-les-Pins. In 1931, aged twenty, he had taken his first photographs of a motor race; now, wielding a camera with a proficiency almost as great as that with which he negotiated hotel discounts and secured lifts to and from races, he was selling his images to *Motor Sport* and *Speed*. He and Dick would become good friends.

A dozen entrants turned up for the 60-mile junior race, including Reggie Tongue in a supercharged 750cc MG. The field was not of the highest class and at half past eight in the morning Seaman roared away from an assortment of Maseratis and Bugattis. He was more than a minute ahead of his nearest pursuer, Ettore Bianco in a Maserati, when he took the chequered flag. 'The crowd was amazed at the wonderful performance of the ERA, which they were seeing for the first time in an Italian race,' *The Autocar*'s correspondent reported. Then Dick could spend the afternoon relaxing and watching the Auto Unions of Achille Varzi and Rosemeyer demolish the challenge of Scuderia Ferrari's six Alfas. That night the English entrants – Seaman, Tongue, Kenneth Evans and Lord Howe – went out for dinner together. Evans, who had been driving an MG, remembered Seaman's insistence on paying the bill. When it came, however, he summoned the waiter and demanded that the police be called. Soon it was re-presented, this time totalling half its original sum.

There was always a price to be paid for success – Lilian Seaman was getting used to her son's increasingly frequent requests for funds to pay the mechanics' wages and the little team's other expenses – but it brought a patriotic response in a *Motor Sport* editorial: 'Continental organisers are ordering new gramophone records of the British national anthem to play at the end of their races, for the ERA is regarded as unbeatable. Maserati and Bugatti – names to conjure with – have been subdued.' The writer also recognised the contribution of the man in the cockpit. 'In Seaman,' he wrote, 'we obviously possess a driver of outstanding ability. It is to be noted that he has wisely used continental road races as his training ground.'

◆

Straight wrote to Dick again after returning from a trip to Denver, Colorado, where he had been examining the latest aircraft and assessing the way in which American airlines went about their business. This time there was a very different kind of message for his former teammate. The man who had encouraged Dick to follow his example by leaving Cambridge for a life on the world's racetracks was now advocating another change of course.

'Lambert is keeping me informed about your motor racing successes – I have just heard that you have won the 1500cc race at Pescara,' Straight wrote. 'I think that is grand, but you must give up motor racing soon, as it does not really lead anywhere, except to a position like that of Lord Howe [the president of the British Racing Drivers' Club], and I think you ought to concentrate your ability on something more constructive.' His conclusion might have been more to Dick's liking: 'I am looking forward to seeing you soon, and for heaven's sake take care of yourself, and don't leave the braking too late!'

Two weeks after the Coppa Acerbo, the team's next

Father and son in 1923: William Seaman, aged sixty two, and ten-year-old Dick, then a pupil at Hillmorton House.

Mother and son in 1929: Dick, now a sixth-former at Rugby, and Lilian Seaman on an outing.

Aldingbourne House in West Sussex, built around 1800, where Dick was born in 1913.

Dick in the MG K3 Magnette, setting the fastest time at the 1934 Inter-Varsity Speed Trials on the Eynsham bypass near Cambridge.

Dick and the Magnette on their way to third place in the Coppa Acerbo Junior at Pescara in 1934.

On pole position in the ERA for the 1935 Dieppe Grand Prix, alongside the cars of Raymond Mays (centre) and Pat Fairfield (right).

Preparing to start the 1935 Coppa Acerbo Junior, his first victory in the ERA, with mechanic Jock Finlayson at the rear of the car.

Off duty in the paddock at Donington Park, Britain's attempt to match the
road circuits of continental Europe.

Pull Court, the Worcestershire pile bought in 1933 for Dick to
inherit, giving him a place among the landed gentry.

A one-off drive in the ex-Scuderia Ferrari Duesenberg, shared with Buddy Featherstonhaugh in the 1935 BRDC 500 at Brooklands.

On the grid with the maestro Giulio Ramponi and the borrowed Maserati 8CM in which Dick won the 1936 British Empire Trophy at Donington Park.

Outside the garage in Ennismore Gardens Mews with Hans Ruesch's
Alfa Romeo 8C-35 before an easy win in the 1936 Donington Grand Prix,
sharing the drive with the car's owner.

At Donington Park in August 1936 during a race that would give him his sixth
and last victory with the Delage.

Dick toasts his victory in the 1936 Junior Car Club 200 at Donington, flanked by two of his mentors: Giulio Ramponi (left) and Lord Howe, the car's former owner (right).

Rolling to the grid for the South African Grand Prix at East London on January 1937, a final and ill-fated outing with the black Delage, attended by flat-capped mechanic Lofty England.

Lilian Seaman's favourite photograph of her son, taken by George Monkhouse
during a journey through the Alps, probably in 1936.

appointment was at Bremgarten, where Dick had driven the Magnette to victory in the previous year's Prix de Berne. The 1935 grid of eighteen cars for the voiturette race included a full house of ERAs, on their first visit to Switzerland: the works trio of Mays, Cook and Rose-Richards, and the private entries of Seaman, Fairfield and Bira. Somehow Dick managed to get around the organisers' insistence that all cars should be presented in their national colours. He might simply have argued that there was no time for a repaint; his mechanics had endured a protracted journey through the Alps, making three-point turns in the Dodge at one hairpin after another while he and Birch sailed through the mountains in the powerful Ford V8.

The voiturettes' practice was delayed by the need to clear up the widely scattered fragments of the Mercedes W25 in which Hanns Geier, promoted from the team's reserves at the start of the season, had crashed at 160mph just past the pits during the final session for the Grand Prix cars. The driver's life was saved on the spot by Dr Peter Gläser, a physician retained to travel with the two German teams; a year in hospital would end Geier's racing career. When the smaller cars were finally sent out, Dick's first laps persuaded him that, as at Dieppe, the fuel supplied to all the teams by the organisers was not producing full power. Keeping the discovery to himself, he again made his own arrangements for an alternative supply, missing a session as a result but finishing fourth fastest in the final practice behind Mays, Bira and Pietro Ghersi's Maserati. By the end of the first lap of the race Seaman had swept past Mays to take a lead he would hold without challenge once the leader of the works team had been forced into the pits for a complete change of plugs. Bira finished second, almost a minute behind, with Howe's light-blue Delage a distant third. For the second year in succession Dick was able to take the applause of the Swiss spectators and a place of honour at the victory banquet in the ballroom of the Hotel Belle Vue.

◆

A week later he was at Freiburg for the German hill-climb championship, where he achieved an even more remarkable result. First he drove up and down the 12-kilometre course – familiarising himself with its 140 corners, six of them hairpins – in the Ford. Then, on a gloriously sunny day in the Schauinsland mountains, in front of a crowd of 40,000, he recorded the class-winning time of 8 minutes 25.1 seconds. And on a road winding through pine forests, its freshly relaid surface quickly breaking up as the racing tyres bit into asphalt softened by the heat of the day, his time was a mere second slower than that recorded by Stuck at the wheel of the mighty 5-litre Auto Union. Mays, who had spun on the way up, was ten seconds further back; his preparation had been disturbed the night before the event when he received a telephone call purporting to be from the local Gestapo headquarters, telling him to go back to England immediately. Choosing to ignore it, he heard nothing more.

It was Stuck who, two years earlier, after his application for a place in the Mercedes team had been turned down, persuaded Hitler to divide the subsidy for a Grand Prix project between two teams. Now his successes on the hills with Auto Union were earning him the nickname 'Bergkönig', or King of the Mountains. A month after his Freiburg victory he would take another win at Feldberg, in the Black Forest, in the last big hill-climb of the European season. At that meeting *Motor Sport*'s Harold Nockolds witnessed something out of the ordinary: 'The event was marked by a vindictive outburst against Stuck. Notices were pinned to trees and hung across the road to the effect that Hans must be spat upon, and that he is a traitor to Hitler – for marrying a Jewess.' In 1932 Stuck had divorced his first wife and married the successful tennis player and writer Paula von Reznicek, who turned out to have a Jewish grandfather. It was only Stuck's friendship with Hitler that saved her from further persecution.

But Nockolds had more to report: 'A few months ago I saw from my hotel window a young Jew being marched through the streets for having walked out with a German girl. One village I passed through had a banner strung across the street bearing the words: "The road to Palestine doesn't lead through this village!" Here are the hill-climb results . . .'

◆

Returning to Britain that September with a string of good performances behind him and as something of a hero, Dick accepted an invitation from the Bellevue Garage to drive one of the Evans family's three MGs entered in the Ulster TT, a 478-mile handicap for sports cars. The race was held on the Ards circuit, laid out over 14 miles of country roads on the coast of Northern Ireland. Given its length, the enterprising Evanses tried fitting the Bellevue MGs with two-way radios so that the drivers could communicate with their pits, an innovation that would turn out to be several decades ahead of its time. Sadly, the system – supplied by Marconi – could not be made to work. Worse, the handicappers had treated the Magnettes unkindly, and Dick could do no better than tenth place at the end of the longest race of his career to date.

Later in September there was another extra-curricular adventure, this time in the form of an invitation to share the wheel of a Duesenberg with Buddy Featherstonhaugh in the British Racing Drivers' Club 500 Miles on Brooklands' Outer Circuit. The big red American car, powered by a 4.4-litre straight-eight engine, had been brought to Europe by the Scuderia Ferrari in 1933. It was acquired the following year by Straight, who planned to use it to beat John Cobb's outright record on the Mountain Circuit at Brooklands. He fell short, an average of 138mph good enough only for a new class record. It must have seemed a fine idea to enter the car, now owned by Jack Duller, a well-known Brooklands figure, for the next year's 500 Miles. But having taken over from his co-driver and lapped at competitive speeds in his first and only outing on the bumpy Outer Circuit, Seaman was forced to retire after seventy-two laps when the fuel tank broke loose, the vibration having snapped its stay. This was to be his last serious outing at Brooklands. He shared Tazio Nuvolari's distaste for a track that bore almost no relationship to the circuits of continental Europe, with their narrow roads, natural contours, demandingly diverse corners and a variety of hazards offering a proper challenge to anyone who wanted to be considered a real racing driver.

The familiar cockpit of the ERA welcomed him back a week later, when he returned to Brno for the Masaryk Grand Prix, the last big race meeting of the year. The 17-mile circuit, laid out over national and local roads, had been resurfaced, and corners had been reshaped to encourage higher speeds. The Grand Prix and voiturette races would be run simultaneously, with the big cars starting at the front of the grid and racing over seventeen laps while the smaller ones would complete fifteen. Despite a warning from Ramponi that moisture beneath overhanging trees would make the track surface slippery, Dick's first practice session ended prematurely when he hit a kerb, bending a front stub-axle. ERA declined to send a replacement part from Bourne, so Ramponi – always well connected – spoke to acquaintances at the Skoda company and used their equipment to straighten it in time for the next day's session, although that one, too, was truncated by complete brake failure. Fortunately it happened in a place where Dick was able to bring the car to a halt without causing further damage. But the accident on the first day prompted the 22-year-old to reflect, in a subsequent conversation with Monkhouse, on his occasional habit of taking a corner too fast, losing control and having to deal with the consequences.

An estimated 150,000 spectators were at the circuit when the cars assembled on the Sunday morning in grid positions determined not by their practice times or, as had sometimes been the case, by ballot, but by the order in which their entries had been received. With twenty-two cars in the two classes lining up on the narrow road in a 2-1-2-1 formation, the secretary of the Czech motor club had to climb a telegraph pole at the starting line so they would all be able to see him wave his flag. Dick, all alone on the twelfth row of the grid, overtook half a dozen Bugattis, Ruesch's Maserati and an MG to take the class lead by the end of the opening lap, and next time around broke Nino Farina's lap record for the voiturettes. He might even have been close enough to the German cars, at least in the early stages, to have his nostrils filled with their distinctive exhaust fumes, described by Mays as 'smelling like boot polish and acting like tear gas'.

'The car went magnificently again,' Dick observed, and so dominant was his performance that he was able to make three pit stops without losing the lead, finishing the race more than three minutes ahead of Veyron's Bugatti. It was the final part of a remarkable hat-trick of wins in continental road races – Pescara, Bremgarten and Brno – that elevated his standing both at home, among the readers of the motoring press, and abroad.

Meanwhile the bigger cars thundered on, with Rosemeyer taking the win in his Auto Union. It was the first Grand Prix victory for the 25-year-old former motorcycle champion, the son of a garage owner from Lower Saxony. This was also the day on which Rosemeyer met his future wife: Elly Beinhorn, an aviatrix whose dramatic long-distance flights had made her a national celebrity, and who was in Czechoslovakia on a lecture tour. After she offered Rosemeyer congratulations at the victory banquet, they danced the night away. By the time they were married the following July, they were Germany's celebrity couple, embodying values particularly prized by the Third Reich: youth, good looks, and a willingness to risk death in pursuit of national glory.

Mercedes had given Brno a miss, but in October they celebrated the season's successes by sending a W25 to be displayed in the window of their London showroom at 110 Park Lane, close to Marble Arch. Placed on a dais bordered with laurels amid their sports and saloon models, it attracted a stream of people wanting a chance to see one of the already legendary Silver Arrows at close quarters. The display coincided with the London Motor Show, at which Caracciola was among the guests of honour. Mercedes arranged a reception for him at Grosvenor House, close to the showroom, where the newly crowned European champion modestly explained that the racing cars of the day, with their independent suspension, were as easy to handle at 200mph as their predecessors at 130. So easy, in fact, that he had been able to enjoy the sight of several pretty girls sitting on a balcony while he was winning a recent race in San Sebastián. He also expressed the hope, warmly applauded by the enthusiasts in his audience, that Britain would soon stage a full-scale international Grand Prix of its own.

◆

In early November, Tommy Wisdom informed readers of the *Sporting Life* that Dick was to drive an Auto Union in the forthcoming South African Grand Prix. 'Mr Seaman will be the first Englishman to drive this type of car – in fact, the first non-member of the German team to do so,' he wrote. 'It was reported earlier in the year that Whitney Straight, the young American driver, would handle one of these cars in South Africa. I understand, however, that Mr Straight is doing no more racing, and that he will be replaced by Mr Seaman, who has driven in his team on previous occasions.'

This was a confection of fact (Straight had been linked with an Auto Union drive a year earlier, and Seaman had been led by Sammy Davis, the sports editor of *The Autocar*, to believe that the German team were planning to sell their 1935 cars at the end of the season) with wishful thinking. Perhaps Seaman gave Wisdom a story in the hope of encouraging Auto Union to sell him a car. Or the journalist may have concocted it at the behest of the South African race organisers, looking for publicity.

But Seaman stayed at home, absorbed in his plans for the coming European season while finding time to attend a cocktail party at the flat of Bira and Chula, an agreeable gathering of racing people including Fairfield and the Canadian-born Brooklands ace Kay Petre, one of the leading women drivers of the era. Also present was Sammy Davis; he and Dick may have discussed the discovery that, although the likes of Alfa Romeo, Maserati and Bugatti were happy to defray their costs by flogging off their old cars at the end of the season, this was not the way the state-subsidised German teams, keen to preserve the secrecy of their technical innovations, went about their business. The request to buy an Auto Union had been flatly turned down. At that moment, the prospect of driving a German Grand Prix car seemed remote.

12

Winter work

On the grid Dick would line up alongside certain rivals, such as Mays, Fairfield and Bira, who wore helmets with hard shells made from layers of linen soaked in shellac: the sort of thing seen on the heads of polo players. Dick, by contrast, stuck with a simple linen or thin leather wind-bonnet, not very different from a flying helmet, offering no protection against an impact even when lined with chamois. When John Dugdale asked about his preference in an interview for *The Autocar*, the response said everything about his ambitions within motor sport. 'I take as my example the crack professional drivers of the continent,' he said. 'Not one of them wears a crash helmet, and, as they are racing every weekend in the season and have been doing so as their job for years, it strikes me they must know all the risks by now.' In other words, Dick Seaman now wanted to be measured not against the chaps at Brooklands but against the real aces on the world stage.

The attempt to acquire an Auto Union had been rebuffed, and there was no point in buying a Maserati that would be left behind in the clouds of dust kicked up by the German teams. He had begun to talk about the dream of racing a British Grand Prix car, but when Dugdale asked him what sort of car he would build if money were no object, he replied: 'I'd go to somebody with plenty of Grand Prix experience. Not an Englishman, I'm afraid.' The immediate task was to find a way of using the 1936 season to prove that Grand Prix racing was where he belonged.

Another year among the voiturettes – a complete season of continental races with a fully competitive car – seemed the best option. First, he needed to move on from the ERA. Mays and his men would be working on their factory-entered cars for the new season, with the aim of finding some new development – more efficient suspension, a better supercharger – that would restore their competitive edge. His own car was bound to get left behind. So it was sold to Jock Manby-Colegrave, a former officer in the Royal Tank Corps, the co-founder of a small company that built Squire sports cars, and a useful amateur driver. Manby-Colegrave paid £1,400 for the black ERA, which he repainted green – a darker shade than the works machines.

For Dick, something different would be required, and it was Ramponi, with his analytical eye, who came up with a solution that initially sounded so unlikely as to be ridiculous. The experienced Italian had been watching Lord Howe's performances in his blue Delage and thinking about the car's potential. This was a paradox, since the machine was already nine years old and seemingly obsolete. Its glory days had come in the mid-1920s and the pace of change had left it behind, along with those it had vanquished in its prime.

Louis Delage's company, founded in a Paris suburb in 1905, had established a fine racing pedigree in the sport's early years, and in 1926 a new model emerged from the factory in Courbevoie: the 15-S-8, with a supercharged straight-eight engine and a low-slung single-seater chassis in which the driver was positioned slightly to the right, alongside the offset transmission instead of above it. Created by Albert Lory, the chief designer of the company's competitions department, it was a car that looked so far ahead of its time that it would still seem contemporary a decade later.

On its debut in 1927, at San Sebastián, the streamlined shape proved its undoing. In extreme heat, no cooling air reached the drivers, who had to be relieved by reserves in mid-race pit stops while the mechanics cut emergency ventilation holes in the bodywork. At Brooklands that year, however, there were no such problems and Louis Wagner and Robert Sénéchal took the car to its first victory. The good form continued throughout the following year, bringing wins for Robert Benoist at Linas-Montlhéry, San Sebastián, Monza and Brooklands again. With four wins in four races, the team were named world champions. At the end of the season, the windows of the four-storey Maison Delage in Courbevoie were hung with banners celebrating their triumph.

Four examples of the 15-S-8 had been built, all of which passed into private hands. In 1931 two of them were bought by Lord Howe: they were the third chassis, which Benoist had driven throughout his triumphant season, and the fourth. Francis Howe, the descendant of an old and distinguished family of English aristocrats, was already forty-seven years old. His debut as a racing driver had come only three years earlier, delayed first by a naval career and then by his election as a Member of Parliament in 1918. A familiar figure on the racing scene, distinguished by the tweed flat cap he wore outside the cockpit, he assumed the presidency of the British Racing Drivers' Club in 1929 and was seen as an elder statesman in the paddock. At the wheel, his ability was demonstrated with wins at Shelsley Walsh and Brooklands in a variety of Bugattis, Alfa Romeos and Mercedes, and in 1931 he won the 24 Hours of Le Mans, co-driving a works-prepared Alfa with Tim Birkin. The purchase of the two Delages was a further sign of his ambition, and he used the ex-Benoist car to win the Whitsun Handicap at Brooklands and the voiturette class of the Dieppe Grand Prix and the Avusrennen. When he wrote it off during the Monza Grand Prix meeting in September 1932 (his polo-type helmet saving him from serious injury), he had the wreckage crated up and sent home. He switched to the fourth chassis, but used it only occasionally over the next three years. He and the Delage

won the 1500cc class in the Eifelrennen in 1933, but it was
the third place in Berne two years later, behind the ERAs of
Seaman and Bira, that persuaded a watching Italian to approach
his employer with a radical notion.

When Ramponi looked at the Delage he saw not an outdated
piece of equipment but something full of possibilities. During
the many discussions about the future held in the garage in
Ennismore Gardens Mews, the chief mechanic put his case. At
first, Dick dismissed the idea. He could see no sense in it. Nor
could his friend Monkhouse, who sat in on the conversations.
In a sport based on rapidly evolving technology, how could a
9-year-old car become the portal to the future? But Ramponi
persisted, and began to explain how he would go about turning
the car into something capable of beating anything their rivals
might have in mind for 1936. Tony Birch, who got the point
before Seaman did, added his weight to the debate.

'We argued with him [Ramponi] until we were almost black
in the face,' Monkhouse remembered. 'We pointed out that the
design was ten years old, the car had seen its best days, it was
heavy, it had poor brakes, etc. Giulio was adamant, and maintained that the engine was of a very sound basic design, and
without impairing reliability the horsepower could be materially increased by raising the compression ratio, the chassis could
be lightened, the brakes and roadholding improved.' Finally
Ramponi lost patience with them. 'If you and Mr Seaman are
setting up as racing-car experts,' he said, 'it seems a pity I've
wasted so many years at Alfa Romeo, where I've obviously
learnt nothing.' They gave in under the weight of Ramponi's
argument, and an approach was made to the car's owner.

As it happened, Lord Howe was moving in the opposite
direction. Having watched at close quarters as the ERAs
started to win races, he decided that he had to get his hands on
one – and thus satisfy his own desire to compete in a British
car. Financially, he had no need to dispose of the remaining
Delage. He was fond of the car, although he had raced it only

three times in 1935 while otherwise occupying himself with Alfa Romeos, Maseratis and Bugattis. And once he had decided that he would let it go, he told Seaman that he wanted the top price – the equivalent of what a comparable new car would cost: close to £2,000.

The £1,400 from the sale of the ERA had not yet been received from Manby-Colegrave, and Dick also had salaries to pay and parts to buy. He went back to his mother for the money to buy the Delage, asking her for £3,000. With his father gone, there might be less resistance. 'I bet you she won't give it to you,' Monkhouse said as they sat in a car outside 3 Ennismore Gardens. 'I bet you she will,' Dick said, and went inside. At first Lilian resisted the idea of paying so much money for an old car, demanding an explanation. He was only too pleased to give it, saying that £1,000 of the money would be spent on the planned modifications. Within minutes he was back in the car alongside Monkhouse, triumphantly brandishing the cheque. It would not be the last.

The next morning he paid the money into his own account at the Westminster Bank in St James's Street and transferred the agreed amount to Lord Howe. The deal was done and in November the blue Delage, with its two spare engines and an ample quantity of spares, many of them scavenged from the Monza wreck, made the short journey from Howe's garage in Pitt's Head Mews, behind his house on Curzon Street in Mayfair, to Seaman's workshop, where Ramponi and his colleagues knuckled down to what would be a five-month project, less the chief mechanic's Christmas holiday with his family in Milan.

◆

On the second day of the new year Dick wrote to the Hotel Bellevue in Davos, where Whitney Straight was skiing with his wife and his brother. He thanked Whitney for the Christmas presents sent to himself and his mother and mentioned that he was off to Paris on a day trip to see Albert Lory at Delage.

'Giulio is coming back this week, so we shall be able to get a move on with the car.' Between shooting trips to Yorkshire and Cumbria, Dick had plunged into a blizzard of correspondence, drafting letter after letter to suppliers, to be typed up on his own new headed notepaper. Occasionally he would pop downstairs to consult with Ramponi while watching the slow transformation of the Delage. The priorities were to replace certain components with better ones – particularly the braking system – and to reduce the car's overall weight, the two factors linked wherever possible.

He wrote to Tom Murray Jamieson, asking for the maximum boost his design of supercharger would give on the Delage. Murray Jamieson had been noted for his work on the record-breaking supercharged Austin 750cc single-seaters, and Dick also mentioned that he had written to Sir Herbert Austin to ask if one of the latest cars could be placed at his disposal for continental races. 'Perhaps you could discuss this with him,' he suggested. Five days later he received a polite refusal from the Austin company, but Murray Jamieson visited Ennismore Gardens and, after inspecting the Delage, told Seaman and Ramponi that the existing supercharger was perfectly adequate. Dick also asked him about the progress of his plan to build a proper British Grand Prix car, something they had discussed at Brooklands in November.

Word of the modifications was getting around, arousing curiosity and a degree of scepticism. Early in the new year the publisher and editor of *Motor Sport*, T. G. Moore, requested an appointment to come and take a look. There was also a letter from Sammy Davis at *The Autocar*: 'I am glad you have got rid of the ERA so quickly, and I hope things are progressing well with the Delage. Would you be able to drive an Aston in the TT, do you think?' Dick's response was swift and positive: 'provided my expenses were paid and I received a percentage of anything which I might win.' As for the Delage, he said, they were at a temporary standstill, waiting for specially made parts to arrive.

Albert Lory had responded to a query about valve clearances and a request for gearbox parts for the car he had created ten years earlier. The designer regretted that Delage only had a spare gearbox for the 2-litre model, which would have to be modified to fit the 1500. Dick wrote back to say he would take it. He enclosed a cheque for 1,000 francs, on condition that if the adaptation could not be made, he would send the gearbox back and expect his money to be reimbursed. There was an extensive correspondence with Hepworth & Grandage of Birmingham, who were being asked to manufacture a set of their Hepolite pistons for the Delage. 'We should be quite prepared to supply you with any special pistons you may require, without cost,' the firm replied, complimenting him on his success in the previous season. Now on the lookout for every available financial saving, Dick sought free spark plugs from Bosch in Acton, free carburettors from H. M. Hobson & Son in Wolverhampton, free or discounted valves from Standard in Northampton, an electron bell-housing and a prop shaft at near cost price (after haggling) from ENV in north-west London, Hartford shock absorbers from T. E. André & Co. of Putney, free clutch and brake linings (and win bonuses) from Ferodo in Stockport, oil and petrol tanks and chassis parts in Dural alloy from Dürener Metallwerke of Cologne, steering-box castings and front axle ends from Laystall of Southwark, and ball and roller bearings from Hoffmann of Chelmsford at 60 per cent off. There were parallel negotiations over tyres with Dunlop in England and Englebert in Belgium, ending up in the favour of the English company, whose win bonuses ranged from £25 for Shelsley Walsh and the Coppa Acerbo Junior to a top rate of £75 for the Mille Miglia, the Tourist Trophy, the British Empire Trophy and the French and Italian Grands Prix.

Sometimes Dick's powers of persuasion fell short: not even the recital of his recent racing record would persuade Superflexit of Slough to let him have free piping. Neither Hepworth & Grandage nor Ferodo took up his suggestion that, for an annual fee of £10, they might like to have their name on the side of the Dodge transporter. Super Line Bodies of Stratford, east London, specialists in sign painting, were commissioned to paint his name in capital letters and Dunlop's name and slogan – 'The Performance Tyre' – on both flanks of the lorry, for the sum of £2 10s. Later a second sponsor would be added: 'Essolube: The 5-star motor oil'. The Dodge was insured with Stafford Knight & Co. of Fenchurch Street, who also covered the Delage – valued for the purpose at £1,200, although much more had and would be spent on it – and two mechanics for a premium of £66 10s.

Tony Birch, meanwhile, was in Germany, exploring the possibility of ordering a new lightweight chassis for the car. He was also talking to suppliers, discussing magnetos with Bosch and negotiating with Zahnradfabrik (ZF) in Friedrichshafen over a self-locking differential and a gearbox in a lightweight aluminium-silicon alloy called Silium. Eventually ZF came up with quotes of RM 495 for the gearbox and 350 for the differential, or about £40 and £28 respectively. After consulting Ramponi, Dick ordered the differential and decided against the gearbox. Perhaps sensing a cool reception in Ennismore Gardens Mews, Birch backed off from an earlier suggestion that the car should be assembled at the Dürener works in Cologne – not least, he argued, because the Nürburgring would be nearby for testing. The scheme for a lightweight chassis was eventually abandoned.

◆

Dick's exploits had begun to attract fan mail. Typical was a letter received in late February from a pupil at the Leys School in Cambridge: 'Dear Sir, As a motor racing enthusiast I am naturally very interested in your activities, and I should be very pleased if you would let me have your autograph. If you could let me have a photograph, I should be even more delighted. Wishing you best of luck with your Delage this season. Yours faithfully, J. Lowrey.'

A week after replying to his young admirer, the frustrations of the previous season were briefly reawakened when the publisher of *Speed* offered him the right of reply to a letter written by Ken Hall, a former ERA mechanic, in response to Seaman's article on his experiences with the R1B in 1935. Hall wrote:

> Mr Seaman's article leads one to believe that until he took his car away from the care of English Racing Automobiles, it was never properly prepared. I consider this attitude most unfair, and a slight on all concerned with the production of this fine car. Mr Seaman did not mention the short time in which his car was built, the work that went on almost unceasingly night and day to finish it in time for his first race, the work that was done at the Nürburgring (by ERA mechanics) to replace the broken piston, when they had more than enough on hand with the works cars to prepare ... As I know Mr Seaman to be a good sportsman, as well as a very fine driver, I am sure that he would not wish any misunderstanding between him and those responsible for his car.

In his reply, Dick disavowed any intention to criticise the work of the mechanics – 'an excellent lot of fellows' – but pointed to Hall's own mention of the time occupied in preparing the works entries. 'This is exactly the reason why, halfway through the season, I decided it would be better to relieve the ERA factory of the necessity of looking after my car,' he wrote. As it happened, Hall left ERA early in 1936 to accept a job with the White Mouse team, working on Bira's cars; so perhaps he, too, had not found Bourne to be the ideal environment.

◆

As if he were not busy enough, Seaman got it into his head to have a tilt at the world land speed record, then held by Malcolm Campbell, who had broken the 300mph barrier the previous September in his *Blue Bird*, powered by a Rolls–Royce aero engine, on the Bonneville salt flats in Utah. Previous records had been set at Daytona Beach in Florida, and when Dick discovered that the Daytona authorities were offering a significant financial reward to anyone who could recapture the record on their measured mile, a plan began to take shape.

The best person to design the chassis, it was thought, would be Dr Ferdinand Porsche, once with Mercedes-Benz but now a freelance designer responsible not just for Auto Union's Grand Prix cars but for the dramatically streamlined machine in which Hans Stuck had recently set a flying mile class record of 199.01mph. Birch, based in Germany, was ideally placed to make an approach. 'I find that the Daytona town council is offering a prize of 100,000 dollars (£20,000) to anyone besting the present record on Daytona sands,' Dick wrote to his manager. 'So will you ask Porsche if the suspension of his car would be good enough to run at Daytona. I suggest that you do not tell him about the prize or he will put his price up.'

Writing directly to Dick, Dr Porsche pointed out that the cost of designing and building such a car, with a new engine of sufficient power, would be 'not far from £100,000'. 'Under these circumstances,' he continued, putting it tactfully, 'we have to ask whether the sum can be raised for this venture.' A much cheaper fallback plan, also suggested to Dr Porsche, was to build a chassis around two 650hp Napier Dagger aero engines, an advanced twenty-four-cylinder design used on the Handley Page Heyford bomber. After visiting Dr Porsche in Stuttgart, Birch reported back: 'The cost will be too large in producing a car with special engine, so he proposes making a 1/10 scale model of a car with the Dagger engines lying flat. He says it will possibly give 350mph. The cost of the model and the testing in a wind tunnel is being worked out and I shall know tomorrow. After the tests he will be able to say with certainty the speeds obtainable, and the cost of a chassis to take the two engines.'

On 16 January Dr Porsche again wrote to Seaman, offering to prepare sketches of the general outline of the twin-engined car, followed by the building of a wooden model in 1:2.5 scale, suitable for assessment in a wind tunnel, at a cost of £850. If Seaman agreed, Dr Porsche added, it might be possible to prepare a costing of the project, excluding engines and testing, by the time of the Berlin Motor Show, four weeks hence. Dick wrote back to say that it would be essential to work out a complete budget for the finished car before spending £850 on a wind-tunnel model. He would not be able to make it to the Berlin show – 'We are very busy building the new 1.5-litre car' – but asked Porsche to press on with a rough estimate of the cost of a car with the Napier engines. Porsche's response was swift: the cost of building such a car would be in the region of £8–10,000. 'This may seem at first glance somewhat high but you have to bear in mind that we are talking about single pieces which are hand-made with extreme care and must undergo the most rigorous testing. Naturally we want to avoid unexpected surprises in the future so set the bar at the top end.' He concluded by observing that his design studio needed to make a small profit on the job, since the business could not live by publicity alone.

Dick had already been harbouring doubts. 'I think we should have considerable difficulty in getting two Daggers on reasonable terms,' he wrote to Birch on 16 January. In his final letter to Stuttgart, on 19 February, he told Dr Porsche: 'I have carefully considered everything, and I have come to the conclusion that the proposed record car should be left until later. In the first place, two record cars are being built in America and it would be better to wait and see how fast they are. Secondly, the publicity would be worth so much more if we could beat the Americans. Therefore I will contact you at a later date.' It was the last word they exchanged on the matter.

There was still time for involvement in Whitney Straight's commercial projects. In January, Dick had resigned from the board of Air Commerce Ltd and sold his five hundred £1 shares to another director for £750. Later that month he bought a thousand £1 shares in Ramsgate Airport Ltd, of which he became a director. Through his association with these Straight-led companies, Dick was also the registered owner of several aeroplanes. It was an arrangement of convenience, made because Straight was still a US national – something that would change during the year, when he applied for and was granted British citizenship. This made Dick the temporary owner of a Leopard Moth and a General Aircraft ST-25 Monospar utility aircraft, and in March he received a letter from Ramsgate Airport, noting the imminent delivery of the company's new Hawk Moth. 'Mr Straight would be extremely obliged if you would allow the machine to be registered in your name,' the company secretary wrote, enclosing the appropriate forms for signature and submission to the Air Ministry. In April, Straight wrote to ask if he 'would mind owning the two new Scions' – a reference to the purchase of a pair of Short Scion nine-passenger seaplanes for the use of one of Whitney's airlines.

◆

While the Delage was being so painstakingly remodelled, Dick had written to Harry Rose, who had bought Straight's black Maserati 8CM, to ask if he could borrow the car for the British Empire Trophy at Donington Park in April. Rose now lived in Grosvenor House on Park Lane and kept his extensive stable of cars in Lancaster Mews in Bayswater, where Ramponi and his business partner Bill Rockall had set up their business. Since he planned to drive an Alfa Romeo at the meeting, he was happy to agree – and to accept Dick's request to modify one of the Maserati's spare engine blocks, reducing the capacity of the car to 2.7 litres for the event in order to take better advantage of a handicapping system based on engine size.

Ramponi, already thoroughly familiar with the car, carried out the work so successfully, using specially made Hepolite pistons, that Dick was able to open his season with a resounding win in the 100-mile handicap race, the Maserati finishing ahead of Fairfield's 1.5-litre ERA. He split the £400 prize money, plus £145 from his petrol supplier, with Rose after paying the entry fee, insurance premium and running expenses himself. There would also be bonuses of £20 from Ferodo – who featured his success in an advertisement on the front cover of the May issue of *Motor Sport* – and RM 300 from Bosch. He wrote immediately to Hepworth & Grandage. 'I thought you would be glad to know that I was successful in winning the British Empire Trophy race yesterday, using the pistons with which you supplied me,' he told them. 'The engine ran extremely well throughout, and on lifting the head afterwards we found the pistons to be in perfect condition. I wish to thank you very much indeed for your co-operation in this matter.'

When the news of the result reached Italy, a telegram was sent from Bologna to Ennismore Gardens: + FELICITAZIONE VIVISSIME BRILLANTE MAGNIFICA VITTORIA = MASERATI +

13

Music to the ears

'The comings and goings between the garage and my house in Ennismore Gardens were terrific during the time that the Delage car was taken to pieces and rebuilt,' Lilian Seaman remembered. 'In a very short space of time, the £1,000 apportioned to rebuild the Delage was exhausted, and Dick stood before me, with further requests for money to pay the mechanics' wages alone each week, to say nothing of the sheaves of bills from motor engineers apparently from all over England. Dick would come round from his garage while I was out and place a pile of accounts on my desk, with a little note in his own handwriting on top, saying, "Would you please sign cheques for these." And there was no choice left to me but to do so. From the first to last of my son's motor racing career, from the time he joined the Cambridge University Automobile Club to the day Mercedes engaged him to race for Germany, Dick obtained from me by easy stages just over £30,000. In addition to this sum he also spent all his racing fees, entry monies and the large sums he obtained from the big advertising firms.'

Eight decades later, the equivalent of her £30,000 would be just over £2 million. There was also a rapidly increasing telephone bill. 'My telephone account for trunk calls by Dick, all over England, and long–distance calls to the continent was truly staggering, but I never offered one word of protest, because the Delage was under way for next season, and it was literally the light of his life.'

In his absences she found herself answering the door to people, often chauffeurs from nearby houses, who had heard about the car and were curious to see it. While knowing that Dick generally declined such requests, she felt it churlish to refuse, and the enthusiastic response as they peered into the garage made her think that she might be getting her money's worth for the original £3,000 cheque.

She recalled, too, the excitement in Ennismore Gardens on the day the rebuilt machine burst into life and Ramponi drove it out of the garage for the first time. When Dick himself took the wheel, the excitement was even greater. An item in *Motor Sport* reported that the car had been driven around the streets of Knightsbridge without the mudguards, lights, silencer and registration plates required by law: 'Perhaps the police purposely averted their eyes, knowing the prestige of the car's young English driver on the continent.' John Dugdale also came to watch – and to listen. The sound of the unsilenced eight-cylinder engine, he said, was 'a joy to hear, real music to the ears of a twentieth-century sportsman'.

Watching the Delage being driven around Princes Gate was the closest Dick's mother would get to seeing it in action. He had always forbidden her to attend his races, saying that the track might be a place for wives and girlfriends, but it was not for mothers. When she joked that she would go to Donington Park in disguise, he gave her another reason, which was that the bond between them would disturb his concentration while he was trying to race. That argument was one she was happy to accept.

◆

In the spring, *Motor Sport* paid an official visit to the mews. 'Seaman has been hard at work all winter rebuilding and revising the 1.5-litre Delage which he has bought from Earl Howe,' the editor reported. 'Converting the car to independent front suspension was found to be too complicated, and the idea has been dropped for the present, but the front springs have now been shifted outside the chassis to lessen the twisting effect of the brakes on the front axle. After the servo locked on him at Monza, causing the car to wrap itself round a tree, Lord Howe changed over to mechanical brakes, and Seaman has carried things a stage further by using Lockheed hydraulic brakes. By fitting light tanks, body and other chassis fittings, the total weight of the car has been reduced from 1,900 lbs to 1,500 (13½ cwt) or about the same as the ERAs. In its original trim the engine gave 150hp, producing a speed of 130mph, but the compression has been considerably raised, so it should develop about 200. Anyhow if anything bursts, Seaman has a brace of spare engines. The gearbox is one of those built for the 2-litre twelves, with five gears.'

In fact the weight savings included a reduction of 70lb by using the five-speed gearbox, 95lb by fitting a new fuel tank, and 28lb by ordering a set of Duralumin wheels. Ramponi had spent hours adjusting the engine's timing, using a protractor against the flywheel to check the tappet settings. Its debut in Dick's hands had been planned for the Prince Rainier Cup at Monte Carlo on 11 April, but even after three months of solid work it was not ready. Ramponi believed that it needed a proper test before exposure to competition, so instead they went to the Nürburgring, where a week of running produced satisfactory results. The engine was now producing a reliable 195bhp, which Ramponi believed to be a higher figure than any of their rivals, and the lightened chassis and new brakes gave Seaman cause for optimism as he thrashed around the Eifel mountains, getting comfortable with the car's characteristics. In his absence the Coupe Prince Rainier was a clean sweep for ERA, with Bira heading Marcel Lehoux, the French star newly recruited to the official team, and the Greek shipping heir Nicky Embiricos.

The rebuilt Delage was unveiled to the world at Donington

Park on 9 May, entered in two events at a meeting run by the Derby & District Motor Club. Onlookers and rivals in the paddock noted that the black-painted car looked sleeker than during its years in light blue with Lord Howe, but they were not impressed when Dick's time in practice was five seconds slower than the mark set by Bira's ERA. Had Seaman and Ramponi outsmarted themselves? The first race, a ten-lap handicap, provided the answer. Headed off the line by the ERAs of Bira and Peter Whitehead, Dick overtook them both within two laps and mopped up the earlier starters with ease. On that bitterly cold spring afternoon the car's potential was underlined in its second outing, when the Delage swept past Whitehead's ERA, this time driven by Peter Walker, to win a five-lap scratch race. *Motor Sport*'s verdict was unequivocal: 'A full justification of Seaman's faith in this ten-year-old car.'

It was with confidence that Dick took the Delage to the Isle of Man for its first long-distance test: the RAC's International Light Car Race, a 200-mile race around a 4-mile course on public roads. He told *Motor Sport*'s correspondent that the job of weight reduction had not been completed: the car was now down to 14cwt, still 56lb heavier than the ERAs. 'The chassis Seaman tells me is more whippy than the English cars, but this helps it to follow the ground, rather in the style of a dachshund. The engine gives very little power below 4,500rpm and the four top gears of the five-speed gearbox are constantly in use. Maximum revs are 7,500, but the exhaust note, strangely enough, is quite low-pitched, rather like a monoposto Alfa.'

Lehoux's ERA recorded the fastest lap in practice over the four-sided course, ahead of Bira and Seaman, but since he was found to have set the time at the wheel of Lord Howe's car, the latter was placed in pole position while the Frenchman was relegated to the fifth row. On the eve of the race, Seaman had dinner with Chula and Bira; when Chula asked if it was true, as he had been told, that the Delage could go the full distance without refuelling, Dick smiled and said he didn't know, after which he proceeded to beat Bira at ping-pong.

Race day, a Thursday, was bright and warm. As the grid formed up on the narrow road in front of a packed grandstand, the Delage faced no fewer than nine ERAs. Howe made a good start, chased by Seaman, who had passed Bira before the first corner. The order held for four laps before the Delage took the lead; a lap later, experiencing fuel-feed problems, Howe stopped long enough to put himself out of contention. Thereafter for Dick it was a matter of slowly increasing his lead over Bira and Lehoux. When he took the chequered flag, he was a minute and a quarter ahead of the first ERA. In two hours and fifty-two minutes the Delage had given him only one scare, around half-distance, when he heard a sudden graunch from the rear axle as he changed down. He slowed, briefly fearing that his race might be over, but on accelerating again the car behaved normally and the problem did not recur.

Four days later Seaman was at Brooklands for the BARC's Whit Monday meeting, leaving the Delage in London and taking the wheel of a 1926 Bugatti Type 37A. This much-travelled, much-modified car had just been sold by its joint owner-drivers, Eileen Ellison and T. P. Cholmondeley-Tapper, to Richard Barklie Lakin, a 21-year-old Royal Navy subma-riner, and adapted to take independent front suspension at Leslie Ballamy's garage in south London. Seaman had raced against the car several times over the previous couple of seasons; he received the invitation from Ballamy, who had sold him the Ford V8 saloon two years earlier. Entered for two handicap races on the Mountain circuit, the Bugatti failed to complete a lap, thanks to a crippling misfire.

The Delage was back in action two weeks later on a European trip that took in the Eifelrennen and the Grand Prix de Picardie. At the Nürburgring, Seaman led the sixteen-strong voiturette field from the start, but in heavy drizzle he left the road at speed halfway round the opening lap while taking the right-handed kink at Adenauer Forst. He restarted and limped back to the pits, but damage to the oil tank forced him to retire, leaving the victory to the Maserati of Count Carlo Felice Trossi, a gifted Italian amateur who had been Europe's hill-climb champion two years earlier. In the afternoon Dick could watch Rosemeyer earning himself an instant promotion to honorary SS Obersturmführer – the equivalent of a platoon commander – by winning the main event for Auto Union, while Charlie Martin, competing during his honeymoon, returned to the pits on foot to report to Marjorie, his new bride, that his 3.2-litre Alfa was upside down in a ditch. The Mercedes team was completely eclipsed, a phenomenon highlighted by *Motor Sport*. 'The cars look all right, sound all right, and go all right,' the magazine noted, 'but they are no longer their supreme selves of 1935.' Alfred Neubauer's frown, it reported, was 'enough to terrify the most hardened interviewer'.

The magazine also made a point that illuminated the rationale behind the desire of Seaman and some of his contemporaries to concentrate on continental races: 'The astonishing fact has to be assimilated that 300,000 people visited the Nürburg Ring for the Eifel race meeting. That it pelted with rain and clouds descended did not detract one whit from the success of the event. In the German mind it is the racing that counts. Would that a similar state of affairs could be reached in Britain! One is forced to the dismal conclusion that the limit of our countrymen's intelligence is to hit a ball about.'

At the post-race banquet, Dick admitted his driving error. 'This was a most agreeable characteristic of Seaman,' Chula, his first biographer, noted. 'Whenever he made a mistake, he just admitted it, without blaming a crash on faulty brakes or other things, as many drivers would do.' Dick's luck did not improve on his next outing, at the Péronne circuit in Picardy, where – after the drizzle of the Eifel mountains – the mechanics had to shelter from a burning sun under umbrellas in the open pits. The triangular circuit, laid out on fast open roads between small towns, had been in use since 1925. Seaman was feeling under the weather when he arrived, his mood not improved by being billeted in an attic room of an unsatisfactory hotel. He considered going home, but thought better of it and got himself ready for a race to be run in the form of two 60-mile heats and a 90-mile final. Fairfield, newly recruited to the ERA works team, set the fastest lap in practice, ahead of Trossi, with Seaman and Bira equal third.

Trossi won the first ten-lap heat, ahead of Fairfield and Bira. In the second heat Howe took the lead, while Mays in his Zoller-supercharged car blasted past the Delage 'so fast on the straight that he [Seaman] felt as if he had been overtaken by an Auto Union', according to Chula. Mays passed Howe, too, before his engine failed. By then Seaman had overtaken Howe and was able to claim a place in the fifteen-lap final. He was still feeling odd when the race was flagged away, allowing Fairfield and Bira to battle for the lead in the early stages while he fought Trossi for third place. On the fourth lap, however, at the end of the 2-mile straight, he misjudged his entry under heavy braking into the sharp right-hander in the village of Brie, bouncing over a sandbank and coming to rest with bent steering and a damaged rear wheel. He sat in the stationary car for some time, ruing another error and counting his blessings that he had not been injured. It was, Chula added, the only time he ever admitted to having frightened himself.

He stayed in France for the following week's French Grand Prix, run that year at the Linas-Montlhéry autodrome outside Paris and restricted to sports cars. This was partly to give a better chance to the Bugattis, which no longer stood a chance in current Grand Prix racing, and also to fill out the entry. The increasing influence of world affairs on sport lay behind the absence of the Italian teams: their government had banned them from entering races in countries that had joined the economic sanctions imposed by the League of Nations after Mussolini's troops had invaded Abyssinia from Italian Somaliland to start the Second Italo–Abyssinian War in 1935. Britain and France, wanting to avoid a war and preferring Mussolini as an ally rather than Hitler, proposed the Hoare–Laval Pact, which would have given Italy certain territories, but the plan was scuppered by haggling over the details. So there were no Alfas or Maseratis competing in France that weekend.

Seaman accepted an invitation to co-drive an Aston Martin Ulster in the 1,000km race, along with the car's owner, Tom Clarke, a fellow Cambridge man who had co-driven a similar machine to eighth place at Le Mans the previous year. On the day, Dick proved to be too fast for the car. He wore out the brake linings and distorted the drums, forcing the car into retirement at half-distance. At least the French were satisfied: Raymond Sommer and Jean-Pierre Wimille took the win for Bugatti.

Two weeks later, with the Delage still under repair, Dick paid his first visit to Spa-Francorchamps, the 8-mile road circuit in the Belgian Ardennes, to partner the Hon. Freddie Clifford, a former Grenadier Guards officer, at the wheel of a works-entered Lagonda LG45 in the 24-hour race. This would be his only experience of a round-the-clock sports-car contest, and it was a successful one. In cold, rainy conditions typical of the region, the winners were Sommer and Francesco Severi in an Alfa entered by the Scuderia Ferrari, but in finishing fourth overall Seaman and Clifford won their class, having covered 1,740 miles at an average of 73mph.

A week later, Dick heard the news that Marcel Lehoux, driving a works 2-litre ERA, had been one of two fatalities at the Deauville Grand Prix, held along the beachfront avenue and around the streets of the fashionable resort on the Normandy coast. The war in Abyssinia had not quite ended, but the League of Nations' sanctions had been lifted, and Lehoux, lying second, had collided with Nino Farina as the Italian was trying to lap him in one of the Scuderia Ferrari's Alfas. Both cars overturned and the drivers were thrown out, the 48-year-old Lehoux, the winner of ten Grands Prix, receiving head injuries from which he later died in hospital. Farina was merely shaken up; this would not be the only such incident in which he was involved during his long career. Earlier in the race Raymond Chambost had overturned his Maserati, suffering fatal injuries. Wimille's Bugatti took a subdued win for France, and motor racing would never return to Deauville's Boulevard de la Mer.

Still filling in time while Ramponi worked away in London, Dick accepted another invitation: this one from Gino Rovere, now a shareholder in the Maserati company, to drive a works-prepared Maserati V8RI car in the German Grand Prix, under the banner of the Scuderia Torino, a semi-works team of which Rovere was president. It must have seemed an enticing prospect, particularly since the V8RI – with its supercharged 4.5-litre engine and its all-independent suspension – had been introduced less than a year earlier as a direct response to the power and handling of the Mercedes and Auto Unions.

This was his first chance to lead a continental team, his first experience of racing alongside full Grand Prix cars, and his first crack at one of the classic Grandes Épreuves counting towards the European championship (the others that season were the Monaco, Swiss and Italian races). But the car arrived at the Nürburgring a day late and never felt right, its power inadequate and its handling deeply unpleasant. A severe vibration made life uncomfortable, causing such damage to the hydraulic brake pipes during the race that after three laps Seaman had virtually no brakes left and pulled in to retire. A poor showing in any circumstances, he felt, but particularly in front of a crowd of 350,000. Five laps later Count Trossi, in the Scuderia Torino's 2.5-litre Maserati, pulled in for a tyre change and courteously offered Dick the wheel for the remainder of the race, enabling him to do something more enjoyable than sit in the pits and watch the Auto Unions of Rosemeyer and Stuck deal another blow to their Mercedes rivals. He managed to finish eighth, his performance in the outclassed car described as 'one of the outstanding features of the day' by *The Autocar*'s Rodney Walkerley, who added that the German newspapers were 'very impressed with Seaman's driving and regretted that he had not had a faster car'.

The size of the crowd indicated the role played by sport in Germany under the 3-year-old National Socialist government. A week later Hitler's Olympic Games opened in Berlin, where the AVUS track would be used for the 50km walk, the marathon and the cycling road race. 'No nation since Ancient Greece has captured the true Olympic spirit as has Germany,' Avery Brundage, the president of the US Olympic committee, proclaimed as the Games opened on 1 August, having seen off the threat of a boycott by American athletes in protest against Hitler's treatment of Germany's Jewish population. During a fact-finding trip to Berlin two years earlier, Brundage – later the president of the International Olympic Committee – had responded to being told that Jews were excluded from German sports clubs by telling his hosts: 'In my club in Chicago, Jews are not permitted either.'

14

The Voronoff Delage

On Dick's desk at home one day in 1936 his mother found evidence that he was planning to invite his motor racing friends to a grand house party at Pull Court. He had prepared a list in which he assigned rooms to his guests: the State bedroom to Chula, the French bedroom to Bira, the Stuart bedroom to Lord Howe, the Tudor bedroom to Mark Pepys, the 6th Earl of Cottenham, who had been Segrave's teammate at Tours in 1923 before becoming a prominent advocate of safe-driving techniques on the road, and so on. The problem, from Lilian Seaman's standpoint, was that the number and quality of staff she had been able to engage would be nowhere near enough to cope with such an event in the required style.

Reluctant to accept the scuppering of his plans, Dick drove around the neighbouring towns with her, visiting employment agencies in the search for suitable staff. He met, she said, the same response everywhere: 'Nothing suitable on their books. The Dole had been their ruin.' The dole – from the Old English word *dāl*, meaning one's allotted portion – had been introduced to Britain in 1920 via the Unemployment Insurance Act. Initially providing thirty-nine weeks of payments to those who had fallen out of work, it quickly became the focus of discontent from left and right: from communists who believed it delayed the prospect of revolution and from landowners who blamed it for the increasing difficulty of maintaining their country houses.

Infuriated, Dick drafted a letter in his mother's name, complaining to the Unemployment Assistance Board in London about the situation that had been created. 'The replies we received from the board were most unsatisfactory,' Lilian remembered, 'and left us with the definite idea that the government entirely approved of and encouraged both men and women to remain out of work, and were enjoying the high taxation inflicted, to bring about this condition of the country.' The words 'house party' never crossed Dick's lips again, she said. 'He had received his lesson in practical politics. And, to my great regret, from that day he lost his interest in Pull Court.'

What was worse in Dick's eyes was the contrast with Germany, where on his racing trips he had seen the effect of the new government's policies. Even the humblest cottage or the smallest farm, he assured his mother, was always in the most perfect order. 'Hitler stands no nonsense there,' he told her. 'He won't have any slackers about. Everybody has got to work. Consequently he has remade and reorganised the country, and that is why they believe in him and rally round him.'

Richard Seaman was hardly alone among members of the English upper middle class in voicing approval of the Third Reich and its works before the naked reality revealed itself. The novelist Anthony Powell would make a minor character in *A Dance to the Music of Time* casually voice a widely held opinion: 'I like the little man they've got in Germany now.' In those days many such people were accustomed to visiting the country, enjoying its opera and its schlosses, and sending their daughters to Munich to be 'finished', as an alternative to Paris or Lausanne. Their impression was of a country that had emerged proud and self-confident, its society stabilised and its culture restored, from the near-anarchy and financial collapse of the Weimar era. The Liberal peer Lord Hankey, formerly Lloyd George's cabinet secretary, had reported during the new regime's first year a sense of 'extraordinary exaltation' among the people: 'clean trams, hot water in the hotels, well-dressed people enjoying themselves, a holiday atmosphere everywhere'. The following year Sir Arnold Wilson MP, who liked to describe himself as a 'left-wing radical Tory', travelled extensively in the country and told an audience in Königsberg: 'During the past three months I have watched Young Germany at work and at play in every part of the country. I admire the intense energy evoked by the National Socialist movement. I respect the patriotic ardour of German youth. I recognise, I almost envy, the depth and earnestness of the search for national unity which inspires your schools and colleges because it is wholly unselfish, it is wholly good.'

In 1936 a Scottish schoolgirl named Ida Anderson visited the Rhineland with a party of pupils from George Watson's Ladies' College in Edinburgh and met a group of storm-troopers in Heidelberg. 'How charming and polite they were,' she observed. A hockey team from Charterhouse School met nothing but 'marvellous friendliness' at a tournament in Cologne. The 17-year-old Joan Stafford-King-Harman came back from Munich, where she had spent a year studying the piano, feeling 'madly pro-Hitler' (later she would work with the code-breakers at Bletchley Park). Tom Neil, a railway man-ager's son from Bootle, was also seventeen when he attended a summer camp in Germany, making friends with a member of the Hitler Youth and enjoying the 'indescribable electricity' of their campfire singalongs (he would still be in his teens when, piloting a Hurricane in the Battle of Britain, he made the first of his fourteen 'kills').

From statesmen to schoolchildren, what they did not see at the time was the method by which Hitler had engineered the revival, sanctioning a large-scale programme of public works by increasing the national debt to a scale that could only be paid back when Germany fought his planned war and plundered the lands they conquered. Similarly, the vast and illegal rearmament programme – initially concentrating on the army and air force, since the Führer anticipated making an alliance with Britain that would see the Royal Navy taking control of the seas – was disguised and paid for by the creation of promissory notes that could be traded between companies and did not appear on the government's official declaration of expenditure. Nor, in the early years of the Third Reich, did many choose to notice Hitler's policies towards Jews, communists, gypsies, homosexuals and the mentally ill.

A pervasive fear that the Russian Revolution would spread its influence westwards had fuelled powerful anti-communist feelings, explicitly conflated by Hitler with the ambient anti-semitism lurking, even at the best of times, only just beneath the surface of European society. To some in Britain – by no means restricted to the members of extreme groups like Sir Oswald Mosley's British Union of Fascists, or fanatical supporters such as Unity Mitford, the daughter of Lord Redesdale and Mosley's sister-in-law, who had successfully expended so much effort and emotional energy on gaining admittance to the Führer's circle – Hitler was seen as a bulwark against what he called 'Judeo-Bolshevism'.

Many years later, Dick's schoolfriend John Dugdale described in his memoirs how they were taken in by Germany under National Socialism. 'One had a sneaking feeling of admiration for their purposefulness,' he wrote. 'Here was a group of people who knew what they wanted and were determined to get it – something democracy can lack. We just hoped it was all a bad dream. How wrong we were.'

◆

To Dick's relief, Ramponi announced that the Delage would be ready at the beginning of August for the Coppa Ciano – a race named in honour of the locally born Fascist politician Count Costanzo Ciano, whose son was married to Mussolini's daughter. One of the spare engines had been fitted, and further small modifications had been carried out as a result of their analysis of the car's performance in its five races to date, which had yielded three wins and two retirements through crashes. But there was frustration when the car was held up for three days at the frontier between France and Italy, arriving in time only for the final hour of practice.

Held in Livorno, a harbour town on the Tuscan coast known to the English as Leghorn, the 1936 edition of the race was run for the first time on a shortened version of the Montenero circuit, cut from 13 to 4.5 miles. Despite the lack of practice time, Dick was able to lead the race for the first three laps until the fuel pump stopped working, requiring him to pump by hand while driving at racing speed. Inevitably he dropped back to finish sixth, four minutes behind Trossi's winning Maserati. Later, watching the Grand Prix cars in action, he saw Nuvolari break the transmission of his twelve-cylinder Alfa on the starting line and then take over Carlo Pintacuda's car to win with what Dick described in a letter to Monkhouse as 'a colossal display of driving' by a man they both admired enormously.

Two weeks later Dick was on the other side of Italy, in Pescara, where the Delage showed its true colours in the Coppa Acerbo Junior. In the absence of the ERA works cars, which were being prepared for the Prix de Berne a week later, Dick's most formidable rivals were Count Trossi, in the only factory-entered Maserati, and Bira's private ERA. To avoid the midday heat, the motley grid – including one local motor dealer in a Fiat Balilla sports car – was flagged away at eight o'clock in the morning. The starter, Prince Adalberto, the Duke of Bergamo, had been greeted by cheers from the grandstands in recognition of his recent feats while commanding an infantry division in the Abyssinian campaign. Dick quickly left the opposition so far behind that he could cruise to victory, completing the six laps almost forty seconds ahead of Trossi after an hour and a quarter of racing.

Two chicanes had been added to the long seafront straight, in an attempt to handicap the powerful German cars and give the Italian teams a better chance in the Grand Prix. Once he had caught his breath, Dick climbed into a Maserati – not the V8RI he had driven at the Nürburgring but an older 3-litre 8CM. Despite that unhappy earlier experience, he had accepted a further invitation from the factory to take the wheel of their only entry in this important race. Again their car performed poorly, giving him no chance of matching the Mercedes and particularly the Auto Unions, whose good form continued as Rosemeyer led a one-two-three for the team ahead of Ernst von Delius, making his debut, and Varzi. Not only was the Maserati uncompetitive, but it had been badly prepared. In the opening laps a mirror fell off and the filler cap kept springing open, dousing Seaman with fuel as he went round corners. With the water temperature soaring and the engine firing on seven of its eight cylinders, after completing four laps he called it a day in a mood of resolute disgust. 'It is,' he wrote to Monkhouse, 'the last time I shall ever drive a works Maserati.' A top Italian racing team had not been able to match the professional standards the 23-year-old Englishman had set himself.

◆

He and Birch broke their journey in the Ford V8 to the next race in Berne with a stop in Biella, north-west of Milan. There they visited the home of Count Trossi, who was keen to show them his celebrated 'special': a 1930 Mercedes-Benz SSK road-ster he had bought in 1932, commissioning new bodywork that featured long faired coverings over the front and rear wheels and an endless louvred bonnet shrouding its supercharged 7-litre engine. With its gleaming black paintwork and black wire wheels, this was one of the most spectacular cars of its era.

But it was Seaman's black single-seater that was making the headlines, leading one British journalist to call it 'the Voronoff Delage' – an amusing reference to Serge Voronoff, a Franco-Russian surgeon who had gained fame throughout Europe and the United States and amassed a fortune in the 1920s and '30s by grafting testicular tissue taken from monkeys onto men's testicles in order to enhance their sexual potency. Ramponi, it was implied, had become the automobile world's leading performance-enhancer. Unlike Ramponi, Voronoff turned out to be a charlatan.

And not everyone appreciated the joke. Dick arrived in Switzerland on course to complete a hat-trick of victories in the Prix de Berne to discover that Ernesto Maserati and Peter Berthon had protested against his win in Pescara, claiming that the Delage must have been illegally fitted with a 2-litre engine. Knowing there were only two races left in the season and that time was short, an infuriated Ramponi convinced the Automobile Club de Suisse and the representatives of the AIACR, the international governing body, that the engine should be sealed until the end of the season and then examined and measured. Then he had to persuade an anxious owner-driver that it would not be necessary to tinker with the engine's innards over the course of the final two events. Voices were raised, but the Italian got his way.

Dick also discovered that the works ERAs had been repainted black, Raymond Mays deciding that the usual light-green colour was bringing them bad luck. Having lost Lehoux at Deauville, the team were represented by Mays, Fairfield and Howe, whose own machine, still painted blue, was now entered by the factory; they were supported by private entries from Bira, Embiricos and Tongue. Trossi's works Maserati was withdrawn, but Dick was worried that the ERAs had used their absence from Pescara to make important modifications. When he and Fairfield posted identical times in practice on the Bremgarten circuit, smashing the existing mark in the process, he was both proved correct and comforted by the knowledge that, whatever they had come up with, the Delage could at least match it.

Dick pushed hard in the first half of the race, while Fairfield, Mays and Bira all fell away and retired. The Delage finished the twenty-eight laps a minute and a half ahead of Embiricos, with Tongue and Howe in third and fourth places. 'Seaman has endeared himself to the Swiss spectator,' *Motor Sport* proclaimed, 'by his fine driving and calm demeanour.' He had also shattered the team with whose principals, Mays and Berthon, his personal and professional relationship had deteriorated so badly; their six entries had been no match for the combination of Seaman and Ramponi.

Afterwards he was able to watch Rosemeyer, Varzi and Stuck finish the Swiss Grand Prix in the leading positions for Auto Union, once again profiting from the unreliability of their principal rivals. For Mercedes, the humiliation was exacerbated when Rosemeyer criticised Caracciola for consistently obstructing him during the early stages; their dispute boiled up into harsh words exchanged in their hotel lobby when the two German heroes encountered each other on the way to the prize-giving ceremony.

◆

Six days later the Delage was at Donington Park for the Junior Car Club's 200-mile scratch race for single-seaters in two classes, voiturettes and cars of unlimited capacity. Held on a perfect summer day in front of 10,000 spectators, with twenty-one entries, it turned out to be one of the most significant contests of Seaman's career, demonstrating the lessons experience had taught him.

Only third fastest in practice, he took the lead from the ERA of the bareheaded Peter Whitehead on the second of the scheduled seventy-seven laps as the voiturettes proved better suited to the twisty road course than the ageing Grand Prix Alfas, Maseratis and Bugattis. Within four more laps it was Howe, driving with great verve, who was chasing him hard, and Dick was lucky to miss a wheel as it rolled across the track after detaching itself from an Alfa Romeo. Once the charging Howe had overtaken him, he was content to hold station behind the ERA, although when he was held up by a back-marker, Ramponi marched along to the stewards to demand that a flag be waved.

Now a game of cat and mouse began. Howe, knowing that he would have to stop for fuel but unsure of whether his opponent would also need a top-up or a tyre change, tried to increase his margin. It was noted that Ramponi and Finlayson had put out a fuel churn and a set of wheels mounted with new tyres on the Delage's pit counter. After fifty laps, with a lead of only eight seconds, Howe arrived in the pits, losing thirty-nine seconds before he rejoined the race. Seaman responded by speeding up, as did *Motor Sport*'s breathless reporter: 'Would the Delage last? Every enthusiast present seemed to echo that question, for the modest Dick Seaman and his veteran lone-hand motor had captured everyone's imagination. Suppose the fuel would not suffice? Would the car stand up, hard pressed as it was, and not stripped since its victories in the Coppa Acerbo and the Prix de Berne?' Each time Seaman passed the pits, Ramponi held up a sign giving his lead in seconds and the number of laps to run in white figures on a small black disc; the Mercedes pit signalling under Neubauer could not have been more meticulous.

Howe, now the only survivor of the front-line ERAs, could make no further impression – and there would be no pit stop for the Delage, which was going faster as its fuel load lightened. The paraphernalia on the pit counter had been a bluff. As the chequered flag fell, the margin of victory was fifty-one seconds. More than just a victory to show the home fans what he had been up to on his continental adventures, this one demonstrated his maturity and racecraft, requiring the strategic disciplines of patience and restraint – and mechanical sympathy for a tired car – as much as sheer speed. Immediately afterwards, as Ramponi had promised, the seals affixed in Berne were removed from the Delage's engine, which was then stripped and checked by the officials. The measurements proved that its capacity was not 2 litres, as Ernesto Maserati and Peter Berthon had claimed, but 1488cc, meaning that it was completely legal.

As Seaman received the large gold cup and a cheque for £350 for his combined overall and class victory, Francis Howe could only admire the use to which his old car had been put in the hands of its new master. Of the nine races in which Dick and the Delage had taken part that season, they had won six. 'Great credit is due to Richard Seaman and his assistants for so successfully incorporating modern improvements in the Delage, improvements which have turned it from a mediocre performer into a strong favourite for every race in which it is entered,' the editor of *Motor Sport* wrote. 'As for Seaman himself, he has shown himself to be the finest road-racing driver in Britain. He possesses all the necessary qualities of the first-rank driver, confidence, cornering skill, judgement and coolness. Given a chance, he would do great things in Grand Prix racing proper.'

Dick's aggregate of eight wins in three seasons of voiturette racing, in three makes of car, would remain unmatched, even though the series continued until 1939 (in the informal final standings, Mays and Bira would be closest to him, with five wins apiece). In terms of proving himself ready for promotion to the top flight of European road racing, there was nothing more he could do. His mother's investment and Ramponi's devoted attentions had been worthwhile. The little Delage had done its job.

◆

The Maserati brothers had anticipated that he would be driving for them in the Italian Grand Prix at Monza in the last big road race of the international season, but his reaction to the dismal experiences at Pescara and Berne, and to Ernesto Maserati's part in the protest against the Delage, put an end to the notion. Instead Dick faced a different battle, the one for the BRDC's Gold Star, an annual award to drivers who collected the highest number of points in national races or who had achieved significant success in international races or had broken world speed records. Howe and Segrave were among those already awarded the distinction, and as 1936 drew to a close the points-table race for the Gold Star was between Seaman and Bira. Both men

duly turned up at Ards in Northern Ireland to race in the RAC
Tourist Trophy, for which points were awarded.

For this 410-mile handicap race for sports cars, run on public
roads, Bira was driving a BMW 328 entered by the firm's British
concessionaire, H. J. 'Aldy' Aldington of AFN Ltd, the makers
of Frazer Nash cars, while Seaman was entered in a works
Aston Martin Speed Model, built specially for the race and
painted black in his honour. Run in heavy rain, the race was
marred when a Riley crashed into the crowd on the streets of
Newtownards, leaving eight spectators dead and fifteen injured:
the worst accident in the history of British motor racing. Dick
led the early stages, but his engine failed after twelve laps, the
result of oil-pressure problems in practice and the lack of time
to run in a set of newly fitted bearings. While he was still
going, *The Autocar*'s correspondent remarked, he was 'putting
up a wonderful run in circumstances that were anything but
enviable, passing other cars being a matter of guesswork, since
the spray reduced the rival machine to a faint, water-enveloped
blur . . .' Bira's seventh place gave him enough Gold Star points
to draw level with his rival. The fatalities meant that the Ards
circuit was never used again.

With characteristic boldness, Dick had written to Alfred
Neubauer at Mercedes-Benz, hoping that his record over the
season justified a request to borrow one of their W25s for
the final races of the season, the BRDC's 500 Miles and the
Mountain Championship at Brooklands and the Donington
Grand Prix, all run for cars of unlimited capacity. He received
a courteous refusal. Mercedes did not lend out their precious
Grand Prix cars. But perhaps a note had been taken of the young
man's initiative.

The alternative was to share an ex-works Alfa Romeo 8C
35 Tipo C recently acquired by Hans Ruesch. Although the
Swiss driver was happy to agree, the car was not available for
the BRDC 500, at which, having returned from shooting
with Tony Cliff in Yorkshire, Dick was reduced to the role of

spectator and amateur paddock photographer. He was back in his racing overalls at Donington to familiarise himself with the car co-driven to victory by Nuvolari and Pintacuda in the Coppa Ciano six weeks earlier. This was an infinitely better machine than Maserati's V8RI, its 400bhp delivered with such impressive torque that the two drivers were able to lap Donington at racing speed while changing down from top gear only for the Melbourne hairpin and Redgate Corner.

As a coda to a marvellously successful season, the race could hardly have been less demanding. Setting the fastest time in practice (although the grid positions were decided by drawing lots), Seaman lapped five seconds under the lap record and four seconds faster than the car's owner. Starting from the middle of the second row, Ruesch took the wheel for the opening stint of the 306-mile race, run in autumn sunshine. After surviving a shunt up the rear from Bira's lapped Maserati, he had opened a useful lead when he pulled in at half-distance to hand over to to his partner. Seaman merely had to stroke the slightly dented car to the line, which he crossed four and a half hours after the start, having driven, in the words of Cholmondeley-Tapper, who watched from the trackside after crashing his Maserati, 'with cool precision and an air almost of being out on a country tour,' and with Charlie Martin's second-placed Alfa not even a speck in his mirror.

It was his last race of the season. He had asked to borrow the Alfa for the Mountain Championship, but Ruesch planned to drive it at Brooklands himself. This presented Bira with the chance to win the Gold Star, which he duly took. Dick gave a somewhat unguarded interview to John Dugdale, in the upstairs office at Ennismore Gardens Mews, in which he spoke of arranging his race schedule according to where he could attract the best starting money. He discussed techniques of overtaking, and offered mild criticism of British drivers for failing to copy the cornering methods of the continental aces. Dugdale showed Birch the resulting story before it was rushed into publication. The manager had already given the journalist his approval when he passed the copy on to Seaman, who hit the roof, believing that it was too personal and showed him in a bad light. He berated his old schoolfriend, and harangued the magazine's editor, too, to no avail. The magazine was already being printed and it was too late to make amendments. An infuriated Dick sent back the fee he had been paid for putting his name to the piece, and it would be some time before he and Dugdale resumed their friendship. But he had already received another piece of paper – one that would change his life.

15

The talent contest

At Dick's request, his mother dealt with the mail that arrived during his increasingly frequent absences. This included letters from members of the public, many of them young women. When she asked him why he was encouraging these admirers, he told her they were simply an occupational hazard for a racing driver and asked her to burn them, which she promptly did. Then one day when she had just returned to Ennismore Gardens from a trip to the Knightsbridge department stores, a telegram arrived in an envelope addressed simply to 'Seaman'. On opening it, she found a message inviting her son to take part in a Mercedes–Benz trial for young drivers at Monza on 20 November. Well aware of its significance, she put it back in its envelope and left it for him to find. When he arrived at the house, accompanied by Tony Birch, he read it with controlled excitement. George Monkhouse, arriving to pick Dick up for dinner at Simpson's in the Strand, was less restrained in his delight.

What Lilian did not know was that her son had already taken part in a preliminary trial at the Nürburgring at the end of October, following the arrival of an earlier telegram – which she had not intercepted – from Alfred Neubauer after the Donington Grand Prix. The Mercedes team manager had invited twenty-nine aspirants to take part. They included several men employed by Daimler-Benz, the parent company, in a variety of occupations, from a mechanic to a salesman. Later Ramponi would claim the credit for the initial approach; through contacts at the Bosch electronics company, he had suggested to Rudolf Uhlenhaut, Mercedes' young English-born technical director, that Dick was worth a trial, although the vigilant Neubauer would certainly have spotted his potential.

Seaman and Ramponi had been discussing the options for 1937. Another season among the voiturettes would prove nothing; now convinced that he could succeed at the highest level, Dick needed to make the final leap without delay. They were thinking about the Bugatti Type 57S sports model that Nicky Embiricos had crashed while battling for the lead in the Tourist Trophy. Just conceivably, Dick may have considered inviting Ramponi to use its powerful supercharged 3.3-litre straight-eight engine as the basis for a single-seater Grand Prix car: the Seaman Special of his schooldays come to life at last. Once Mercedes had shown an interest, however, all other possibilities faded into the background.

'We were searching far and wide for young talent,' Neubauer wrote in his autobiography, 'but natural racing drivers don't exactly grow on gooseberry bushes. We hit on the idea of starting a school. There was no shortage of applicants.' Once the idea was made public, he was flooded with letters from young hopefuls, 'mostly attracted by the fat prizes, fame or just speed – or a combination of all three. And it's surprising how many of those letters contain the same sentence: "I am not afraid of death." My answer invariably is: "It's not dead drivers but winning drivers that I'm looking for."'

The young candidates for the 1937 team were first sent out in 2.3-litre Mercedes road cars, which had a top speed of 75mph, and told to complete three laps of the very demanding 14-mile circuit at the seemingly modest average speed of under 40mph, which meant a lap time of twenty-two minutes. At that stage,

Neubauer was not looking for heroics but for competence, consistency, and the ability to act on a simple instruction. 'Anybody who completes a lap in less than twenty-two minutes can pack his bags,' he told them. Among the hopefuls was Hermann Schmitz, a 21-year-old from the delivery department, who had saved enough money to buy a BMW motorcycle and was in the habit of revving it noisily outside Neubauer's office window. Sent out in the sports car, he came back to the pits after completing two laps in twenty-eight minutes each, was patted encouragingly on the cheek by Neubauer, and went out again. This time he crashed at the Karussell, the long, deceptively tricky banked left-hander, and was killed. Another candidate, who had turned up for the test wearing an SS uniform, crashed at the Foxhole and disappeared from the scene altogether, leaving behind only a torn black sleeve.

The fourteen most promising performers during the initial test were then sent out in a pair of 2-year-old W25 Grand Prix cars. Twelve of them were German; the other two were Christian Kautz, the Swiss son of a Deutsche Bank director with an English Literature degree from Oxford University, and Richard Seaman, both of them twenty-three years old. Sitting in the pits as the others went out, Dick was able to appreciate the unearthly wail of the supercharged Mercedes straight-eight engine: an intimidating sound unlike anything else in motor sport. The two young drivers who most impressed Neubauer were the non-Germans: Kautz and Seaman. Particularly Seaman. 'As soon as he started,' Neubauer said of the Englishman, 'I realised that he had real talent. His first lap was excellent, and his best lap time was 10 minutes 03 seconds. A good driver does the Nürburgring in 10 minutes 15 seconds. An ace will do it in under ten minutes.'

Many years later, Neubauer would recall that the first round of testing had been a disaster. 'One of the candidates had been killed. Our sole consolation was that we had found one driver of world class: Dick Seaman.'

◆

For Mercedes, 1936 had been a season so catastrophic that they had been briefly forced to withdraw from competition in order to avoid further humiliation of the sort that, given the source of their funding, would court official displeasure. At the Nürburgring that summer, *Motor Sport* had summed up their plight: 'A cloud hangs over the Mercedes-Benz camp. Apart from the fact that the cars are not completely reliable, all is not well with the personnel. Perhaps a too-rigid discipline has resulted in a smouldering resentment, but whatever it is, the team does not seem to pull as a team. Some people say that Caracciola is favoured above the rest of the drivers, and we all know that Fagioli has been a "rebel" in the past. Chiron does not like the behaviour of the cars – he practised in one of the old type when he signed his contract. Von Brauchitsch seems to lose all interest as soon as his car gives the slightest trouble. Hermann Lang, the youngster of the team, is the only member to appear at all happy.'

It was Neubauer's responsibility to find a solution. The abrasive Fagioli and the underperforming Chiron would be leaving the team. There were arguments going on with von Brauchitsch over the financial terms of a new contract. It was time for fresh blood, and at the Monza test the most promising of the young drivers were assessed more rigorously: Heinz Brendel, Walter Bäumer, Heinz-Hugo Hartmann, Kautz and Seaman, the Englishman arriving on a flight from Croydon to Milan. A sixth man, the Italian driver Freddie Zehender, also took part; he, however, was a known quantity and had already been retained for 1937.

The five candidates – competing for two positions as reserve, or 'cadet', drivers – took turns in a pair of 1935 W25s. There was no real yardstick for them, apart from each other, given that Mercedes had missed the most recent Italian Grand Prix and that the circuit's layout had been modified from the one used the previous year, with the chicanes reprofiled and the total length extended by 110 metres to almost exactly 7 kilometres. The fastest lap in the 1936 Grand Prix had been set by Rosemeyer's Auto Union at 2 minutes 56 seconds.

The official chart of the day's activities showed that Dick was the only driver to be sent out in both cars. His times, after the out and in laps were removed, demonstrated not just his speed but a remarkably consistent progression. In the first car, on a circuit entirely unfamiliar to him, his seven flying laps were timed at 3 minutes 15 seconds, 3:13, 3:12, 3:07, 3:06, 3:05 and 3:05. In the second car he recorded 3:08, 3:05, 3:05 and 3:05. That was the sort of thing to impress the most demanding team manager. Kautz was the next best of the batch. For comparison, the Swiss driver's flying laps in the second car were timed at 3:25, 3:25, 3:24, 3:19, 3:18, 3:23, 3:20, 3:19 and 3:19. When the day was over, the fastest laps for each of the five drivers stood thus: Brendel 3:24, Bäumer and Hartmann 3:20, Kautz 3:18 and Seaman 3:05.

The young man in the all-black outfit had given Neubauer plenty of food for thought on his return to the Mercedes factory at Untertürkheim, a suburb of Stuttgart, where the *Rennabteilung* – the racing team – had set up a new headquarters and Uhlenhaut was now leading a technical team ambitious to produce something capable of winning races again.

◆

To his mother's dismay, Dick announced that he would not be spending Christmas at Pull Court. Instead, while waiting for news from Germany, he would be making a second trip to South Africa, to take part in a three-race series that included the country's Grand Prix. Whatever the future held, he had already negotiated to sell the Delage to Prince Chula for Bira to drive in 1937, settling on a price, according to Chula, that more than covered not only the amount Seaman had paid Howe for the car but also the considerable development costs. As part of the deal, Chula agreed that Dick could race the car for the last time in South Africa.

He left Southampton on 4 December. During the voyage he and his fellow passengers would learn of the abdication of Edward VIII and of the newly retitled Duke of Windsor's departure from Portsmouth in a Royal Navy destroyer, accompanied by Wallis Simpson, an American divorcée, en route to exile in France.

Dick's fellow passengers on the first-class deck of the Union Castle line's lavender-hulled *Winchester Castle* included his pal Tony Cliff; Pat Fairfield, who had won the previous year's race for ERA in the country where he had grown up, and his English wife Jean; and Kay Petre, formerly the holder of the women's record for the Brooklands Outer Circuit. Two missionaries and a group of Hungarian circus acrobats were also on board, along with the 19-year-old jockey Bill Rickaby, a prodigy who had ridden the first of what would be more than a thousand winners at Sandown Park five years earlier and was now on his way to a three-month spell working in South Africa. In tourist-class berths were the mechanics of various teams, including Lofty England, who was looking after the Delage, and whose 6ft 5in frame might have found what was effectively the third-class accommodation a little cramped.

In the first-class quarters, the Seaman party had another member: a young woman later described rather vaguely by Cliff as 'one of my cousins' and 'Dick's first serious girlfriend'. 'I had a suspicion that she always intended to get after Dick, and he was certainly interested in her,' he would tell the journalist Chris Nixon, without giving her a name, 'but it was transitory and I don't think it meant a good deal.' George Monkhouse, too, could not come up with her name when he mentioned to Nixon that he had seen Dick and the same 'attractive, dark-haired girl' together at a National Sporting Club event at Grosvenor House.

Her name was Ann Hunter and if she was indeed Cliff's cousin, she was a very distant one. Twenty years old, she lived with her mother at 10 Exhibition Road, a South Kensington apartment block five minutes' walk from Ennismore Gardens. Her Scottish-born father had served in the Great War as a major in the Warwickshire Regiment before working as a land agent on the Rothschild estates in France; he had died in 1932 in Saint-Briac, a seaside village in Brittany, leaving an estate valued at £11,977 9s. 2d. to his wife, Sybil, and their two daughters. Ann's elder sister, Betty, aged twenty-six, was now the director of a fashion studio, living in a flat in Earls Court.

Like Dick, Ann was booked to leave the ship at Cape Town. 'He was obviously quite keen on her,' Monkhouse said of the relationship. Ramponi, he added, was not pleased by the idea of his driver taking a girl along on what he saw as a work trip. But in this matter, as in others, Dick's mind was not to be changed.

Most of those involved in the programme of South African races were heading for East London, where the first event would be held. A good time was had on the voyage, with games of cricket and deck tennis (won by Fairfield, a fine all-round sportsman) and parties with the officers. 'Someone threw the captain's special dining room chair overboard and we were blamed for it,' Dick wrote to Monkhouse, 'and the captain himself promptly had a heart attack and retired to bed for the rest of the voyage.' Dick and his companion disembarked in Cape Town on 18 December. Christmas Day was spent in Port Elizabeth before his arrival on 26 December in East London, where he stayed at the Beach Hotel. There was time for a little shark-fishing with Rosemeyer and von Delius, who had arrived with the Auto Union team; the only catch, a baby hammerhead, came Dick's way.

The South African Grand Prix took place on New Year's Day: a 211-mile handicap race, it had attracted a strong field from Europe, led by a pair of Auto Unions. Like Seaman and the Delage, however, the Germans were poorly favoured by the handicappers. Victory went to Fairfield's ERA, ahead of a couple of Rileys, with Rosemeyer down in fifth place, between

Ruesch's Maserati and Howe's Bugatti. To overcome his handicap, Dick was forced to drive the Delage so hard that one of its tyres blew in the closing stages, forcing him to limp back to the pits on the rim. After a wheel change he went out again, only for the weakened hub to break. Very quickly he cancelled his entries for the forthcoming two races, partly to avoid further risk to the car for which Chula was paying him a good price but also – as he told the organisers with some asperity – because he did not enjoy being handicapped out of contention. This, he decided, was the last time he would take part in such an event.

He returned to Cape Town, where he stayed at the St James Hotel in Kalk Bay. On 12 January, four days before the second race was due to be held, he boarded the *Winchester Castle* for the two-week voyage home via Madeira. Ann Hunter stayed on until 3 March, returning on the sister ship, the *Warwick Castle*; there would be no further recorded sightings of the couple together. A few months later, she and a group of girlfriends bought an old ambulance and drove it to Barcelona to help treat the wounded of the Spanish Civil War.

Once back in London, Dick ensured that the Delage was safely delivered to Chula, along with its spare engines and other parts, before closing down his racing team. Ramponi and Rockall would continue their race-preparation business from premises in Bayswater. Lofty England would move with the Delage to the White Mouse team. Finlayson was now Hans Ruesch's chief mechanic. And the Dodge van had been sold to Nicky Embiricos for £125. The decks had been cleared.

PART THREE

1937–38

16

Silver Arrows

The offer was for a thousand Reichsmarks a month – the equivalent of almost exactly a thousand pounds a year – plus expenses, plus prize money. In terms of pay, there was no thinking or arguing to be done. Even after Birch's 10 per cent had been deducted, it was more than acceptable. In terms of what it offered Dick, the arrangement was everything for which he might have hoped.

To the British, seasoned fans and schoolboys alike, German supremacy on the racetrack had long been a thing of wonder and the object of admiration. Peter Ustinov – whose father, Jona von Ustinov, served as a press secretary in the German embassy in London after the Great War while also working for MI5 – remembered from his days at Mr Gibbs' school that 'when Caracciola won a race in his supercharged white Mercedes-Benz, I was congratulated as though I had been at the wheel, whereas when the team of green Bentleys won, I received formal condolences'. By the mid-1930s, the German domination of Grand Prix racing was absolute.

Adolf Hitler had bought his first Mercedes-Benz in 1923 from a fellow Austrian, Jakob Werlin, the manager of the firm's Munich dealership, which shared its premises with the company that printed the Nazi Party's newspaper, the *Völkischer Beobachter*.

This was the first of many such Mercedes of increasing size supplied by Werlin, who became one of the leader's confidants and was made an officer of the SS. The chairman of the Daimler-Benz board of trustees, the banker Emil Georg von Stauss, had given significant support to the National Socialists; when the company's managing director, Dr Wilhelm Kissel, received a letter from Werlin reporting on a meeting with Hitler in 1932, he responded: 'He will be able to rely on us in the future, as in the past.' A year later, the announcement of the project to fund a Grand Prix car prompted Kissel to ask the government for a budget of a million Reichsmarks.

Kissel fully expected to be the sole recipient of this public subsidy, but his plans were disrupted by a challenge from a new consortium of four German manufacturers. Audi, Horch, DKW and Wanderer had combined to enter Grand Prix racing under the name Auto Union. They had signed a contract with Dr Ferdinand Porsche, the designer of successful sports cars for Mercedes in the 1920s, to supervise the building of his single-seater, a radical rear-engined design initially known as the P-Wagen, at a new racing department within the Horch factory in Zwickau, a mining town in Saxony. Much to Kissel's chagrin, the influence in Berlin of leading National Socialists sitting on the board of Auto Union meant that the pot would have to be shared between the two companies.

The complexity of the arrangements by which Daimler-Benz and the Auto Union consortium became involved in other government work – much of it to do with rearmament – would make it difficult for posterity to untangle the respective budgets. One historian, Eberhard Reuss, suggested that over the six years from 1933 to the outbreak of war, the two teams received around RM 6.5 million between them in direct government subsidies for their racing activities. Thanks to Hitler's indulgence towards a firm that was also building engines for the Luftwaffe, Mercedes took a slightly greater share than the company whose contracted designer was also turning the

Führer's idea of a 'people's car' into reality and from whose drawing board the blueprints for the Wehrmacht's armoured vehicles would emerge. Eventually the two concerns made common cause in their appeals to the government for increasing support, channelling their requests through the NSKK, the *Nationalsozialistisches Kraftfahrkorps* (National Socialist Corps of Motorists), a paramilitary organisation whose responsibilities included the training of tank drivers for the German army. Other factors, such as money from equipment suppliers and organised donations from the public, enabled them to increase their budgets substantially. Reuss calculated that Mercedes spent RM 20.5 million (£1.65 million) on racing over that period, against Auto Union's RM 15.5 million (£1.25 million). Eighty years later, the sterling equivalents would be £105.5 million and £80 million.

They were quick to turn such resources – unparalleled in the previous history of motor sport – into success on the track. The new Mercedes W25 – initially painted white, Germany's national racing colour, as its predecessors in earlier phases of the company's racing activities had been – was presented to Hitler in January 1934. Two months later the Auto Union made its public debut. Dramatically different, with a twin-supercharged 4.3-litre sixteen-cylinder engine housed behind the driver and cloaked in bare aluminium bodywork, the futuristic machine caused a sensation among the thousands of Berliners who turned up to watch as it screamed around the AVUS track, breaking several world records in the hands of Hans Stuck.

By the time the Mercedes W25 made its first appearance in competition, at the Nürburgring that June, its white paint had been stripped off, almost certainly with the aim of helping the car to get beneath the 750kg maximum weight limit imposed on Grand Prix cars under new regulations introduced that year. The legend of the two Silver Arrows teams, racing head to head for the glory of Germany, was born and would not be slow to flourish. In that first season Mercedes entered eight

Grands Prix, winning four. Auto Union entered nine and won three. In 1935 Mercedes won eight times to Auto Union's two. In 1936, with the arrival of Rosemeyer, the balance shifted: six victories for a much-developed Auto Union, now with a 6-litre engine, to two for Mercedes' ageing W25. In 1935 and '36 only Nuvolari's Alfa Romeo had punctured their dominance, winning four races out of the twenty-two in which one or both of the German teams participated, and only one of the classic Grandes Épreuves.

There had been some discussion with Dr Karl Feuereissen, Auto Union's team manager, about the possibility of Dick being given a test drive with a view to a Grand Prix seat in 1937, but the team had been slow to get in touch with him. Their young-driver trials had taken place at the Nürburgring early in October, resulting in a place in the team alongside Rosemeyer, von Delius and Rudolf Hasse for H. P. Müller, the newly crowned German 500cc motorcycle champion. Walter Bäumer, who had set the second-fastest time (and had also tested for Mercedes), was named as the reserve. Dick was not impressed by their poor organisation and communication, which made such an obvious contrast with Neubauer's meticulous approach. By the time he returned from his South African trip at the end of January, the monthly magazine *Speed* had published a story that he was about to sign a contract with Mercedes-Benz, congratulating him 'on the very considerable compliment that has been paid to him – and through him paid to his country – by his inclusion in the Mercedes équipe this year'.

The story did not mention that the appointment required the personal approval of Adolf Hitler, or suggest a reason why it might have been granted. This was a time when the German leader, although still not admitting the true nature of his ambitions, was hoping that a friendship with Britain would be useful once northern and eastern continental Europe had been conquered, and the cordial response of members of the British establishment had given him every reason for optimism. The arrival of an Englishman in an otherwise all–German team might become a helpful symbol of that relationship.

For Seaman, the unacceptable alternative to taking up Mercedes' offer would have been to settle for driving something inherently uncompetitive in major Grands Prix, but he understood the implications of aligning himself with a symbol of a resurgent and potentially belligerent Germany. Twelve months earlier Louis Chiron had faced criticism in France when he signed up with Mercedes, and Dick's position now was delicate enough for him to seek advice. Among those he consulted was Lord Howe, an aide–de–camp to George V in the Great War and a Conservative MP from 1918 to 1929. Howe knew all shades of political opinion, and his deep involvement in racing gave him an understanding of the ambitious young driver's dilemma.

In Britain, the reaction to Hitler's Germany ran from fervent admiration to deep hostility. Howe would certainly have been aware of the outbreak of violence in the Whitechapel district of London a couple of months earlier, when 20,000 anti-fascist demonstrators – a mixture of Jewish, socialist, communist and anarchist groups – confronted 2,000 uniformed Blackshirts led by Hitler's most prominent British supporter, Sir Oswald Mosley, thwarting their intention to march through the heart of the East End, with its large Jewish population. Mosley's own admirers included Malcolm Campbell, the great record breaker on land and water and a national hero, not least to the crowd at Brooklands. In terms of attitudes to far–right regimes, the leading newspapers were divided between, on the one side, the *Daily Mail*, whose proprietor, Lord Rothermere, had visited Hitler and written an article headlined 'Hurrah for the Blackshirts', and on the other, David Low, the coruscatingly anti-Nazi cartoonist of the *Evening Standard*. Eventually Howe concluded that the prestige of having a British driver in one of the world's two best Grand Prix teams outweighed the potential drawbacks, which included the possible use of Seaman's successes to burnish the image of the new Germany. He gave Dick his blessing.

A draft contract arrived at Ennismore Gardens, and in the last week of February Dick and his manager flew to Stuttgart. They were shown around the Mercedes headquarters at Untertürkheim, where 32,000 workers – up from 4,958 in 1932, at the nadir of Germany's financial crash and the height of the unemployment crisis – had turned out 22,994 passenger cars and 9,218 trucks and commercial vehicles the previous year, the annual growth rate now running at 25 per cent. In 1933 the number of cars produced had been a mere 7,617; that year's turnover of RM 100.9 million for the entire Daimler-Benz organisation had almost tripled to RM 295.1 million three years later. In the racing department, no fewer than 380 people, including designers, engineers, fabricators and mechanics, were solely engaged in the work of building and running the Grand Prix cars.

When he showed his mother the contract, she noticed the paragraphs dealing with insurance and compensation in the event of his serious injury or death. The most significant of the sums mentioned – RM 100,000 (about £8,200 in 1937, worth just over £500,000 eighty years later) payable in the event of his death – was not what dismayed her. It was the simple reminder once again of the risks inherent in his occupation, and she wondered briefly if she could still find a way to dissuade or prevent him from taking this latest step. But that was, she decided, a pointless thought. Any objection she might make would only antagonise him.

For Birch, on a percentage of Dick's earnings, the deal represented a fine arrangement. Since he already lived in Germany with his family, there would be no problem with currency restrictions. For this reason, too, it was agreed that it would make sense for Dick to live there, in reasonable proximity to the Mercedes headquarters. The days of stuffing wads of Reichsmarks up the exhaust pipe of a racing car and crossing fingers while going through border checks were over.

◆

Dick's new employers were also playing their part in another
aspect of the German revival. As well as the motorisation
project, the National Socialist government promoted a mas-
sive increase in the size of the German armed forces. At first
half-concealed, this violation of the detested post-war Treaty
of Versailles was brought into the open in 1935, when Hitler
revealed the existence of 2,500 warplanes and a standing army
of 300,000 men. From the French and the British, who had
imposed the disarmament terms in 1919, there was no significant response. In effect, Hitler could now do as he liked.

In February 1937 the first production versions of the
Messerschmitt Bf 109, the single-seater aircraft that would
become a mainstay of Germany's fighter squadrons, were delivered to the Luftwaffe. The prototype, which made a display
flight at the Olympic Games in Berlin the previous summer,
had been powered by a Rolls-Royce engine. Once in production, it was fitted with a Daimler-Benz DB 600, an inverted
V12 engine of 33.9 litres, delivering about 1,000 horsepower.
Later in the year it would be replaced by the fuel-injected
DB 601; in November a special racing version, the DB 601R,
enabled the Messerschmitt's chief test pilot to reach a speed of
379.92mph, a new world record. The 109's engines were manufactured at Daimler-Benz's factory in Marienfelde, a southern
suburb of Berlin, and later at a new plant in Genshagen, a few
kilometres further south, concealed in woodland. Very soon
the first 109s − the first of a total of 33,000 − and their pilots
would be sent by Air Marshal Hermann Göring to join the
Condor Legion in Spain. This large contingent of German air
and land forces was fighting on the side of General Franco's
Nationalists in the civil war, testing new weapons and tactics
for a larger conflict to come. In the Battle of Brunete that July,
pitted against the rugged but outdated Polikarpov biplanes
that had been supplied by Russia to the Republican air force,

the Messerschmitt was able to give its own demonstration of German supremacy.

◆

On Dick's visits to the Mercedes headquarters he stayed at the Hotel Graf Zeppelin, in the centre of Stuttgart, close to the main railway station. But among the tasks for which Tony Birch volunteered that spring was finding a permanent place for him to live, somewhere that suited his love of the outdoors. The Starnbergersee seemed perfect. Germany's largest lake, 30 miles in circumference, 150 miles south-east of Stuttgart and 25 miles south of Munich, it was known to some English-speakers through a mention in the opening passage of T. S. Eliot's *The Waste Land*, first published fifteen years earlier: 'Summer surprised us, coming over the Starnbergersee / With a shower of rain ...' It offered swimming and boating off the wooded shores, a view of the Alps to the south, and a mixture of local people – mostly farmers and fishermen – and wealthy citizens of Munich seeking weekend tranquillity.

In the hamlet of Ambach, on the eastern side, Birch found Haus 12, a spacious villa set just above the narrow road running along the shore, with a boat house on the lake below. This was ideal for Dick, who would have plenty of room in which to put up his friends from England – and just the thing, too, for Birch, who also enjoyed a house party.

In Untertürkheim, where the *Rennabteilung* occupied a group of buildings behind the imposing twin main blocks, Dick was entering a world run by men with motor sport in their blood. Kissel had come up through the commercial side, but Max Sailer, the director with responsibility for the racing programme, had briefly led the 1914 French Grand Prix for Mercedes, the last big race before the Great War. The 46-year-old Alfred Neubauer, who reported to Sailer, had raced in the early 1920s, albeit without notable success, before joining Daimler in 1923, soon giving up his own racing ambitions in order to show his ability as a shrewd organiser who looked after the team, in Hermann Lang's words, 'like a hen with its chicks'. Dick got on well with all of them, but one of his key relationships was with the young man in charge of design and development of the latest Grand Prix car, a man with almost no racing background at all.

Rudolf Uhlenhaut's English was much better than Dick's German, thanks to a childhood in England, where his father was a director of the Deutsche Bank's London office. Born in Muswell Hill, he was eight when the Great War broke out and the family returned to Berlin, where he attended school until his father was posted to the Bremen office. In 1926, already fascinated by trains, cars and motorcycles, he enrolled as a student in mechanical engineering at Munich's Technical University. After his father's death in 1928 the bank supported the family, enabling Rudolf to complete the remaining three years of his studies.

On his graduation in 1931, his late father's friends secured him work at Untertürkheim as a paid-by-the-hour technical assistant in the test department of a company formed five years earlier when the country's first car manufacturer, Daimler, merged with Benz, the maker of the world's first internal combustion engined truck. His aptitude was quickly recognised by promotion to a staff position and a rise through the ranks. At thirty years of age, on the eve of Dick's arrival, he was assigned by Fritz Nallinger, the head of the research and development department, to work with Albert Heess, the engine specialist, and the chassis designer Max Wagner on a car capable of reviving the racing team's fortunes.

Among Uhlenhaut's gifts was a natural talent at the wheel: he had twice represented Mercedes in the 2,000km Tour of Germany, driving the firm's powerful sports cars. In August 1936, having cancelled their Grand Prix programme for the remainder of the season, the team devoted a week to intensive testing at the Nürburgring, trying to find out exactly what was wrong with the W25 and how they might move forward. After the designated drivers, Caracciola and von Brauchitsch, had gone home at the end of the second day, Uhlenhaut took over. This was his first experience in a single-seater: he spent three days lapping the track at competitive speeds, recording his findings in detailed technical notes that became the basis for the car's successor. After that, the drivers knew they could never pull the wool over his eyes; and by giving them the equipment they needed to win races, he commanded their respect and trust.

When Dick arrived, Wagner, Heess and Uhlenhaut were working flat-out on the new machine for 1937. Their resources were virtually unlimited. 'I could have as much as I wanted,' Uhlenhaut would remember. 'Nobody said I was spending too much. I didn't even know what was spent.' The W125 had a lower centre of gravity, an entirely new suspension system based on soft springs and stiff shock absorbers, new front and rear axles, an oval-tubed frame providing much greater stiffness, and sleeker bodywork covering a supercharged twin-cam straight-eight engine of 5.8 litres. The result would be a transformation of performance and results.

◆

Dick's new teammates were a mixed bunch: Rudolf Caracciola, thirty-six years old, the son of a hotel keeper and wine dealer from Remagen, near Bonn, already a winner of the European Grand Prix championship; Manfred von Brauchitsch, thirty-one, a member of a Prussian military family and the nephew of a man rising rapidly through the upper echelons of Hitler's armed forces; and Hermann Lang, twenty-seven, a local man who had started his working life as a mechanic. All of them were enrolled – as a matter of form for German racing drivers – in the NSKK, given honorary ranks and membership cards signed by the organisation's leader, Korpsführer Adolf Hühnlein, a member of the anti-Bolshevik Freikorps immediately after the Great War and a veteran of the 1923 Munich Beer Hall Putsch.

As head of the *Oberste Nationale Sportbehörde* (ONS), the national sports ministry, the irascible and self-important Hühnlein was also the man directly responsible to Hitler for Germany's sporting success.

NSKK membership would not be required of Dick Seaman. Caracciola, however, was NSKK member No. 54, with the rank of Sturmführer. The debonair former European champion, known as 'Caratsch', walked with a limp as a result of a bad crash in the 1933 Monaco Grand Prix; the accident had shortened his right leg by 2 inches. Motor-mad from childhood, he became an apprentice at the Fafnir car factory in Aachen and competed in motorcycle endurance events before driving a works-entered Fafnir to his first four-wheeled victory at Rüsselsheim. In 1922 a fist fight with a Belgian soldier, part of a unit still occupying that part of Germany, forced him to flee to Dresden, where he worked as a salesman for Fafnir before moving to a similar position in Daimler's local showroom. He continued to compete, and was soon promoted to the company's racing department as a junior driver. Many victories in smaller races preceded a win in the 1926 German Grand Prix at AVUS and a prize of 17,000 marks, which he invested in a Daimler-Benz dealership in the Kurfürstendamm, Berlin's most glamorous shopping street. His success also enabled him to marry an attractive divorcée, Charlotte 'Charly' Liemann, the daughter of a Berlin restaurateur.

In 1929, after the financial crisis had forced him to close his Berlin dealership, he took Charly to live in Switzerland. His successes mounted up, including the 1930 European hill-climb championship and the 1931 Mille Miglia. When Mercedes withdrew from racing, he switched to Alfa Romeo, racing first for the factory and then for a private team set up jointly with his friend Chiron. There were more successes in 1932 – although the crowd at AVUS booed their once-adored Caratsch for driving a foreign car, albeit painted white – before he smashed his leg in Monaco.

He was in a plaster cast for six months. When it was removed, Charly took him back to their alpine chalet in Arosa for the winter. In February she went off for a day's skiing with friends, but when he went to meet her train he discovered that she would not be returning: an avalanche had killed her. He mourned in seclusion for a while before Chiron's girlfriend, Alice 'Baby' Hoffmann, arrived to try to console him. The two couples had been close friends, and Baby, the popular American-born ex-wife of the heir to the Hoffmann-LaRoche pharmaceutical company, took on the job of rescuing Rudi from his gloom. She succeeded so well that he made a well-received demonstration run during the race weekend at Monaco twelve months after the accident, having been given a new contract by Mercedes.

In 1935 Caracciola had the best of years, fending off a pair of combative teammates, Fagioli and von Brauchitsch, to win six Grands Prix – including three of the seven Grandes Épreuves that counted towards the European championship that season, thus taking the title for the first time. The following year Chiron joined the team but could not get on terms with the latest version of the W25. And young Rosemeyer had arrived at Auto Union, his capture of the 1936 European title threatening to end the long reign of Caracciola as Germany's top driver.

Von Brauchitsch lacked Caracciola's finesse at the wheel but made up for it with a furious aggression which sometimes exacted a heavy price. He had followed his father into the army as an officer cadet before fracturing his skull in a motorcycle accident, requiring a long convalescence. It was the end of his military ambitions, but a holiday with a cousin in a castle near Leipzig presented him with an alternative. The cousin had a powerful Mercedes SS, and during the visit von Brauchitsch watched a newsreel containing film of a motor race. He was soon entering his first hill-climb at the wheel of his cousin's car.

His entry into the public consciousness came at AVUS in 1932, when the conventional bodywork of the Mercedes was replaced by dramatic streamlined panels, under the supervision of Neubauer, in order to extract maximum benefit from the long straights of the Berlin circuit. His duel with Caracciola's works Alfa forced the Mercedes management – who had refused a request for official backing – to take notice of his talent. Modest factory support in 1933 was followed by a works drive alongside Caracciola for 1934; he won the Eifel GP but then broke a number of bones a month later at the Nürburgring.

Several weeks of mountain air in Davos restored his fitness in time for the 1935 season, but good performances were often cut short by misfortune, leading him to acquire the nickname *Pechvogel*: the bad-luck bird. He was leading the German Grand Prix, after dicing on equal terms with Caracciola, Rosemeyer and Nuvolari, when Neubauer decided against bringing him in to replace his worn tyres, knowing that a pit stop would hand the win to Nuvolari in his obsolete Alfa. When a tyre blew on the last lap, it gave the Italian one of the most celebrated underdog victories in the sport's history. Von Brauchitsch limped across the line in fifth place, his tyre in shreds, with sympathetic applause in his ears and tears streaming down his face.

In 1936 he was chosen to deliver the welcome address to Hitler at the Berlin Motor Show. 'If, in the last few years, German racing cars have sped from victory to victory, if today we in motor sport stand at the head of all nations,' he told his Führer, 'then the credit goes not so much to us or to our industry – the achievement is principally yours. You have given us back a belief in the future of Germany, a belief in ourselves.'

A few weeks earlier he and his brother Harald had been involved in a drunken scuffle at the Hotel Post on the Walchensee, in the Bavarian Alps, with Baldur von Schirach, the head of the Hitler Youth movement. Von Schirach had reacted to a perceived insult by whipping the brothers, after which von Brauchitsch demanded the satisfaction of a duel with weapons, but was refused. The dispute may have caused the uncertainty over his continued place in the team for 1937, but he was well connected – Hitler had lent his uncle, General Wilhelm von Brauchitsch, RM 80,000 to pay for a divorce and was about to make him commander-in-chief of the army – and a contract was signed in time for him to join the preparations.

The third member of the first-choice team was a newcomer, promoted entirely on his own merits. Born in Bad Cannstatt, near Stuttgart, Lang had been brought up in straitened circumstances after his father's early death. He began his working life as an apprentice mechanic in a motorcycle garage, where he was eventually allowed to take out a machine for a Sunday ride, beginning a progression to amateur racing and leading to victory in the 1931 German sidecar hill-climb championship. When the collapsing economy cost him his job in the garage, he was offered the chance to drive a diesel locomotive to and from a gravel pit. Bicycling to work each day, he passed the Daimler-Benz factory. Through a friend, he managed to secure a job in the engine-testing department just as work was about to begin on the W25.

In 1934 he became one of the racing team's engine fitters; his duties included sharing the driving of one of the transporter lorries as they travelled in convoy around Europe, each with a two-man crew. 'We had a firm arrangement,' he remembered. 'Nobody was to sleep while the column was on the move, otherwise the driver might drop off, too.' On the day before they left the factory for each Grand Prix, Max Sailer would pay a visit to the workshops and put the mechanics of each car through a wheel-changing test; the fastest won a cash prize that was put towards an end-of-season outing for their families. In 1935 Lang was made head mechanic of Fagioli's car. During the pre-season test weeks at Monza, he and Frau Neubauer shared the job of cooking meals for his team at the circuit. When he served up his steak or chicken with noodles, the drivers would wander over to share the mechanics' feast.

The chance to drive the Grand Prix cars from their garages to the circuit, or to bed in new brake linings on an adjacent strip of public road, helped to fire his ultimate ambition. Late in 1935 he was given the chance to drive in the Eifelrennen, finishing fifth in one of the previous year's cars after spinning in the rain and being pushed back onto the track by spectators. The following year he became the team's official reserve driver and led the German Grand Prix briefly until the pain from a broken finger forced him to hand his car over to Caracciola. He had done enough to be given a full contract for 1937.

Alone among the drivers, Lang was a member of the National Socialist Party: less from conviction, it seemed, than out of the feeling that not to join might harm his career. Neither Caracciola — a national hero whose birthday greetings to the Führer elicited a personally signed postcard of thanks — nor the well-connected von Brauchitsch would have needed the reassurance a party card provided to an ex-mechanic married to a local girl he had known since his days as an apprentice in the motorcycle garage. As it was, Caracciola and von Brauchitsch seldom missed a chance to put him in his place. Once, on a night out in Berlin with the team, von Brauchitsch was said to have addressed a waiter at the fashionable Roxy bar in Schöneberg with the order: 'A bottle of champagne for Herr Caracciola and myself — and a beer for Lang . . .'

As a group, they embraced the kind of internal competition beloved of all team managers, particularly those in charge of dominant teams. Your most important opponent, racing drivers often say, is your teammate: since you are in supposedly identical machines, he is the only one against whom your own performance can be judged with any precision. For a man in Neubauer's position, this kind of competitive tension could be the source of a successful team's energy. But if the ego and the ambitions got out of control, the consequences could be lethal.

17

The wall of death

The formalities of Dick's contract were not completed in time for the new recruit to join a parade during the Berlin Motor Show at the end of February, when the Mercedes and Auto Union teams lined up their cars and drivers to be presented to Adolf Hitler outside the Reich Chancellery. Thousands marvelled at the sight and the sound as Caracciola, von Brauchitsch, Rosemeyer and Stuck drove the Silver Arrows through the Brandenburg Gate, down the Charlottenburger Chausee and all the way to Adolf-Hitler-Platz, the square close to the exhibition halls, a 5-mile drive along a dead-straight boulevard that was intended to become, in Hitler's dream, the meridian of a new imperial Berlin.

A month later Seaman and Birch flew to Milan to meet up with the rest of the team. They were quartered at the Hotel Principe e Savoia, close to the city centre: a sign of the first-class conditions in which Seaman would now be going about his work. His upbringing had made Dick more than a social match for Caracciola and von Brauchitsch. But his months of work with Ramponi, Finlayson and England rendered him equally comfortable in the company of the genial and sympathetic Lang and the team's mechanics. Uhlenhaut, who was used to receiving little or no constructive information from his two leading drivers, appreciated the feedback from a pair of eager young men keen to play a role in improving the cars' performance.

One of the new W125 machines had been brought down to Monza, along with a couple of the older W25s, on three of the *Rennabteilung*'s fleet of dark-blue diesel-engined Mercedes trucks, with a fourth carrying spare parts and tools. Dick was able to report to Monkhouse that 'the new car seems quite promising, although it is a bit early to be over-optimistic'. Uhlenhaut and the mechanics worked on the car over the Easter weekend, enabling the non-technicians to have some time off. Neubauer and his wife headed for the coast at Rapallo, while Caracciola went off to Lake Garda. Seaman and Birch took a day trip to Como, where they admired the Villa d'Este, a lakeside hotel that had begun life as the summer residence of a sixteenth-century cardinal.

Work resumed following the break with such intensity that there was no time to go into the town for lunch, so the Neubauers and Lang cooked meals for the assembled company on an electric stove in the workshop lorry. But on the Friday, after the new car had been returned to Stuttgart for further work, Dick was out practising in an old W25 when he gave the car too much throttle coming out of one of the chicanes at around 70mph. The rear end swung round, he overcorrected, and the car left the track and hit a large tree before he had the chance to take further action. He was thrown out and found himself sitting on the grass with a pain in his left knee. The engine, having detached itself from the chassis, was lying in the road. The wreckage was starting to burn, but he managed to get himself to a safe distance, hampered by what turned out to be a fractured kneecap. It was a sharp reminder that he was making the move from the 180 horsepower of the Delage to more than double that figure in a car of roughly the same weight.

If he was expecting a rocket from the team manager, he was to be pleasantly surprised, as he told Monkhouse in a letter written from his hotel bed: 'Neubauer did not seem to mind too much; in fact he seemed to think it was rather funny, and consoled me with the information that Caracciola, Fagioli and Brauchitsch had all crashed when they started driving these cars in 1934, i.e. too much gas after a corner. Well, one lives and learns!' Neubauer's attitude might have been a little less relaxed had Seaman destroyed one of the latest cars.

'I have come to the conclusion that one is always apt to get caught out at the beginning of the season,' Dick told Monkhouse, 'for one tries to dice in the same way as one had been doing at the end of the previous season, without realising that one is very lacking in practice.' He also mentioned going back to examine the scene of the accident and picking up pieces of the Mercedes' alloy bodywork: 'I must say I was absolutely amazed at the lightness of the material they use. It is much lighter than anything I've ever felt before, and is obviously something rather special.' In his reply, Monkhouse correctly speculated that the metal in question was probably magnesium alloy. He also mentioned that the publication of his first book of photographs, *Motoraces*, to which Dick had contributed a short essay titled 'What is Grand Prix racing?', had been delayed by problems with the paper supply.

After a plaster cast had been put on his leg in a Milan clinic, Dick wrote to his mother, mostly in reassuring terms but also pointing out that he had recently sat down to a meal at a table of thirteen, that his hotel room number was 113, that he had used cabin number thirteen at a swimming baths, and that the accident had taken place on a Friday. Perhaps he was not aware that in Italy, where the crash happened, *fare tredici* is considered a sign of good fortune. More cheerfully, there was an enjoyable rendezvous with Chula and Bira, visiting Milan, although they told him over lunch that their early experiences with the expensively acquired Delage had been disappointing, Bira finding the engine response slow and the gearbox tricky.

Discharged from the clinic with his leg still in plaster and his cuts and bruises healing, Dick took the train to Munich before being driven to Ambach. Birch's wife, Barbara, an army officer's daughter, was acting as housekeeper while also looking after their young son. The owner of the house, who lived in a property next door, sent her maid over to them with food while a new boiler and kitchen sink were being installed. Nine days later, following a return to Munich for the removal of the plaster, Dick was deemed fit enough to join the Mercedes party setting off for Tripoli and the start of the team's season.

◆

Although Dick had been engaged as a reserve driver, Neubauer chose to thrust him straight into the action in a four-car entry for the lucrative Grand Prix at the Mellaha circuit, laid out on a salt lake outside the Libyan capital. First held in 1925, the race had close links to the Italian national lottery and in 1933 had been the subject of rumours that a group of leading Italian drivers had conspired to fix the result.

For the government in Rome, keen to promote a sense of empire and also to exploit the potential for tourism along Libya's Mediterranean shore, this was an important event. The governor general, Marshal Italo Balbo, having helped bring Mussolini to power, had been given the job of building up the air force before being charged with consolidating Italy's power by merging the territories of Tripolitania, Cyrenaica and the arid Saharan region of Fezzan into one country. His support of spectacular displays of Italian prowess in the air, including massed transatlantic flights of flying boats, had brought him worldwide fame, making him a natural impresario of the Grand Prix.

The four drivers made their separate ways to Naples, where they and the transporters carrying the cars – five of the new W125s, including a spare – would be taken on board the *Città di Palermo*. Dick drove down in his new black team-issue 2.3-litre Mercedes saloon, making a side trip to Pompeii before joining the party for the thirty-hour voyage through the Strait of Messina and across the Mediterranean to Tripoli, where they were given rooms in the Uaddan Hotel, a handsome seafront complex of buildings designed by a prominent Italian architect in the Moorish style. Opened the previous year, containing a casino, a 500-seat theatre and a Turkish bath, and with just fifty guest rooms, it was described by an American reporter as 'the Waldorf Astoria of North Africa'. The Uaddan was also part of Balbo's scheme to promote Tripoli as a tourist destination, which included backing archaeological projects – such as the excavation of the basilica at Leptis Magna and the restoration of the Temple of Jove in Tripoli itself – intended to highlight the legacy of the Roman occupation.

Arriving a week before the race, Dick and his teammates were shown the sights; the track, too, made an impression. Eight miles long, lined with palm trees, it played to the German teams' strengths, and the 1935 and 1936 races had resulted in wins for Caracciola's Mercedes and Achille Varzi's Auto Union. 'Balbo has made the circuit probably the finest, and certainly the fastest, road circuit in the world, and provided it with a magnificent concrete grandstand, surrounded by lawns and brilliant flowering shrubs,' Dick would write in a post-race article for *The Autocar*. 'The pits . . . are done on a lavish scale, all in snow-white concrete, and all very spick and span. In fact, it is the Ascot of motor racing circuits.' But its high average speed would, as he observed, exact a price in terms of tyre wear. In the forty-lap race, some drivers would need to change their tyres half a dozen times or more. During the practice sessions Dick found that his swollen left knee was still not flexible enough to allow him to get the sole of his foot on the clutch pedal properly; instead he was forced to use his heel. Luckily a lap of Mellaha required few gear changes. The new car, he was pleased to find, matched the top speed of the Auto Unions but had the advantage of better acceleration and braking and, thanks to Uhlenhaut's work on the suspension, superior roadholding.

Before the start, the final arrangements for the lottery were made. Many thousands of tickets had been sold all over Italy at twelve lire each, with a first prize of 6 million lire (about £30,000, or almost £2 million today). A few days earlier thirty tickets had been drawn from the total entry, and their owners invited, with great publicity, to Tripoli. Immediately before the race each ticket and the number of each of the thirty competitors were paired in a draw made by a blindfolded member of the Italian youth league. In order to avoid collusion of the sort that had brought previous editions of the race into disrepute, the draw was made after the cars and their drivers had assembled on the grid, where they were guarded by ranks of Askari, the African troops who were now part of the Italian army and who, according to Lang, were so startled when the engines finally started up that they broke ranks and scattered.

The start was enlivened for Seaman when, in the row ahead, the hubcaps of Lang's car and von Delius's Auto Union touched as they accelerated away. They slowed, Dick slowed in reaction, and so, just behind him, did Nuvolari, who needed to perform a lurid manoeuvre to avoid an accident. Caracciola, Stuck, Rosemeyer and von Brauchitsch swapped the lead in the early stages before tyre changes shuffled and reshuffled the order. By half-distance, as the cars screamed past the tall white timing tower that stood opposite a modern cantilevered grandstand offering shade to ten thousand spectators, Lang had moved into what would prove to be a decisive lead. His delicate touch meant he needed only two pit stops on his way to victory while he sweated off four and a half pounds in the extreme heat. Both Caracciola and Seaman were hindered by problems they put down to sand blowing into the air intakes and clogging their superchargers; they finished sixth and seventh respectively, behind four Auto Unions. Von Brauchitsch's split radiator made him the only retirement of the eight German cars. Uhlenhaut later admitted that Seaman's problem had actually been caused by a mechanic's rag left under the bonnet: a most untypical oversight.

Seaman was discussing the disappointment with Caracciola

in the pit lane when Fagioli, who had finished fifth in an Auto Union, charged up to them and began shouting at Rudi, claiming to have been baulked. Picking up a copper-headed wheel hammer from the pit counter, he hurled it at his former teammate, narrowly missing both Mercedes drivers, before being dragged back to his own pit, still bellowing accusations.

After Lang, in ecstasy after his first Grand Prix victory, had received his trophy from Marshal Balbo, he was engulfed by the spectators. Among them, ready to bestow a kiss on his cheek, was a butcher from Piacenza: the winner of the lottery, now a rich man (although Lang recorded in his memoirs that the beneficiary of his victory subsequently closed his business, gambled the millions away and ended up in a mental home). A lavish party followed the race. Never imagining that he would win, Lang had neglected to pack formal clothes. He and his wife stayed in their hotel room out of sheer embarrassment until Neubauer arrived to summon them. Lang tried to persuade his team manager to take his place, pleading a lack of suitable attire. 'You'll be there,' Neubauer told him, 'even if you're only wearing your bathing trunks.' As fate would have it, once they had made their way to a floodlit government palace through ranks of Askari guards, the lounge-suited Lang was seated at the banquet opposite Hans Stuck, who was resplendent in a perfectly tailored set of white tails.

◆

After a two-day drive back from Naples, Dick got to grips with a new toy: a 12-foot International Class sailing dinghy he had bought to use on the calm waters of the Starnbergersee. 'Like most things it's quite easy at first, but very difficult to do properly,' he told Monkhouse.

His next racing appointment was in Berlin, where Mercedes had entered a five-strong team in the Avusrennen. The drivers had been booked into the Hotel Savoy on Fasanenstrasse, just off the Kurfürstendamm and close to one of Berlin's largest synagogues, which had been closed twelve months earlier on the orders of the Nazi authorities. Also staying at the Savoy was Charlie Martin, who had entered his ERA in the voiturette race, and their friends John and Desbo Cornwall, a London stockbroker and his Greek wife. In the lobby Seaman and Martin bumped into Dugdale, and that night they all went out together.

Seaman and Dugdale arranged to go boating the following morning, before practice for the Grand Prix cars. Dick drove them to Gatow, on the Havelsee, where they hired rowing boats and watched a light plane circling over the lake: it was the famous single-engined, four-seater Messerschmitt Taifun belonging to Elly Beinhorn and containing her husband, Bernd Rosemeyer. There was time for a lunch of iced chicken soup, cold roast beef with salad, and vanilla ice cream with chocolate sauce before they set off for the circuit.

The last kaiser had still been in power when the foundations of AVUS – the *Automobil Verkehrs und Übungsstrasse* (automobile traffic and training road) – were laid by Russian prisoners during the Great War; the original plans had been made as part of a scheme for a national motorway, long before Hitler launched his autobahn project. Its layout could hardly have been simpler: a dual carriageway with a strip of grass down the middle, with a shallow-banked loop at one end and a hairpin at the other. Opened in 1921, it became a public toll road between Berlin and Potsdam when not being used for race meetings. No race was held in 1936 because work was under way to give the circuit its defining feature: a 43-degree banked turn at the north end, 60 feet high and surfaced with bricks, with no lip or retaining barrier. Pathé News called it the Wall of Death.

This new theatre of speed, devised to ensure that Germany had a circuit faster than Tripoli, encouraged Mercedes and Auto Union to bring to circuit racing the theories of streamlining used in their record attempts. They were helped by Korpsführer Hühnlein's decision to lift the normal weight and engine restrictions governing Grand Prix racing, freeing the German teams to exploit their advanced technology to the full. Their cars arrived at the track with swooping bodywork that enclosed all four wheels, making them look even more impressively futuristic. Mercedes entered five cars: a trio of the streamliners for their three leading drivers and a pair of conventional open-wheeled models for Seaman and Zehender, the cars of von Brauchitsch and Zehender having twelve-cylinder engines. Each car had a swastika in a circle painted on either side of the tail, behind the drivers' headrests. Their rivals from Zwickau entered two Porsche-designed streamliners and two open-wheeled cars. Zehender was sidelined during practice when his engine blew up as a result, it was said, of changing to first gear instead of third, while Seaman discovered that the open-wheeled bodywork cost him around 12mph against the top speed of his teammates' streamlined cars, despite the extra weight of their panelling.

On the morning of the race, Seaman invited Dugdale to breakfast in his hotel room. 'It was difficult to realise as we looked out at the fresh green garden below,' the journalist wrote in his diary, 'that within an hour Dick would be racing at 200mph, passing and repassing at fantastic speeds with only about thirty feet of road to share. He showed little sign of strain (he never did), but perhaps he was quieter than usual.'

Joseph Goebbels, Hitler's propaganda minister, was the guest of honour on race day, arriving with his wife, Magda, in a large open Mercedes, surrounded by columns of NSKK motorcyclists. Among the hors d'oeuvres was a race for voiturettes, won by Martin, the only British entrant. When Hühnlein placed the laurel wreath around his neck and 'God Save the King' was played over the public address system, the vast crowd responded by raising their right arms. 'Poor Charles,' Dugdale recounted, 'always rather bashful, was quite overcome by his reception and walked self-consciously down the huge expanse of concrete, acknowledging cheer after cheer until his arm became quite tired of giving the Nazi salute.'

The streamlined Grand Prix cars had been reaching top speeds on the straights of an unprecedented 240mph in practice, and average lap speeds of around 170mph made the teams nervous about tyre wear. From time to time Lang had noticed an alarming phenomenon: when he approached top speed, the nose of his streamliner would start to lift. Holes were cut in the bodywork in an attempt to allow trapped air to escape and keep the car on the ground. Rosemeyer, who had been testing on the track before the meeting began, set the fastest time in practice at 4 minutes 9 seconds, well over 170mph; Dick's time was twenty seconds slower.

The race was to be run as two seven-lap heats and an eight-lap final. Fearful of bad publicity from the inevitable humiliation on such a high-speed track, Alfa Romeo had withdrawn their official entries. That left the contest to eight German cars, two private Maseratis and one private Alfa. Five cars started the first heat, Caracciola finishing first with Dick fourth, sandwiched by the Auto Unions of Rosemeyer and von Delius. The pace, Seaman noted, had not been high, since no one wanted to risk a blow-out. Von Brauchitsch won the second heat from Hasse's Auto Union, with Lang relegated to third following a tyre change. After Neubauer protested that Hasse had obstructed Lang, the order of second and third was reversed. For the final, the team manager concocted a strategy. Caracciola would set the pace, expecting to make a tyre stop. Von Brauchitsch and Lang would try to go through non-stop, as would Seaman, who would be hoping to keep the open-wheeled Auto Unions behind him. But von Brauchitsch retired before half-distance with no oil in his gearbox, followed by Caracciola with a similar problem: heat retained inside the streamlined bodywork had melted the solder on a pipe, and the oil had leaked away. Lang's newer car had the pipe to the gearbox attached by a flange, with no soldering; now he was leading the race, with Seaman close behind, but the Englishman needed a pit stop when his overheated tyres started throwing their treads. Back on the track he fought for a while with Rosemeyer, who had also made an early stop, but the effort put too much strain on the new tyres and he threw another tread on the final lap, forcing him to slow drastically. Lang won his second race in a row, driving – in his own words – 'like a tightrope walker' as he nursed his tyres. Dick trailed in fifth behind the Auto Unions of Delius, Hasse and Rosemeyer, ahead only of the last finisher, the Maserati of the wealthy Hungarian amateur László Hartmann. Why had his car's tyres disintegrated while Lang's remained intact? The team's explanation was that the extra speed of the streamliner, compared to the open-wheeler, meant that its driver could operate at a reduced throttle opening. 'Extremely interesting,' Seaman said, sounding unconvinced. 'What a pity they didn't think of it before.'

The crowd of 380,000 – packed along the sides of the autobahn and not at all bothered by the absence of serious competition for their teams – had enjoyed a magnificent spectacle and Mercedes had won an important victory in front of the assembled dignitaries. Magda Goebbels presented Lang with a trophy so big and heavy that it would take two mechanics to carry it away. The winner's average speed of 162mph made it the fastest road race ever held, a distinction it would retain for twenty years.

This had been the apotheosis of a certain idea of motor sport, the poster image for an entire philosophy: gleaming projectiles with blood-red numbers on silver bodywork, created by boffin-geniuses in shapes drawn from science fiction, driven at seemingly impossible speeds by Übermenschen in white uniforms and dark-lensed goggles around a purpose-built track of such daunting splendour that it seemed part of Hitler's plans for a majestic metropolis. Here was a hint of the *Welthauptstadt Germania* – the world capital of the new German empire – of Albert Speer's drawings, for which the 1936 Olympic Stadium had been a first step. At AVUS the chariot races of imperial Rome were being remade for the twentieth century, leaving a worldwide audience awestruck and conveying a message of unanswerable technological superiority: when our cars can do this to the opposition, just imagine what else we might do.

After a ceremony at the restaurant in the modernistic new circular building next to the banked North Curve, Dick returned to Berlin. He had arranged to meet his friends, including Martin, Birch, Dugdale and the Cornwalls, in the rooftop restaurant of the Eden Hotel, opposite the main entrance to the zoo. Late in the evening, as they ate strawberries and cream, the roof slid open to reveal the summer night sky. They went on to the Ciro Bar on the Rankestrasse, a short walk away. It was one of those Berlin night clubs where jazz-tinged music was played in defiance of Nazi disapproval. The band's singer was an English girl known to Birch – 'of course', Dugdale remarked, rather pointedly. There they also encountered the Rosemeyers and Nuvolari – who, despite not being involved in the race, had turned up to watch while enjoying a weekend away with 'his cutie', as Dick put it. The Italian maestro led the dancing, at one point clearing the floor to give a solo exhibition.

18

A night in Harlem

It was Lilian Seaman who had advised her son to retain the services of Tony Birch, 'for companionship and a steadying influence' as well as the usefulness of his fluent German and his wife's domestic skills. But as Lilian continued to sign cheques in the first half of 1937, she began to feel some disquiet. When she discovered that Birch had charged Dick's racing account for four air tickets to Germany – one each for Dick and himself, plus two unidentified young women – and that the party had spent a few days in Paris en route, her view of the manager began to change. And having sounded out her son's friends and associates, including his former mechanics, on the subject, she did not enjoy what she heard about Birch's social habits.

'I put them under such a searching cross-examination,' she wrote, 'that eventually I was informed of all the activities of the previous racing season, and how Mr Richard was one of the quietest of young men if left to his own inclinations, was not over-addicted to social activities, and it was Mr Birch who liked parties and the gay life, provided always it was at other people's expense. In fact he was one of those men who could not live without it.' Setting aside any suspicion that her son was not necessarily averse to an active social life, she decided to take action against the man she believed to be leading him astray.

The first step was to close two of Dick's three accounts at the Westminster Bank, into which she put the funds for his racing activities and over which she had control. The third account, into which his income from trust funds was paid, had to be left open. Before informing Dick, she placed a call to Birch in Germany, during which she told him what she had discovered and what she had done about it, which included ending his right to sign cheques on her son's accounts. When he was silent after being ordered to close the Ambach villa and leave her son's employment, she put the phone down. Then she sent Dick a telegram.

His reaction was furious. He flew to London to confront her, but it became obvious that she would not order the accounts to be unfrozen until he promised to sever his relationship with Birch. That would not be easy, given that he had signed a piece of paper – which he had not bothered to read properly – giving Birch another year's contract, meaning another large chunk of his earnings. When he eventually gave in to his mother's demands, it was in the knowledge that she would find it hard to check whether he had expelled the manager or not, and Birch stayed on for a little while after the ultimatum had been accepted and the assurance given. Dick's progress in his German lessons, along with Uhlenhaut's perfect English, meant that the need for the manager's assistance was in any case greatly diminished. But he had regained access to his mother's funds, and that was the main thing.

◆

Two weeks after the AVUS race, the team made its way to the Nürburgring for the Eifelrennen. Five cars had been entered in the 150-mile race for Grand Prix cars, with Kautz replacing Zehender. Auto Union, stung by Mercedes' two big early-season wins, had been putting in extra tests at the circuit, and entered five cars of their own. All the W125s experienced fuel-feed problems, Seaman's petrol pump breaking altogether after only four practice laps. Once mended, it was given to von Brauchitsch, whose own car had failed. A message was sent to Stuttgart and on the Saturday evening another car was put onto a high-speed transporter and driven through the night to the track. Seaman dragged himself out of his bed in the Eifelerhof Hotel in Adenau at five o'clock in the morning in order to drive a couple of laps to make sure everything worked. Practice was also interrupted when von Delius, approaching Bergwerk at high speed in his Auto Union, was hit in the face by a bird and crashed heavily, shaking him up without causing serious injury.

Dick returned in time to watch the sports-car race at midday, won by the Frazer Nash-BMW of A. F. P. Fane, a friend and a shareholder in the British sports-car manufacturer. An Anglo-Indian, born Alfred Fane Peers Agabeg, the winner celebrated by installing Adolf Hühnlein in the car's passenger seat for his lap of honour around the 14-mile circuit. 'Very sporty of the old chap,' Dick observed, referring to the Korpsführer, with whom he got on quite well once he had penetrated the officious surface to discover a layer of joviality ('Seaman told me that he had two very pretty daughters,' Monkhouse remembered).

The race for Grand Prix cars was a disappointment. In front of 300,000 spectators, Dick was holding sixth place on the second lap when the fuel-feed problem recurred and halted him at the Fuchsröhre. He could do nothing but sit and watch as Caracciola, the early leader, was challenged by Rosemeyer, the two Germans duelling furiously until the Mercedes driver was forced to stop for a tyre change. Faster pit-work by the Auto Union crew, combined with repeated fuel-flow problems for the Mercedes, settled the result in Rosemeyer's favour.

The observant would have noticed that Kautz's car sounded different. It was fitted with an alternative type of supercharger, which sucked fuel through the carburettor instead of forcing compressed air into it. When fitted to the W125, the result was not just more power but a complete absence of the unique high-pitched scream associated with Mercedes since their return to Grand Prix racing in 1934. Soon the new supercharger would be fitted to all the cars, silencing forever that banshee noise.

◆

The first half of July saw a clash in the racing calendar. In Europe, the Belgian Grand Prix was being held at Spa-Francorchamps. But on the other side of the Atlantic, the Vanderbilt Cup offered a rare opportunity for publicity in the United States. Both Mercedes and Auto Union decided to split their teams between the two events. Showing the significance they placed on success in front of an American audience, Neubauer and Uhlenhaut crossed the Atlantic accompanied by Caracciola, their most famous driver, and Seaman, who would be able to speak to journalists and broadcasters in their own language. Von Brauchitsch, Lang and Kautz went to Spa. Dick obtained a new passport, issued by the British consulate in Munich, in which a temporary US visa was stamped.

In 1904 the inaugural Vanderbilt Cup, held over a 30-mile circuit of public roads on Long Island, had become the first international road race ever held in the United States. Gradually it had adapted itself until, by 1937, it was being run at the Roosevelt Raceway on Long Island, an artificial 3.3-mile track on an old airfield. Not only was the prize money considerable – $20,000 for first place, down to $1,400 for tenth – but the prestige value to the visitors, both for the winning manufacturer and for the international reputation of German engineering, was potentially enormous.

The teams embarked at Bremerhaven on an ocean liner that, four years earlier, had held the Blue Riband for the fastest Atlantic crossing. Between its two funnels, the SS *Bremen* of the Norddeutscher Lloyd line featured a catapult to launch a small mail-carrying Heinkel seaplane, which could be sent off to arrive at the destination port several hours ahead of the ship itself. Two years earlier, anti-Nazi demonstrators had stormed the ship at its pier in New York and torn down its swastika flag, throwing it into the Hudson River.

Rudolf Caracciola came on board when the *Bremen* docked in Cherbourg, accompanied by his new wife. Since Chiron refused to propose, Baby Hoffmann had accepted Rudi's offer of marriage. A most elegant couple, they were married in Castagnola, on Lake Lugano, where they were settling into a new villa. 'He had kept it very quiet, though I knew they were pretty friendly,' Seaman wrote to Monkhouse. 'Personally I think it will make an excellent match, for she is a very intelligent and charming lady and I think they are well suited to each other.' She had already shown herself to be a practical asset to the team, adept as a timekeeper in the pits, manipulating stopwatches and keeping a lap chart up to date.

The Auto Union party included Dr Feuereissen, Bernd and Elly Rosemeyer, Ferdinand Porsche and Professor Robert Eberan von Eberhorst, the designers, with Dr Porsche's son, Ferry, and Ghislaine Kaes, his nephew and secretary. Other occupants of the first-class cabins were Bodo Lafferentz, a Nazi official who, as leader of the *Kraft Durch Freude* (Strength Through Joy) movement, was a co-director with Porsche of the People's Car project; Jakob Werlin, Hitler's car dealer and now a Daimler-Benz director; the Stuttgart-based journalist Eberhard Hundt, said to have been the first to apply the term *Silberpfeil* (Silver Arrows) to the German cars; and the film director Friedrich Stollsteimer (also known as Erich Stoll), there to capture for posterity this German invasion of the New World, accompanied by a cinematographer, Hans Scheib, who had been one of the cameramen on *Olympia*, Leni Riefenstahl's documentary of the 1936 Games.

The voyage had barely begun when Dick received the news of Pat Fairfield's death at Le Mans. His friend had been taking part in the twenty-four-hour race for the first time, sharing the wheel of a Frazer Nash-BMW, and became involved in a pile-up that started when a French amateur lost control of his Bugatti in the Maison Blanche curves and was hit by a German-entered BMW. The Bugatti and its driver's dead body were lying in the road when Fairfield arrived at high speed, unable to avoid a collision. Thrown clear, he stood up but soon collapsed and lost consciousness. He died in hospital two days later.

When the ship stopped at Southampton, Seaman posted a letter to his mother, asking her to send a wreath, calling Fairfield 'a really good driver and also a good sportsman ... I was very friendly with him.' On her son's behalf, Lilian attended the funeral in Sevenoaks, Kent, where Fairfield was mourned by his wife, Jean, whom he had met while at Cambridge, and their 5-year-old daughter. At the start of the season, Fairfield's family had urged him to give up the sport; his response said much about what had been happening in Europe, particularly since Hitler's remilitarisation of the Rhineland in March 1936 and the growing clamour for Britain to invest in its ability to defend itself. 'I don't know why you worry so much about my getting hurt or killed,' he told them. 'There is going to be a war, and if I don't get killed driving I shall probably get killed fighting, and I should rather die doing something I love than be killed doing something I loathe, and I should loathe to have to kill.'

News of another tragedy arrived on the ship carrying the other European entrants, the Scuderia Ferrari, from Le Havre to New York. On 27 June, while on board the SS *Normandie* of the Compagnie Générale Transatlantique, Tazio Nuvolari – the much-fêted winner of the race a year earlier – received a radio message from his wife, Carolina, to inform him that the elder of their two adored sons, 18-year-old Giorgio, had died of myocarditis, an inflammation of the heart muscle, at their home outside Mantua.

At Southampton Dick was able to pick up his evening clothes, which he had asked his mother to send down from London, enabling him to dress for dinner at the captain's table. The onboard facilities included a cinema, a casino and various other games; a guided tour of the *Bremen*'s impressive steam-turbine engines particularly interested Dr Porsche. At the end of the five-day crossing, the passengers disembarked in New York amid heavy rain but to a warm welcome from the race organisers and a posse of reporters and photographers.

The management and drivers of the Mercedes team were booked into the modern fifteen-storey, 500-room Hotel Gladstone on 114 East 52nd Street, close to such fashionable midtown night spots as El Morocco and the Stork Club. Their first outing, however, was to the circuit. On the 25-mile journey to the outskirts of Westbury, a small town on Long Island, Seaman was struck by the American system of concrete highways with bridges, viaducts and clover-leaf junctions, the layouts giving him an explanation for the soft handling and sluggish performance of American road cars. 'There is no question at all that for proceeding along a smooth concrete road, with no corners to speak of, at 40mph among myriads of other cars, the only hazard being lots of traffic lights, they are quite ideal,' he wrote to Monkhouse. The provision of a chauffeured Cadillac for the rest of the trip was, he concluded, 'extremely comfortable and ideal for the conditions'.

The track was wide, and bordered by a low wooden fence. There were two long straights and no really fast bends, although the banked turn at the end of the lap looked spectacular, but the absence of external features – no trees, houses or other signs – made it hard for the European drivers to pick out braking points. Forewarned by Lord Howe, who had taken part the previous year, Dick spent much of the time in practice trying to find the best lines, following the American ace Rex Mays, who was driving the Scuderia Ferrari's spare Alfa Romeo from 1936, a 2-year-old eight-cylinder model.

Of the thirty-strong field, the other American competitors included Wilbur Shaw, who had won the first of what would be three victories in the Indianapolis 500 five weeks earlier, now driving a Maserati V8RI. The rest of the local drivers were mostly mounted on two-seater Indy-style specials or dirt-track machines, some of them home-built. Their crude suspension and two-speed gearboxes would put them at a disadvantage against the Europeans. For the visitors, an exception was made to the American Automobile Association's regulation requiring the drivers to wear hard-shelled crash helmets; they were allowed to retain their leather or linen windcaps. The authorities would not, however, lift the ban on women in the pits, which meant that Alice Caracciola had to sit with her stopwatches on a small platform in the infield. Since the organisers had asked the foreign entrants to display their national emblems, the German cars also appeared with black swastikas on white roundels in red rectangles – recently confirmed as the official flag of Germany – on the tails of the Mercedes and the cockpit sides of the Auto Unions; this was something the teams rarely did in Europe, and never outside Germany. One technical feature, however, made the Mercedes cars less easy to identify: now that a new type of supercharger had been fitted to the W125s, Seaman immediately noted with relief the absence of the old distinctive wail. It may have thrilled spectators but it was something, he told Monkhouse, that he had 'always found extremely tiresome when driving'.

In the days leading up to the race, which was to take place over the Fourth of July weekend, Dick noticed that, unsurprisingly, Nuvolari's heart did not seem to be in it. In the American fashion, qualifying times were taken as the average speed over nine consecutive laps, with each driver allowed three attempts at the 30-mile distance. Caracciola was fastest, with an average of just over 85mph. Behind him came Rosemeyer, who pleased the press photographers by wearing lederhosen between practice sessions, while Mays surprised the Scuderia Ferrari with third place in their old car. Seaman was fourth, and Nuvolari and Farina were fifth and sixth in the Scuderia's latest twelve-cylinder Alfas. The race had been scheduled for the Saturday, but a downpour half an hour before the planned start led to a postponement. While standard practice in the US, this was a

novelty to the Europeans, who were used to competing whatever the conditions.

The 300-mile race was finally rescheduled for the Monday,
the last day of the holiday weekend, in front of 80,000 spectators
who had made the trip out to Long Island. Before the start, the
competitors were introduced to the crowd and the announcement of the only Englishman in the field was preceded by a brief
tribute to Fairfield, who had finished fifth a year earlier. From a
wooden platform high above the start line, the flag was dropped
by Ralph DePalma, the recently retired Italian-American driver
whose long career had included an estimated 2,000 wins on all
kinds of tracks.

Neubauer had told Seaman to let Caracciola battle it out with
Rosemeyer and wait to see what transpired as the ninety laps
ran their course. After spending the first ten laps sitting behind
Mays, he diced with another American, Billy Winn. Eventually,
after eight laps of watching Winn's Summers-Miller taking the
bends in long slides, Dick went through into third place when
the dirt-track machine's crankshaft broke. Caracciola's retirement elevated him to second place, thirty-eight seconds behind
Rosemeyer. He cut twenty seconds off the Auto Union's lead
before coming up to lap von Delius, who made it hard for the
Mercedes to get past, thus allowing the leader to pull away again.
After the first round of pit stops von Delius, in contrast to the
gentlemanly behaviour of the American drivers, held him up
again and Rosemeyer was able to take the chequered flag with a
lead of fifty seconds. Seaman had taken no risks, conscious of the
responsibility of being the only Mercedes left in the race. Mays
finished third, ahead of von Delius, whose tactics were reckoned
by Dugdale to have cost Dick ten seconds twice over.

Second place was a satisfactory result, but a memo from
the Mercedes management to Korpsführer Hühnlein back in
Germany put a slightly different interpretation on the team's
defeat by Auto Union in such an important race: 'In the 89th lap
Seaman stopped suddenly, to everyone's surprise, as he thought

the race was over. By the time it had been explained to him that he had made an error, costly seconds had passed which could not be regained before the end of the race.' This seems to have been an amended version of reality. Seaman certainly made a very late stop, lasting only fifteen seconds. Accepting that he could not challenge Rosemeyer for the victory, he took on a splash of fuel that would ensure his tank did not run dry in the final miles.

Dick was impressed by Alice Caracciola's expertise with a lap chart. 'What she doesn't know about motor racing after ten years with the "wily fox" [Chiron] just isn't worth knowing,' he told Monkhouse, 'and she has given me a lot of useful tips.' Afterwards there was a female encounter of a different kind. Ralph Vickers, a friend and contemporary from Trinity College, was living in New York while studying the methods of Wall Street, having recently joined his father's stockbroking firm. A Bugatti driver in his university days, Vickers was living, quite by coincidence, at the Gladstone, and going out with a well-known beauty. That night he took Dick up to Harlem to visit the clubs; not the celebrated Cotton Club, which had moved to midtown two years earlier, but perhaps Monroe's Uptown House, where the 22-year-old Billie Holiday was a regular attraction, or the Shim Sham on 113th Street, run by Dickie Wells, a celebrated Harlem figure who combined the roles of gigolo and entrepreneur for a clientele including Tallulah Bankhead and Joan Crawford. During the evening, Dick added, Vickers 'introduced me to a very nice cutie'.

Whatever may have transpired, it was destined to be brief, for the next day was his last in New York. In between a prize-giving reception, a press conference and a dinner hosted by the German ambassador, Dick squeezed in a trip to a record store, partly in answer to Monkhouse's request to 'collect a few records for me while you are over there, particularly by Dorsey Brothers, Benny Goodman and Adrian Rollini, or for that matter, any of the really good swing bands. Naturally, I would pay you for these.' Dick responded by bringing back 'quite a good selection' of 78s.

There had been anti-German protests during their stay in New York, and as the teams prepared to set off for home on the SS *Europa*, the *Bremen*'s sister ship, they might have seen the cartoons in the *New York Times* and the *Daily News*, satirising their lavish and meticulous style of preparation: cars and swastika-bedecked pit counters surrounded by squads of overalled technicians giving Hitler salutes and saying things like '*Ja, alles in ordnung!*' Disembarking five days later at Bremerhaven, they were ushered into a reception at which Korpsführer Hühnlein eulogised the victorious representatives of the Third Reich.

19

The goddess of speed

Encouraged by a warm reception for *Motoraces*, Monkhouse and Seaman had cooked up a scheme for George to spend a season with Mercedes, photographing the Grand Prix circus from the inside. Dick, who had shown a copy of the book to Karl Kudorfer, the team's publicity chief, advised his friend on how to make a formal approach and what to say in his letter to Dr Kissel. The response was positive: clearly Monkhouse was a highly proficient photographer with a real knowledge of motor racing, and his employment in a senior position with Kodak would have acted as a further guarantee of a serious approach to the assignment. Permission was granted, and George's boss at Kodak, who had previously run the firm's German office, was happy to keep him on full pay.

George's regular presence would also give Dick greater opportunity to spend time studying his friend's photographs in detail. This was the habit he had acquired since discovering that by comparing George's shots of different drivers taking the same corner, he could analyse the differences between his own driving style and those of his rivals – an example of the studious approach he had brought to bear on improving his personal performance since the earliest days of his racing career.

Monkhouse's first official rendezvous with the team was at

the Nürburgring, where a place in the line-up for the German Grand Prix was Dick's reward for his result in the United States. Accompanied by Tony Cliff, who was staying at Ambach, he picked up George from Cologne airport and they drove to the Eifelerhof. George brought with him Dick's raincoat, which had been left in the Bentley sometime earlier in the year, and received a tin of Four Square pipe tobacco in exchange. In three days of poor weather, the practice times had provided a less-than-exact guide to form, although Rosemeyer was fastest, ahead of Lang, von Brauchitsch (who had to be pacified by Neubauer on discovering that, as a Nürburgring specialist, he had been outqualified by the former mechanic), and Caracciola, with Seaman a modest eighth on the grid.

At the end of the first of the twenty laps Dick was down in tenth place, but climbed up to seventh on the next round, scrabbling past Nuvolari's Alfa on the inside of the turn after the pits before accounting for Kautz and Hasse. On the following lap he went by Müller and von Delius, the crowd's attention now gripped by his rapid progress, and by a quarter distance Mercedes were holding the first four places, with Caracciola, von Brauchitsch and Lang ahead of their English colleague. On the sixth lap, however, Seaman failed to come round. Von Delius, in a desperate attempt to repass him just after the second of two humpback bridges on the long straight, had come up alongside him on the narrow road as they approached a left-hand curve at about 150mph. The German brushed the hedge on the left side of the track, lost control, slewed back in front of Dick while trying to straighten up, was struck by the Mercedes and shot off through a hedge and a wire fence, down an embankment and across an adjacent public road before finally coming to halt in a field. Dick had been unable to avoid clipping the Auto Union; his car hit the hedge on the right-hand side, struck a metal post and spun, ejecting the driver, who landed face-first on the track, suffering scrapes, cuts and bruises to the left-hand side of his face, a broken nose and a broken left thumb. Despite his injuries, Dick got up and helped a group of Brownshirts to push the battered car off the course.

Dugdale was among a group of British reporters who left the press box, jumped into a car, and drove down the Koblenz road, which ran parallel to that section of the circuit, to find the crumpled wrecks of the two cars. Both drivers were taken to Adenau hospital as the race continued, Caracciola and von Brauchitsch taking a Mercedes one-two ahead of Rosemeyer. Dr Kissel descended from the grandstand to congratulate the drivers and the mechanics as Caracciola received the winner's trophy: a large bronze head – the Goddess of Speed – given in Hitler's name. On their way to an uproarious victory party at the Eifelerhof, Neubauer, Kautz and Monkhouse visited the hospital, where they found Seaman heavily bandaged around the head but fully conscious and grateful, he said, for his good luck in having escaped much worse injury. Dugdale and Cliff, too, found their way to his room. 'Come in,' he whispered through the aperture in the bandages covering his face. 'Let's have a party. Order some beer!' He was being overoptimistic.

He had been told nothing of von Delius's condition. The diminutive German driver had also been hurled from his car. Conscious enough to shout at the ambulance driver to slow down on the way to the hospital, he survived the evening while doctors diagnosed a fractured skull, a broken leg and several broken ribs and a double fracture of the spine, along with serious facial injuries. At four o'clock in the morning, he succumbed to bleeding on the brain.

On the morning after the race Caracciola and von Brauchitsch flew from Cologne to Berlin in a plane sent by Hitler in order to attend a special ceremony at which they received the Führer's congratulations. Privately, the two drivers were coming to an agreement to do everything they could to ensure that Lang, whose talent was now impossible to ignore, would find it difficult to get the better of the men who did not consider him to be their equal. Lang himself stayed on at the Eifelerhof until the Thursday, visiting the hospital several times to see Seaman, who had not been told about von Delius's death. 'Although he seemed to be in the best of spirits,' Lang wrote, 'he was certainly a most hideous sight, having two enormous black eyes, very swollen lips, and a steel catapult device on his thumb to keep it straight. He still maintained his appetite in spite of the fact that his feeding aperture was somewhat restricted.'

◆

Since the death of her husband, Lilian Seaman had developed the habit of placing a phone call to the London office of the *Sporting Life* after Dick's continental races, asking how he had got on. She had become known to some of the night-duty journalists, but an unfamiliar voice came on the line when she called from Pull Court to ask about the German Grand Prix. After being given the names of the first three finishers, she thanked her informant and was about to put down the phone, thinking that her son must have finished further down the order, or had perhaps retired with some problem. But then the man said, 'Don't you want to hear anything about Dick Seaman, our own English driver?' 'Yes, please,' she replied. 'Seaman has met with an accident,' he told her.

She went cold. And colder still when he gave her what he knew of the details. 'Severe facial injuries. Broken arm and wrist. Feared internal injuries not yet diagnosed. So far as known retains his sight. Still under anaesthetic.' Her cry of horror startled her informant, prompting him to ask if, perhaps, she had some connection to the driver. Yes, she said, he's my son. He promised to ring her back when more details arrived.

She paced around the house, looking at the moon shining through the leaded windows in the Great Hall, unable to stop herself imagining that the worst had happened. And then, during the night, she did indeed receive a call – not from a journalist but from the hospital, giving her details of the accident. After putting down the phone she looked out of the drawing-room windows at the parkland in front of the house, where her son had often landed his Gipsy Moth, and wished that an aeroplane could be there to take her to him now.

By the time dawn broke she had decided to go to London and catch a flight to Germany to be with him, even though she had never flown before. Her driver took her to Evesham, where she caught the first train. From Paddington she was taken to Ennismore Gardens. There she spoke on the telephone to the *Sporting Life*'s motoring correspondent, Tommy Wisdom, who reassured her that her son had not lost his sight and was making good progress. He gave her the address of the hospital, to which she immediately sent a telegram telling Dick of her intention to be with him as soon as possible.

Before her preparations for the journey could be completed, a telegram arrived by return. The message was plain: PLEASE DO NOT TROUBLE TO COME OUT STOP PLEASE ACCEDE TO MY REQUEST STOP BETTER FOR YOU NOT TO SEE ME NOW AS FACE HEAVILY BANDAGED STOP AM FAIRLY COMFORTABLE STOP WRITING SOON STOP LOVE DICK. Reading and re-reading it, she thought back to the time when he was six years old and had scolded her for coming to meet him outside Mr Gibbs' school. Again she bowed to his demand; it would be months before she saw him again.

◆

Dick would not be fit to return to the team either for the Monaco Grand Prix or for the Coppa Acerbo. Instead he occupied himself with his correspondence. He wrote to Fred Craner, the secretary of the Derby and District Motor Club, about Craner's desire to see the German teams compete in that October's Donington Grand Prix. Keen for his home crowd to see him at the wheel of a Mercedes, Dick had been trying to persuade Sailer and Neubauer to enter the race. Now he was writing on Neubauer's behalf, asking Craner to raise the winner's prize from the previous year's £400 – he suggested £500 – and to offer starting money that would at least cover the cost of sending a team to England; eventually Craner would agree to the sum of £100 for each car entered by the two German outfits.

Even with his left arm still in a sling, before going home to Bavaria to continue his recovery Dick had insisted on driving a lap of the Nürburgring in the 3-litre Mercedes on loan to George. In Munich, a doctor told him that plastic surgery would be necessary on his disfigured face. In his absence the team had another good day, this time in the Monaco Grand Prix. With Lang also missing through illness, von Brauchitsch led home Caracciola and Kautz in a Mercedes clean sweep. The winner had angered Neubauer by ignoring his increasingly frantic signals to slow down and let a faster and very frustrated Caracciola past on the tight street circuit. Defying the man who had invented team orders, von Brauchitsch insolently stuck out his tongue when Neubauer frantically waved his red and black flag as he sped past the pits.

Monkhouse had attended the race and was preparing to set off on the drive to Munich the following day when a telegram arrived. It was from Seaman, announcing that – thanks partly to Lang going down with influenza followed by a kidney infection – he had been told by Neubauer to report for duty in Pescara. Monkhouse promptly changed his plans and headed for Italy. Not having been booked into a hotel by the team, he had to find his own lodgings on the holiday weekend, ending up in a room also occupied by mosquitoes and bedbugs. (Later, Earl Howe told him that he never travelled to Pescara without mosquito netting and a supply of Flit sprays and ointment.) George found Seaman restored to fitness, if still the worse for wear around the face – 'his nose was a hideous sight as it seemed to have absorbed large pieces of the road' – and with a big blister on his left thumb left by the contraption that had helped the broken bone to set.

During the first practice session, Dick's right front brake locked as he slowed for one of the chicanes. It sent him off the track, without damage. Worse was to come the next morning, when the left front brake locked as he was going through the village of Cappelle sul Tavo, up in the hills, at around 100mph. Trying desperately to slow the car enough to make it through the right-hand bend that began the long flat-out descent back to the seafront, he ran straight into the side of a house, pushing the left front wheel back and fracturing the chassis, leaving the stricken car stranded across the narrow road amid a scattering of dislodged kerbstones. Luckily, he emerged unscathed, but the car was a mess and required the help of a group of policemen and soldiers to push it out of the way. Since Mercedes had brought only three cars for their trio of drivers, Dick was out of the race, except as a reserve: a serious disappointment at a place where he had won twice. In Saturday's ferocious heat Rosemeyer amused the spectators by removing his shirt and recording the fastest lap wearing just his wind helmet, gloves, sandals and a pair of shorts.

The supporting voiturette race on the Sunday morning was notable for a hideous accident on the opening lap. Pasquino Ermini was attempting to force his Maserati past the similar car of Luciano Uboldi when he hit a marker stone and collided with Reggie Tongue's ERA before spinning into the crowd. Four spectators were killed, one of them a Blackshirt and two – according to Monkhouse – having their lower limbs completely severed. The race continued, as races always did. Afterwards Tongue had to defend himself against a charge that he had caused the accident by being under the influence of drugs. Someone had seen him pouring white powder into his pre-race glass of orange squash. It was Glucodin, a glucose-based energy supplement.

Dick was sitting in the pits in his racing gear – a short-sleeved shirt helping him to cope with the extreme heat of the Ferragosto weekend – when the Grand Prix cars left the starting grid. Rosemeyer took the lead from Caracciola on the opening lap and extended it until he swiped a kilometre stone halfway around the circuit, limping into the auxiliary pit on three wheels and a rear brake drum before resuming after repairs. Caracciola, however, came into the pits at the end of the eleventh lap, running on seven cylinders. The mechanics fitted new plugs and he was sent back out, but he returned at the end of the next lap for Seaman to jump in and take over. Dick also had a bad moment when a small fire broke out in the engine compartment, but he stopped until it had extinguished itself and restarted to finish the race in fifth place, with Rosemeyer winning ahead of von Brauchitsch.

After the race Dick and George left for Milan, where they stayed for a couple of nights. Then they set off through the Alps towards Berne for the Swiss Grand Prix, stopping for lunch at a hotel on the Furka pass, where the staff yodelled for them in four-part harmony. 'I have heard yodelling many times before,' Monkhouse noted, 'but never anything as beautiful as this.' Somewhere in the mountains, in the rain, Dick managed to lose control of the Mercedes on the wet road as they entered a village, the car smashing backwards into a group of fruit barrows. After picking up the fruit and making good the damage, they resumed their progress.

On arrival at the Bremgarten circuit they were surprised to find Nuvolari ensconced in the Auto Union pit. Alfa Romeo had abandoned the Scuderia Ferrari a few weeks earlier, entering their new twelve-cylinder car under their own banner at the Coppa Acerbo, from which it quickly retired, and now their finest driver had left them to line up alongside Rosemeyer, Stuck and Fagioli. At Mercedes, Seaman had been demoted to reserve, a disappointment in the light of his hat-trick of voiturette wins at the circuit, with Kautz stepping up to join the regular drivers. Dick was allowed a couple of laps in practice but had to watch as Caracciola, Lang – who had lost a great deal of weight during his illness, and had to fight to overcome dizziness at the wheel – and von Brauchitsch completed a Mercedes sweep. Afterwards Dick and George were among the guests at a celebration for the team and the Mercedes hierarchy hosted by Dr Kissel in his villa at Überlingen, on the shores of Lake Constance, where beer, wine and champagne flowed.

◆

During a party that went on into the small hours, Monkhouse noticed the presence of Peter Gläser, the doctor who travelled with the two German teams, and his fiancée, Laury Vermundt; they had become friendly with Dick during their travels to races, and would be among those who came to stay with him in Bavaria during the two weeks before the Italian Grand Prix. The guests at the Ambach house party that August also included a young stockbroker named Hubert Sturges and another friend, Tony Bell, who had just begun a distinguished career with Lund Humphries, the publishers of illustrated art books; they had travelled from London with Dugdale in the journalist's Ford V8, bought in rather battered condition from Reggie Tongue.

John Dugdale encountered Dr Gläser while staying with Dick that summer, during a drinking session at the inn at Ambach. 'He was an interesting and intelligent man,' Dugdale wrote. 'His gossip about the racing world was illuminating but his job, although taking him to all the gala spots in Europe, had its disadvantages. Being up at the Nürburgring for weeks on end in the cold weather for the early spring practising was, he told us, rather dull, on duty for the emergencies they all hoped would never come.' It was Gläser who had saved the life of Hanns Geier, so badly injured when his Mercedes crashed at Berne in 1935 that he was forced to stop driving and take a job assisting Neubauer in the racing department. 'Dick owed much to him. He restored confidence to Seaman and Kautz after crashes, talking to them in his quiet voice and watching them steadily with his dark eyes.' But Dugdale was particularly struck by the doctor's companion, a widow in her mid–thirties.

'It must have been her colouring that gave one such a vivid first impression of her,' he wrote of Laury Vermundt. 'She seemed all pale blues and roses because she was wearing the Bavarian country dress, the dirndl – all frills and apron and full skirt, puffed sleeves and shepherdess hat. The face was strong, the hair blonde.'

She also made an impression on Dick, becoming one of several women, including Marjorie Martin and Alice Caracciola, with whom he established close, relaxed and platonic relationships – although not everyone believed that his friendship with Laury Vermundt was entirely innocent.

While Dick and his guests were enjoying themselves on the shore of the Starnbergersee, elsewhere in Bavaria 140,000 Nazi faithful were assembling for their ninth annual rally. Among those listening to the speeches in Nuremberg was Sir Nevile Henderson, the newly appointed British ambassador to Germany, who had already bonded with Hermann Göring over a shared interest in hunting as well as a fondness for sartorial extravagance (Henderson became known to Adolf Hitler as 'the man with the red carnation'). The ambassador reported to the Foreign Office in London that 'we are witnessing in Germany the rebirth, the reorganisation and unification of the German people. One may criticise and disapprove, one may thoroughly dislike the threatened consummation and be apprehensive of its potentialities. But let us make no mistake. Germany is now so strong that it can no longer be attacked with impunity, and soon the country will be prepared for aggressive action.' After a private conversation with Hitler at Nuremberg, however, he reported that the German leader sought an Anglo–German understanding based on 'reasonableness'.

An attempt to halt Germany's Grand Prix steamroller was being made in Italy, whose teams were being humiliated as Mercedes and Auto Union amply fulfilled the Führer's desire to use motor sport as a symbolic expression of technical resources, willpower and aggression. The Italian Grand Prix was moved from Monza, its ultra-fast home since 1922, to Livorno, where it was hoped that a circuit on tight, narrow streets would suit the slower but supposedly nimbler Italian machines. Nuvolari, too, was back in an Alfa Romeo again, giving the home fans an extra reason for hope. At Mercedes, Dick was restored to the starting line-up at the wheel of a fifth car. After crashing in Pescara on his return from convalescence, he resolved to take it steadily and was eighth fastest in practice.

As the grid formed up, each car was pushed to the start by three mechanics, accompanied by a sailor carrying the national flag. All the drivers were expected to give the fascist salute as they marched past the grandstand where the dignitaries were installed. A huge crowd spilled onto the track near the first corner, ignoring the police's attempts to persuade them back into their positions and delaying the start for so long that Neubauer ordered the mechanics to reinstall soft plugs in the engines and warm them up all over again. To Dick, it was the most bizarre incident he had experienced at a big race. He started from the middle of the third row, between the Alfas of Nuvolari and Trossi, and found himself in a scrap for sixth place. At the front Caracciola and Lang were having a furious battle, the younger man taking the lead and refusing to give it back despite Neubauer's frantic signals and a stern lecture during a pit stop. Resuming in second place, Lang did his best to retake the team's senior figure but was held at bay on the narrow roads, the two cars finishing four-tenths of a second apart. Seaman won an enjoyable dice with the Auto Unions of Müller and Varzi to finish in fourth place: the sort of solid supporting performance that would have done him no harm in the eyes of his team manager, who now had his hands full with an outbreak of internal warfare.

Two weeks later it was Kautz's turn to be dropped as a quartet of Mercedes arrived for the seventh Masaryk Grand Prix in Czechoslovakia, run over the 18-mile circuit at Brno. They faced only two Auto Unions, driven by Rosemeyer and

Müller. Hasse was ill, Varzi had gone home with a hand injury, and Stuck had been sacked by Dr Feuereissen, who had grown tired of his complaints about his car, the excuse for his dismissal probably coming when he boasted about the details of his very favourable contract to Rosemeyer, who promptly demanded more money from the management. Lang took an early lead but had relinquished it to Rosemeyer by the time he slid wide at high speed on dirt and gravel thrown onto the road by other cars, his car hitting a low stone wall, somersaulting twice and landing in a ditch, killing two spectators while injuring a dozen others.

The sudden transformation of a racing car into an instrument of slaughter was hardly an uncommon occurrence in those years. The drivers knew and accepted the risks – and so, they believed, did the spectators, who turned up in the expectation of seeing men flirting with mortal danger. In this case the dead and injured had been watching from a prohibited area, sitting on the edge of a ditch on the outside of the fast right-hand bend. When Lang, having been taken to hospital for treatment to a cut on his head, learnt of the consequences of the accident, he was naturally shocked. But however genuine his sympathy for the casualties of the crash, he was not prepared for the insults he received from the injured who had also arrived at the hospital, and who, once he had been pointed out to them, blamed him for the tragedy. His conscience, he felt, was clear. It was an accident, and they had been in the wrong place.

Rosemeyer also crashed, leaving Caracciola unchallenged ahead of von Brauchitsch. Dick finished an unspectacular fourth, winning an early battle with Nuvolari's Alfa but being passed on the last lap by a charging Rosemeyer, who had taken over Müller's car at the final pit stop. Neubauer was advised by the race organisers to get Lang out of the country as quickly as possible, before the local police could take an interest in his accident. Eventually the bereaved and the injured joined forces to bring a case against him, alleging that he had hit a trackside stone earlier in the race and continued in a dangerously damaged car. Lang firmly denied it, and there was no evidence to support the claim, but the case would spend several years in the courts before being dismissed. Meanwhile, as the team left Brno, there was another race only a week away.

20

In an English garden

On the day after the race in Czechoslovakia, the Mercedes management and drivers took off from Vienna for London in one of Lufthansa's three-engined Junkers Ju 52s, flying via Munich, Frankfurt and Brussels to a rainy Croydon airport. A small reception committee was waiting for them, including Charlie and Marjorie Martin, Tommy Wisdom and Bill Boddy, the new young editor of *Motor Sport*. To the disgust of Boddy – an admirer of the German approach to racing – no representative of the RAC, the British Racing Drivers' Club or the organisers of the third Donington Grand Prix had turned up to welcome these distinguished visitors on their first trip to England; nor was the road to London lined with fans. 'I suppose one cannot hope that the British public will show the enthusiasm and curiosity for the racing aces that they do for long-distance aviators or sex-appealing film stars,' he wrote.

Four German-registered Mercedes saloons were lined up outside the terminal building, ready to take the team on the 12-mile journey to the Grosvenor House Hotel on Park Lane, a few doors away from the company's London showroom, for an overnight stay. The saloons had been driven from Untertürkheim, like the two convoys of lorries that had already arrived at the circuit, carrying four fresh W125s plus the equipment and the mechanics required for the 1937 Donington Grand Prix, while the equivalent cars, material and personnel used in Czechoslovakia were making their way back to the factory. Only Caracciola was missing; always reluctant to fly, he had elected to travel by boat train, arriving with Alice at Victoria station the next day, before joining the party for the drive up to Donington Park.

First there was a formal tea arranged for them at the Dorchester and hosted by Jakob Werlin, Hitler's confidant on the Daimler-Benz board. Afterwards Dick went to Ennismore Gardens to visit his mother. Once she had recovered from the shock of his very visible facial cuts and bruises, they sat in front of the log fire and he talked about his life in Germany. As far as he was concerned, he told her, he had always tried to represent what Britain stood for and to encourage friendship between the two countries. The Germans had treated him with kindness. They had felt down and out after the war, and who could blame them for trying to rise again? But that was no reason why England should go on so blithely disarming and giving the dole to everyone who asked for it while Germany was arming itself to the teeth. 'Can you wonder,' he said, 'that they laugh at us?' He left at one o'clock in the morning, telling her that he would have to be up early in the morning, in time to join the team for the drive up to the Midlands.

They were billeted in Nottingham, at a ninety-room hotel called the Black Boy, built in the 1880s by the celebrated local architect Watson Fothergill with a typically eccentric Bavarian-style gabled and colonnaded red-brick facade that made it a distinctive feature of the city centre. In the mornings they would be awakened in the city of Robin Hood by the deep clang of Little John, the 10-ton bell in the clock tower of the adjacent Council House. Australia's Test cricketers, staying at the Black Boy while playing Test matches at Trent Bridge, had made regular efforts to get the clock silenced, to no avail.

When the man from *Motor Sport* got up to Donington, his

first sight of the German teams in a British environment had a significant impact. 'The outstanding impression,' Bill Boddy wrote after the first day's practice sessions, 'is one of profound respect for the thorough way in which Germany goes about this serious business of motor racing – and that, in turn, reflects very favourably on the entire outlook of the Germany of today.' His colleagues on the local papers were delighted when the Mercedes personnel distributed lavish press packs including profiles of the drivers and details of the cars' technical specifications. Some of the English competitors were astonished to see the Germans using thermometers to take the temperature of their tyres when the cars came into the pits during the practice sessions.

The visiting teams had mixed feelings about Britain's attempt to create a proper circuit in a country where racing on public roads was banned, and where the rather down-at-heel Donington Hall had housed German prisoners of war twenty years earlier. A new half-mile loop had lengthened the circuit to just over 3 miles, but they were unhappy about the narrowness and rough surface of the older sections of the track. The spectators, however, were enthralled by the spectacle of these futuristic monsters leaping into the air at the top of the steep rise after the Melbourne Hairpin with all four wheels off the ground, by the ear-splitting scream of the V16 and straight-eight engines, and by the distinctive smell and eye-watering effect of the blend of methyl alcohol with nitrobenzol, acetone, ether and high-aromatic petroleum spirit that produced such phenomenal power.

The four Mercedes and three Auto Unions were garaged in the outbuildings of Coppice Farm, where spectators gazed in awe on their meticulous preparations. When the cooling system in one of the W125s sprang a leak, a specialist welder from Unterturkheim arrived the next day to fix the problem. There were no works Alfas to put up the semblance of a challenge to the Germans, and the eight British-entered cars completing the mixed field of Grand Prix cars and voiturettes – five ERAs (including the works cars of Mays, Howe and Arthur Dobson), two Maseratis and a Riley – might as well have been in a different contest altogether. One entrant, a young Londoner named Arthur Hyde, recognised as much. After posting lap times consistently twenty seconds slower than the favourites over the three days of practice, he very honourably withdrew his Maserati in the belief that he would only obstruct the German cars and thereby present a danger to everyone.

Von Brauchitsch took pole position with a lap in 2 minutes 10.4 seconds, with Rosemeyer a second slower. Lang and Seaman filled the remainder of the four-abreast front row of the grid on the widened finishing straight, with Müller, Caracciola and Hasse on the second row. Then came the home-based competitors, the Riley of Percy Maclure last of all, alone on the fifth row. There had been time in the evenings for Ludwig Sebastian, Rosemeyer's chief mechanic, to watch Derby County play a friendly against Hearts at the Baseball Ground, while other members of the Auto Union team – including Rosemeyer himself – went in the opposite direction, attending a Friday-night greyhound race meeting in Nottingham.

◆

On the day of the race a crowd estimated at 50,000 began to assemble, having jammed the roads from Nottingham, Derby and Leicester as they approached the circuit. Only seventeen policemen were thought necessary to control such a well-behaved throng. On-course betting, a regular feature of major race meetings at Brooklands, was much in evidence before the start of the Grand Prix. The bookmakers knew less about international motor racing than about thoroughbred horses, but enough to offer the shortest odds on the Mercedes drivers: Caracciola 4-1, Lang and Seaman 5-1, and 6-1 against von Brauchitsch, whose unlucky reputation had clearly gone before him. When the Auto Union mechanics saw the odds of 5-1 against Rosemeyer and 10-1 against Müller and Hasse, they rushed out to place their bets on their drivers. Many of the notable personalities of British racing had turned up for this unprecedented event, including one no longer active. The familiar figure of Whitney Straight was on the grid, nine months after his last race, he and Lady Daphne chatting with Seaman and Rosemeyer before watching the race from the pits, his three-piece Prince of Wales check suit matched by his wife's elegant dark suede two-piece and – appropriately, for Nottingham – a feathered hat in the style of Robin Hood.

When the flag was dropped to start the eighty-lap, 250-mile race, Lang showed the fastest reactions, followed by Caracciola, von Brauchitsch and Seaman, then the three Auto Unions. Soon Rosemeyer passed Seaman, and Müller was trying to do likewise on the inside of Coppice Corner when he ran into the back of the Englishman's Mercedes. His own car was unscathed but Seaman's suffered damage to the petrol tank and a rear shock absorber. He came into the pits for a diagnosis before going back out and limping round at greatly diminished speed until the twenty-ninth lap, when the shock absorber finally broke and he gave up the struggle, much to his disappointment as well as that of the crowd.

After a dozen laps in the lead, Lang felt something go awry with the handling of his car and came in to discover that a front shock absorber had failed, putting an end to his day. Von Brauchitsch took over the lead, but a burst tyre brought him in for a pit stop, enabling Rosemeyer to snatch the win ahead of the two surviving Mercedes, with Müller and Hasse fourth and fifth, and Bira's ex-Straight Maserati leading home the rest of the field as the excited crowd swarmed across the track. None of the English entries was classified as a finisher, since none had completed the full distance within fifteen minutes of the winner's time. Somewhat mysteriously, the German national anthem was not played during the victory ceremony – at which, because the ceremonial bottle of champagne had also gone missing, an exhausted Rosemeyer had to drink lemonade. There was a fuss, too, when the Auto Union mechanics, expecting a handsome extra payout from their flutter, were scandalised to discover that the bookmakers had disappeared, taking their money with them. The race organisers quickly agreed to compensate them in full.

A dinner-dance at the Friary Hotel in Derby that night featured a well-received speech from Lord Howe before his wife – the former Mary Curzon, once described by the photographer Cecil Beaton as 'a perfect specimen of English beauty' – presented the prizes and 'Deutschland über Alles' was finally played, marking the end of a European Grand Prix season in which, once again, the German teams had laid waste to all opposition.

The next morning, after Dugdale had interviewed the drivers on their impressions of the race, the German teams returned to London. On the Monday the winning car went on display at Auto Union's showroom on Great Portland Street, while one of the W125s adorned the window of Mercedes' Park Lane premises, surrounded by large prints of George Monkhouse's photographs. The teams also visited the British International Motor Show, held for the first time at the new Earls Court Exhibition Centre. That night the British Racing Drivers' Club hosted a cocktail party for the German drivers at the Hotel Splendide in Piccadilly, opposite Green Park. Dick was among the 120 in attendance, all gathered to celebrate the greatest motor racing spectacle ever seen in Britain.

21

Royal highness

While his teammates returned to Germany, Dick stayed behind. A week after the Grand Prix, the W125 was removed from the Mayfair showroom and taken – by a crew of mechanics who had also delayed their journey home – to the Crystal Palace circuit in south London. There it was demonstrated to a crowd of enthusiasts who were suitably awed by the noise of the super-charged straight-eight engine, even at part-throttle on the tight little track, and by the presence of its famous driver.

At *Motor Sport*'s offices, the magazine's editor was composing his assessment of the man he admired so much. 'How proud we should all be of Richard Seaman,' Bill Boddy wrote. 'So many moneyed young sportsmen have bought a racing car, partly to take up motor racing and partly to have a lot of fun attending races in various parts of the world, when they are frequently out-classed, and so often the fun they have detracts from their giving their best. Seaman might so easily have followed in their footsteps. Instead he took his well-deserved place in the Mercedes-Benz team, submitting himself to the rigid discipline and long periods away from home that such a move necessitated – proof positive of his overpowering love of motor racing. In addition to which his charming personality makes one glad that it is this particular young Englishman who carries our racing colours abroad.'

After spending a few more days in London, Dick was back in Germany by the time those words were printed. On 19 October he had received a telegram from Mercedes, instructing him to return in time for the arrival of the Duke of Windsor at the factory. The former Edward VIII was on a twelve-day visit to Germany with Wallis Simpson, whom he had married that summer in France, six months after abdicating the throne. Told by his brother, the new George VI, that his handsome allowance would be forfeited if he set foot in England again, the Duke and his wife had gone into exile in Paris, where they lived in a suite at the Meurice, Lilian Seaman's favourite of the city's hotels. Their visit to Germany was of greater symbolism than substance, even though the Duke considered himself still capable of averting a war between Britain and Germany. The news went down badly in Britain and the government's chargé d'affaires in Berlin was instructed not to meet the couple.

Dick left London without telling his mother the reason behind his departure. Perhaps he did not want her going around London telling her friends that her son was meeting so controversial a figure. Perhaps, too, he was uneasy about it himself. Germany, however, felt differently. The couple, given enormous publicity in the German press, were fêted with the pomp of a state visit and a warmth that must have reminded the Duke of the enormous popularity he had once enjoyed among his own people. Everywhere they went, the Duchess was greeted as 'Your Royal Highness', a mode of address denied her in Britain. Her husband was sympathetic to Germany: he had studied at Oxford under a celebrated professor of German language and literature, had made two visits to the country before the Great War, and shared the views on Jews and communists of much of the British upper class. Mobbed by a cheering crowd in Berlin on 11 October as they arrived by train and stepped into a Mercedes limousine, the couple responded by giving Nazi salutes. Hitler's personal train was put at their disposal as they travelled the country to fulfil a schedule that included visits to a mine, a school, a light-bulb factory, a winter relief centre and a concert of classical music for factory workers. They saw U-boats being built at the Krupp works in Essen, watched a Hitler Youth training camp and inspected an *SS-Totenkopfverbände* (Death's Head Unit) in Pomerania. They dined with Joseph and Magda Goebbels; Hermann Göring gave them tea and showed them his model railway and his collection of looted art.

The Duchess opted out of the visit to Untertürkheim, where her husband toured a factory that was one of the jewels of German technology. And who better to join the welcoming committee than a well-bred young Englishman? This, perhaps, was where Dick's experience as an aide to Prince Rupprecht of Bavaria six years earlier would come in useful. In a dark suit, white shirt and dark tie, hair as always neatly brushed, with the corner of a pressed white handkerchief protruding from his breast pocket, he stood next to Lang in the receiving line, smiling and bending forward slightly as the Duke, a full head shorter than his young compatriot, extended his hand at the start of the factory tour.

The next day, 22 October, the Windsors' trip reached its climax with an unofficial meeting at the Berghof, Hitler's retreat in the Bavarian Alps. While the Duchess took tea with Rudolf Hess, Hitler's deputy, the Duke and the Führer had a long conversation in private. The warmth of the encounter was reflected in Albert Speer's recollection of Hitler's verdict on his guest: 'I am certain through him permanent friendly relations could have been achieved. If he had stayed, everything would have been different. His abdication was a severe loss for us.'

◆

Two weeks after his brief encounter with the Duke, about which – since the Windsors' visit was barely reported in the British press – Lilian Seaman remained in ignorance, Dick returned to London. Over tea, he told his mother that the reason for his trip had been to meet the Mercedes team's insurers, to discuss the plastic surgery he needed in order to repair some of the damage to his face. After settling all the expenses for his stay in the Adenau hospital, they had been reluctant to pay for further surgery, which he wanted to be carried out in London. He had argued fiercely. 'Do you think,' he told them, 'that I'm going to go around with a face like this for the rest of my life?' His mother said that she would have been happy to pay for the operation. That, he replied, was not the point. There was a principle at stake. And he had won the argument. They would pay for the surgery.

When, finally, he mentioned that he had been introduced to the Duke of Windsor during his visit, Lilian Seaman was astonished and naturally eager for a full account. 'And what did you think of the Duchess?' was her first question. Dick replied that the former Mrs Simpson had not been part of the visit to Mercedes – although, since the couple were staying at his hotel, he had caught sight of her. All he could add was that she looked just like her pictures in the newspapers. The Duke, he said, had seemed nervous to start with, constantly tugging at his tie, but relaxed as the visit went on and had engaged Dick over cocktails in a conversation about motor racing and life in Germany. Dick's impression was that his life in exile – 'three meals a day, knocking a few golf balls about and accompanying his wife to the hairdresser and dressmaker' – would not satisfy him for long.

It was a Thursday evening, and Lilian was expecting Dick to spend the weekend with her at Pull Court. No, he said, that would not be possible. On Sunday night he was due to report to the London Clinic, where Sir Harold Gillies, a pioneer in plastic surgery, would perform the operation the next morning. When she responded that she would cancel her plans, he told her that he would rather not have the fuss. She was welcome, he said, to come and see him on the Monday evening, when it would be all over.

Gillies had been knighted in 1930 for his work on wounded soldiers in the Great War. Born in New Zealand, he studied medicine at Cambridge, where he was a member of the 1904 Boat Race crew. An expert golfer, he was a regular competitor in the Amateur Championship. He would certainly have known something in advance about the international sportsman whose face he was charged with reconstructing.

After a fretful weekend in the country, Lilian Seaman was at the London Clinic on the Tuesday morning, pleading with the ward sister to be allowed to see her son, who was still unconscious after a lengthy operation. What she saw when she finally talked her way into his darkened room did not dispel her anxiety. 'His face was swathed in cotton wool and lint dressings, and his left arm was heavily bandaged,' she remembered. Blood had seeped through the dressings. When she bent her head close to his, she was relieved to hear him breathing. She sat there for two hours, fretting about the draught from an open window, until he woke, still drowsy, and appeared to register her presence.

She returned the next day to find that he was still affected by the anaesthetic, but on the Thursday, arriving with clean pyjamas, she discovered the nurses in the process of dressing his arm, which was badly swollen and bleeding. They shooed her away, and when she was allowed to return he was fully conscious. Telling her that another operation on his arm had been arranged for the following day, he asked her to bring a copy of A. J. Cronin's latest novel, *The Citadel*, on her next visit. This was an interesting choice: Cronin, a Scot, had practised medicine in the pit villages of South Wales after the war and studied the effects of lung disease on colliers for the Ministry of Mines. *The Citadel*, his fourth novel, had been published earlier in 1937 and quickly became a bestseller on both sides of the Atlantic. Drawing on his experiences, Cronin described a world in which there was one standard of healthcare for the rich and another for the poor to such powerful effect that the book's sensational success led to calls for a universal national health service.

When Lilian returned, fearing that Dick's arm might have

been amputated, she discovered him unconscious again but in possession of all his limbs. On her next visit he was awake and able to tell her that the second surgery had been not on his arm but on his leg. In the first operation, skin had been taken from his arm and grafted onto his face. In the second, skin from his leg had been used on his arm. There was a third operation to come. After that he began to recover and to accept visitors in addition to his relieved mother. Ramponi was among the regulars, as were Monkhouse, Dugdale and Roland King-Farlow, the leading statistician of British motor racing. Cards and flowers arrived in profusion.

On 23 November, however, six days after the third operation and against the advice of the medical staff, he discharged himself and went home, promising to return every day to complete a programme of recovery treatment. After three days of staying indoors, apart from the short daily drive to the clinic, he suddenly announced to his mother that they were going to lunch at Claridge's. Instead of asking for her usual table, from where she could see everything that went on, she requested a quieter spot, so that he could keep his bandaged face away from the crowd. Nevertheless, friends came over to wish him well, and the waiters were particularly attentive. Afterwards he announced that they were going to the cinema, to see *The Life of Emile Zola*, starring Paul Muni, on its way to being named best picture at the 1938 Academy Awards.

Barely two weeks after coming home he shocked his mother again by telling her that he was off to Switzerland to try some skiing. Caracciola, he said, had told him it was the best remedy for the winter blues and a good way of staying fit. She was horrified, thinking of the effect of cold alpine air on the newly grafted patches of skin, which had been settling down well in the gentle regime of life at Ennismore Gardens. She was also saddened by the realisation that he would be away at Christmas for the second year running. He told her that he would come home for the holiday before returning to the slopes for the

New Year. Slightly mollified, she said goodbye to him on 7 December.

In Davos, a small town of about 10,000 people located 5,000 feet up in the Landwasser Valley, he joined the Martins, keen members of a British fraternity who had played a leading role in the popularisation of skiing as a winter recreation. The Martins had not allowed themselves to be handicapped by the birth of their first child, another Charles, earlier in the year. Dick ventured out each day with his leather boots and wooden skis for his first lessons. But the nursery slopes could not hold him for long, and by the time he returned to England fourteen days later his sessions with a private instructor had turned him into not just a competent but a committed skier.

He could afford the indulgence after what had been, from the point of view of his earnings, a good year. In addition to the RM 11,000 of his retainer from February to December, he had received RM 17,865.75 for his second place in the Vanderbilt Cup, RM 2,285.95 for fourth place in the Italian Grand Prix, RM 2,383.90 for fourth at Brno, RM 1,500 for fifth in the Coppa Acerbo, RM 2,166 for seventh in Tripoli, and bonuses ranging from RM 1,000 to 2,000 for races in which he had failed to finish or simply acted as a reserve. All that added up to RM 45,201.60, or about £4,000. (The equivalent eighty years later would be around £270,000.) It did not come close to what the team's number-one driver was earning – it was not even halfway there – but it was enough, along with his trust fund, to give him a comfortable life in Germany.

22

A pretty good joke

Back in London for Christmas, Dick found his mother preoccupied by a legal dispute concerning the future of the Ranelagh Club. Two years earlier, as its first woman director, she had involved herself in an attempt by the members to prevent the development of part of its extensive grounds after what she described as ·the 'secret purchase' of shares by 'a foreign Jewish syndicate'. Now she was about to go for a meeting with Sir Stafford Cripps, who had been engaged by the members as their leading counsel in a High Court action to halt the sale and revoke the planning permission given by the local authority.

Originally founded in Fulham in the middle of the nineteenth century, the Ranelagh had made an ambitious move in 1894. Its new home was 120 acres of parkland in Barnes, on the south bank of the Thames, formerly the site of a country mansion given by Elizabeth I to her favourite, Lord Walsingham, whom she was able to visit there in secret. A consortium of members of London's leading gentlemen's clubs had devised an ambitious plan to set up first-class facilities there, principally for polo – introduced from India in the 1870s and enjoying a surge of popularity – but also for tennis, cricket, football, croquet, archery, swimming and other sports. Aristocrats and the ultra-wealthy made up the committee: the Earl of Dudley was its chairman, while the founders included William Waldorf Astor, the Earls of Chesterfield and Portland, the Marquess of Cholmondeley and Alfred de Rothschild. Soon its four polo grounds, 5,200-yard eighteen-hole golf course, swimming pool, fishing lake stocked with trout, open-air theatre, Saturday-afternoon performances by the Band of the Royal Horse Guards, ice rink in winter, and other attractions had brought it 2,000 members – including George V and a 'limited number' of women – paying an annual membership fee of ten guineas.

'Ranelagh is a great place for pretty girls and smart women,' one magazine observed, and to Lilian its future was important enough for her to join the efforts to thwart the serious threat arising from the sudden and unanticipated sale of the freehold of the land by its owners, the Church Commissioners. The purchasers – the 'Jewish syndicate' of her description – were Isaac Behar and his son David, carpet merchants based in Glasgow. Isaac had arrived from Istanbul in 1920, taking a shop in Sauchiehall Street; soon there were a dozen more shops in Scotland and two on the south coast of England. When the Behars moved into property, their eyes fell on Ranelagh's potential. But while it was gently declining in popularity, the club still enjoyed the patronage of members of sufficient influence to bring a legal action challenging a sale and permission for development agreed without members' knowledge. Questions were asked in the House of Lords and letters published in *The Times*. Sir Stafford Cripps prepared his submission to the High Court.

Lilian's son, she was pleased to note, had been concerned to hear all the details during the three years in which the proceedings were in and out of the courts. She had been nervous when Cripps's name was proposed as a replacement for their original counsel, thinking of him as 'a red-hot socialist', but Dick reassured her not just of his acceptable background – Cripps was a Wykehamist – but of the high regard in which his eloquence was widely held. When she met the great man, she found herself agreeably surprised by his polished demeanour and noted approvingly the swiftness with which he grasped her points. She was present at the court hearings, sometimes accompanied by Dick. 'Let this be a warning to you,' he told her as they listened to Cripps's presentation of the members' case. 'Never form your impressions by what you read in the papers.'

◆

After a week with his mother in London and Worcestershire, Dick returned to Davos, taking Tony Cliff and Ray Lewthwaite with him in the Ford V8 to stay at the Parsenn Sporthotel, a small and comfortable establishment run by the Fopp family. Both experienced skiers, Cliff and Lewthwaite were astonished to discover how much technique their novice friend had acquired in so short a time.

On 28 January, however, came the shocking news of Bernd Rosemeyer's death. (Lilian, seeing a newspaper billboard in London reading 'Famous Racing Driver Killed', immediately assumed that it must be her son.) The German teams had again set up camp by the Frankfurt–Darmstadt autobahn, bringing the latest versions of their streamliners. On the first morning, Caracciola went out at eight o'clock in the Mercedes and set a new class record of 268mph. When Rosemeyer emerged, it was in a strikingly different Auto Union, embracing a visionary concept of aerodynamics, its bodywork shaped so as to channel air under the chassis, creating a low-pressure area that would suck the car down onto the ground.

By the time the mechanics had warmed up the car's new 6.6-litre engine, the wind had risen slightly, blowing from the right. Coming in after his first runs, in which he touched 276mph, Rosemeyer mentioned that he had noticed the effect on one stretch of road in particular. Most of the measured section was protected from the wind on both sides by trees or earth banks, but there was a gap in the cover of about 100 yards where he had felt the car moving off its line. Ignoring suggestions that he should wait for the wind to drop, he climbed straight back in. He was running at top speed when a gust came through the gap, blowing the car sharply over to the left of the carriageway and towards the central reservation. When he tried to correct it, the car went into an uncontrollable broadside and somersaulted, tossing its driver out of the cockpit and into a wood as it cartwheeled, stripping off its bodywork, until the remains were halted by a concrete bridge. The European champion's dead body was found resting against a tree.

The whole of Germany had adopted Rosemeyer and Elly Beinhorn as a model couple: the laughing blond daredevil and the intrepid aviatrix who, only ten weeks earlier, had given birth to their first child, a son. In a statement, Hitler addressed a nation in mourning: 'May your grief be lessened by the thought that he fell fighting for Germany.' Against his widow's wishes, Rosemeyer was given a full SS funeral in Berlin, his Hauptsturmführer's cap placed on the flower-bedecked coffin. Representatives of both teams were in attendance, including Lang, whom he had tried to persuade to join him at Auto Union that winter.

As speeds rose, with no compensating concern for safety measures of any kind, motor racing was becoming an increasingly dangerous sport, one in which fatalities were seen as part of the bargain made by anyone who got behind the wheel of a competition car, whether to win a race or break a record. Among the roll call of the dead were such prominent figures as Gaston Chevrolet, killed at Beverly Hills in 1920, Jimmy Murphy at the New York state fairgrounds in 1924, Antonio Ascari at Montlhéry in 1925, J. G. Parry-Thomas on Pendine Sands in 1927, Pietro Bordino at Alessandria in 1928, Frank Lockhart at Daytona Beach in the same year, Gastone Brilli-Peri at the Tripoli circuit in 1930, Clive Dunfee at Brooklands in 1932, Giuseppe Campari, Count Stanislaus Czaykowski and Baconin Borzacchini at Monza in 1933, Guy Bouriat at Péronne and Otto Merz at AVUS in the same year, Hugh Hamilton at Bremgarten and Guy Moll at Pescara in 1934, Pat Fairfield at Le Mans in 1937 and Marcel Lehoux at Deauville in 1936. By any standards, however, Rosemeyer's death was particularly shocking both to the public and to his rivals. 'I suppose it is the worst motoring fatality since Segrave's death,' Seaman wrote to Monkhouse. 'Anyway his death was as dramatic as his life, and he can't have known much about it at that speed.' He suggested that George should put together a book of his photographs of Bernd that they could present to Elly.

◆

Dick and his friends spent a few days on the slopes in St Anton am Arlberg before Charlie Martin accompanied him on a trip to Munich and Stuttgart; they stopped en route for a day's skiing in Garmisch-Partenkirchen, the site of the 1936 Winter Olympics. In Stuttgart, Dick had a meeting with Neubauer to discuss the programme for the new season. And then, after a few more days in Davos, came an event over which the Rosemeyer tragedy had inevitably cast a shadow.

The Berlin Motor Show opened on 17 February in the complex of exhibition halls near AVUS, with the soaring Funkturm – the 490ft steel radio tower from which the world's first regular television programme had been broadcast two years earlier – as its signpost. Along with the other drivers, Dick listened to Hitler, who had arrived to open the proceedings with a speech celebrating five years of the motorisation project. The People's Car had been delayed, he said, by the need to reduce the cost of synthetic materials, but he could point out that since he came to power, car ownership among the German people had already gone from one in forty people to one in twenty-four, and the 2,000th kilometre of autobahn had recently been completed on schedule. Within the nine halls, pride of place was given to a display by Mercedes-Benz and Auto Union, each with a streamlined record breaker and a Grand Prix car, and a similar mix of motorcycles from NSU, BMW and DKW. In deference to Rosemeyer's memory, there was no parade. Afterwards Dick returned to Davos, where the spring sunshine made the slopes treacherous and he had his first outing on cross-country skis, quickly deciding that he preferred what he referred to as 'downhill dicing'.

On 12 March, five and a half months after telling an audience in Berlin that Germany needed greater 'living space', Hitler sent the German army across the Austrian border. The progress of the *Anschluss* was unexpectedly lumbering – some of the tanks had to be delivered on trains – but nevertheless welcomed by cheering crowds. Three days later Hitler arrived in Vienna, where the ardour of the reception to his speech from the 200,000 listeners gathered in the Heldenplatz persuaded him that there was no need to grant Austria a separate administrative identity. 'We have come not as tyrants,' he said, 'but as liberators.' Within a week reports were arriving in Paris and London of action being taken against Jewish shops, theatres and music halls. The British and French governments had taken no action, but Neville Chamberlain's government reacted to the growing tensions by announcing a rapid rearmament programme, with a defence budget raised, amid widespread protests, from £82 million to £106 million. The people of Leicester were chosen to take part in a blackout exercise, and in London all schoolchildren were to be issued with gas masks.

◆

In Untertürkheim, the designers were putting the finishing touches to the cars for the coming season. Eighteen months earlier the sport's governing body, the AIACR, had announced that the 750kg formula would be replaced from the start of the 1938 season by regulations intended to reduce speed and technical complexity, thereby giving other teams a chance to race on equal terms with the Germans. The new rules stipulated maximum engine capacities of 3 litres supercharged or 4.5 litres unsupercharged, with a minimum (rather than, as before, a maximum) weight limit of 850kg. Work had begun immediately on a new generation of cars. Uhlenhaut's design team and Eberan von Eberhorst – recently installed as chief designer at Auto Union following Dr Porsche's departure to concentrate on the People's Car – arrived at similar conclusions: their respective Grand Prix contenders would both be powered by supercharged 3-litre V12 engines, albeit still at opposite ends of the chassis.

When the Mercedes drivers were given a first look at their new car, they were instantly impressed by the W154's low-slung lines. Testing at Monza started on 16 March in shirt-sleeve weather, Uhlenhaut himself shaking the car down before handing it over to the team's drivers. The results immediately suggested that, although in theory a half-sized engine in a bulkier car should result in slower lap times, the new design would rival the performance of its predecessor, thanks to a lower centre of gravity, better suspension and brakes, a five-speed gearbox and an engine delivering around 450bhp.

In the second week of April the Mercedes team travelled to Pau, where two W154s were sent for Caracciola and Lang. What had been intended as little more than a trial run around the streets of the town on the edge of the Pyrenees turned into an unexpected humiliation. Lang's car destroyed its clutch in practice and Caracciola was beaten in the race by the new unsupercharged 4.5-litre Delahaye of René Dreyfus – a rare and warmly received home victory for the French over one of the German teams. The key to the outcome was fuel consumption: the Mercedes drank a gallon of fuel every 3 miles, whereas the Delahaye's 7–8 miles per gallon meant that Dreyfus could go the whole distance non-stop. When Caracciola came into the pits to refuel at half-distance, Lang took over with instructions to attack, but the car was simply not fast enough to recover the deficit around the tight circuit; at the finish there was a gap of almost two minutes. Neubauer and Uhlenhaut returned to

Stuttgart in a chastened mood, knowing that development work was urgently needed.

◆

Given the rest of the month off, Dick returned to England. In London his mother hosted a dinner for him at one of his favourite restaurants. Luigi's, opened on Jermyn Street in 1936 by two Italian immigrants, had become a favourite of the smart set. Less formal than Simpson's, the Savoy or the Ritz, it offered better value, too. Deborah Mitford, the future Duchess of Devonshire, reported with approval that 'a minute steak and all that went with it, including a bottle of wine, cost a guinea'.

The plan was for Lilian and Dick to motor up to Pull Court. But instead of using one of the family's Daimlers, he surprised her by picking her up in a brand-new Mercedes-Benz 540K, on loan from the London dealership. A rakish machine selling in Germany for the equivalent of around £2,000 (£130,000 today), the car was designed for fast long-distance touring, the potency of its 5.4-litre straight-eight engine advertised by the prominent exhaust pipes that snaked out of the sides of a long bonnet. Lilian was, in all senses, swept away as Dick drove up to Worcestershire, no doubt making the most of the car's 110mph top speed. 'Conservative as I am,' she wrote, 'even I was struck by its wonder, and extreme grace and beauty, and it went forward like a bird ... and it was so comfortably sprung that you hardly realised you were sitting in a car at all.' Wherever they stopped en route, a crowd would quickly gather around it.

At Pull Court she showed him a stained-glass medallion bearing the Trinity College coat of arms, which she had bought at an auction and installed in a window in the Great Hall. He put on some old clothes and went outside to prove that he could cut the lawns with the motor mower faster than the regular gardeners. On what would be their last holiday together, they went for several rides in the countryside – through the west of England and even into Wales – before he returned to London to attend the Easter Monday meeting at Brooklands. A week's yachting off the south coast with the Martins preceded his return to Germany.

Frustrated by the lack of opportunities to race Mercedes' Grand Prix cars, he had responded readily to a suggestion from Aldy Aldington to take the wheel of a Frazer Nash-entered BMW in the forthcoming Tourist Trophy at Donington Park. Max Sailer, the director in charge of racing, wrote to BMW in Munich to clarify the position: 'In addition to our three German drivers, we still have as our fourth and reserve driver the Englishman Richard Seaman. Since only three drivers may be entered under this year's rules, our Herr Seaman is unlikely to be used. This fact is known to Seaman, who now tells us that in England he was approached to drive a BMW car at the Tourist Trophy. Before releasing him for this purpose, we would like to inform you of the above and ask you to tell us whether Herr Seaman's statement is correct. We would be grateful for your decision as soon as possible. Heil Hitler! – Sailer.' Eventually, perhaps out of sympathy for a young man who was spending too much time kicking his heels, his request was granted.

On the day Sailer wrote to BMW, the British parliament approved Neville Chamberlain's Anglo–Italian agreement, intended by one side to prevent an alliance between Mussolini and Hitler and by the other to drive a wedge between Britain and France, who had just signed a joint agreement to defend Czechoslovakia against possible German aggression. The Prime Minister described it as heralding a 'new era', but Anthony Eden, his Foreign Secretary, resigned after criticising the policy of appeasing Mussolini, and the Labour Party called the agreement 'a sell-out to Fascism'. In a letter to Monkhouse, Dick gave his view of the political situation: 'England is becoming a pretty good joke, especially in the Fascist countries, for her flannel-footed behaviour politically and we are rather looked upon as a lot of decadent old women. A successful British Grand Prix team would be a very good way of dispelling this idea!'

On 6 May he was again a member of the Mercedes party setting out for Tripoli, as a reserve to the three German drivers. The new Auto Unions were not ready, so the principal opposition came from the latest cars produced by Alfa Romeo, Maserati and Bugatti, and from Dreyfus's Delahaye, the victor at Pau. To make up the field in the numbers required to run the annual lottery, seventeen Maserati voiturettes were added to the race. Although the teams were restricted to three cars each, Sailer and Neubauer noticed that Alfa Romeo had sneaked a fourth car into the line-up by entering the Frenchman Raymond Sommer as an independent. The Mercedes management offered to paint their spare car British racing green – an extraordinary concession – if the organisers would allow Seaman to start on a similar basis, but permission was denied.

The final day of practice in Tripoli coincided with an international football match in Berlin. A crowd of 110,000 assembled in the Olympic Stadium to see Germany attempt to beat England for the first time, in the presence of Hess, Göring and Goebbels. The home side had spent a fortnight together at a training camp in the Black Forest, practising a new formation. But the first challenge for England's players was a very different one: should they follow their hosts' example by giving the Nazi salute during the German national anthem? On the morning of the match, the chairman of the FA's international committee, Charles Wreford-Brown, and Stanley Rous, the association's secretary, met the British ambassador to discuss what had become a highly contentious issue. 'When I go in to see Herr Hitler,' Sir Nevile Henderson told them, 'I give him the Nazi salute because that is the normal courtesy expected. It carries no hint of approval of anything Hitler and his regime may do. And if I do it, why should you or your team object?' When Wreford-Brown and Rous conveyed that message to the players, they received a mixed response. The captain, Eddie Hapgood, Arsenal's experienced left back, was said to have led the protesters, but eventually he and the others bowed to the officials' insistence. When the anthem began, English arms were raised as straight as those of their opponents. The spectators roared their approval. Their enthusiasm gradually drained away, however, as England won the match 6–3. At the final whistle, the Nazi leaders did not stay around to applaud the victors.

In Tripoli, the Saturday practice times suggested that even though all the cars had been freshly designed to a new set of rules, little had changed in the competitive standings. Lang was fastest, followed by von Brauchitsch and Caracciola. There was a delay when Marshal Balbo arrived half an hour late, and a mood of disorganisation enveloped the start. Half the grid obeyed the lights, while the other half reacted to Balbo dropping the ceremonial flag. As a result, a couple of the voiturettes actually went into the first corner ahead of Caracciola, who had been on the front row. Eventually the three Mercedes established themselves in the lead, taking it relatively easy to save their tyres, with von Brauchitsch at the front until a misfire forced him to let Lang by. The only challenge came from Count Trossi, who briefly led in the new works Maserati before its transmission broke, allowing Lang to take the chequered flag ahead of Caracciola and von Brauchitsch. During a pit stop, the winner's overalls had been doused with a bucket of water after fuel gushed out of the filler and over his back.

Two fatal accidents had marred the race: Eugenio Siena, in one of the new Alfas, ran off the track and into a house while trying to avoid Franco Cortese's Maserati, the impact killing him immediately, while László Hartmann died in hospital the next morning after breaking his back when his Maserati collided with Nino Farina's Alfa – 'perhaps as well', Seaman observed, noting that the Hungarian would otherwise have been permanently paralysed in both legs. Dick blamed the accidents on the decision to run the fast cars together with much slower ones, and on the circuit's loose sand verges. 'I have never known the drivers so unanimous in condemning the dangers of a track,' he said, happy for once to have been a mere spectator.

The accidents led the organisers to cancel the prize-giving banquet. Mercedes held a small celebration of their own, attended by Korpsführer Hühnlein, no doubt delighted that the German cars had again shown up the Italians. 'He was in terrific form,' Dick reported, 'and it was a close thing as to whether he or Neubauer became the merrier.' Whether it was from the effect of the drink or his habitual seasickness, Neubauer was unable to eat his evening meal after the ship had set off across the Mediterranean that night. By the time they went ashore during a brief stop in Palermo, he had regained his appetite and led a lunch party with the Caracciolas, von Brauchitsch, Seaman and the journalist Eberhard Hundt. 'You can imagine the sort of meal he ordered,' Seaman reported to Monkhouse, 'consisting of lobster, asparagus, strawberries and cream, and a particularly noxious red wine followed by the usual espressos and cognacs.' The team manager was sick again that night, and all through the last leg of the voyage. When they docked in Naples he had to be helped off the ship before being driven gently back to Stuttgart, hoping to recover in time for a visit to the *Rennabteilung* by Adolf Hitler, who congratulated Lang and inspected the latest Silver Arrow to add to the glory of his regime.

◆

When Dick returned to Ambach, it was with Peter Gläser and Laury Vermundt as his house guests. Strolling in the evening warmth, amid the smell of mown grass and freshly cut logs, they could watch cormorants drying their wings in the sun and flights of geese covering the length of the lake, with a reef of distant mountains on the southern horizon and the sound of church bells floating across the water, accompanied by the creak and slap of small boats at anchor. The idyll was disturbed only by the need to report to the Nürburgring, to spend a few days seeing how the W154 performed there in advance of the team's most important race of the year, the German Grand Prix in late July.

Increasingly, too, the tranquillity of the lake was disturbed by the buzz of a speedboat engine. To add to the dinghy moored by the bank, Dick had bought a mahogany-bodied two-seater Chris-Craft. Dr Gläser or another friend would drive it as Dick rode behind on a pair of waterskis sent out from London: a complete novelty to the watching Germans. 'He was the first water-skier in Germany, so far as I know,' said Ernst Henne, Germany's 500cc motorcycle champion, who had joined Auto Union for 1938. Henne had a house across the water at Garatshausen, and they had become friendly. After Dick showed him the rudiments, Henne commissioned a pair of his own waterskis from a local boatbuilder. Among Henne's guests was Manfred von Brauchitsch, who crossed the lake to visit Dick several times and started making plans to build his own chalet on the Starnbergersee.

Another visitor to Ambach in those long, too-lazy summer weeks was Monkhouse, who brought along a passenger: his father, getting a look at continental Europe from the passenger seat of George's beloved 4.5-litre Bentley. Their luggage included, at Dick's behest, some Champion spark plugs for the Chris-Craft, a bottle of Listerine mouthwash, a packet of tea and a bottle of Skol sun lotion. He had originally asked George to drop into Sydney Lewis's shop at 27 Carburton Street, just north of Oxford Circus, to check up on his order for specially made leather helmets (two guineas each) and mesh-backed gloves (8/6d.), ordered with tighter elastic around the wrists for a closer fit, but they had already been despatched. George had also brought his fishing rods. The Starnbergersee's population of two dozen species – including carp, perch and zander – had long attracted devotees of another sport in which George and Dick were now taking an interest.

PART FOUR

1938–39

23

The girl and the prize

On the night Dick met the love of his life, he was the only man in the room not wearing evening dress. The invitation had come unexpectedly. Aldy Aldington was running a trip to Germany for his customers and members of the Frazer Nash-BMW Car Club. Aldington had a warm relationship with Franz Josef Popp, BMW's general director, who had supervised the growth of the company after the war; their sports cars and motorcycles were now race winners and record breakers. The British visitors would drive to the Nürburgring to watch the Eifelrennen and be let loose on the circuit the following day. After that they would drive south to Munich, where BMW would host a dinner-dance for these important foreign clients at the Preysing Palais, a baroque mansion in the centre of the city, on 15 June.

As it turned out, that year's Eifelrennen was cancelled. Undeterred, the Frazer Nash tourists went ahead with their trip, of which the dinner-dance was a highlight. Realising that Dick was living not far away, Aldington and his business partner A. F. P. Fane sent a telegram inviting him to join them. For them, naturally, the presence of the Mercedes-Benz team's British driver would be a coup as well as a gesture of friendship. They would also have the chance to discuss the plans for Dick to drive one of their cars in the Tourist Trophy.

He had just flown back from London, where he had spent a few days with his mother. What Aldington and Fane had omitted to mention was that formal dress was required. So when Dick parked his car in the Odeonsplatz after the half-hour drive from Ambach to Munich and made his way up the grand staircase in the eighteenth-century palace built for the Counts of Preysing, he was wearing a tweed suit. Amid the dinner jackets and ball gowns, not to mention the semi-nude plaster nymphs attached to the marble pillars of the staircase, he would hardly have stood out more in his racing overalls.

A business obligation prevented Franz Josef Popp from attending the ball. Instead he sent his two daughters, Eva and Erica. As they took their seats at the top table, it was Fane who introduced Erica to Dick. The attraction was immediate and mutual. He was a 25-year-old racing driver, tall and good-looking, despite the evidence of his recent facial injuries. She was a slender, neat-featured beauty, barely a month past her eighteenth birthday, with an excellent command of English. She responded to his relaxed charm, while he noted her lively, flirtatious spirit. An orchestra played, and many eyes were on them as they danced together, the racing driver in the completely inappropriate suit and the gorgeous girl in a dress that swept the floor.

The following day Aldy and his brother Bill were invited to visit Ambach. In the afternoon they took one of the boats over the lake to Ernst Henne's house, where – as Erica had mentioned to Dick – the Popp family were visiting the man who had been racing their motorcycles and sports cars with great success. Eventually the whole party set off back across the lake to Haus 12, where Dick entertained them.

He was already beguiled, and soon he was learning more. Erika (as she was christened) Elfriede Popp had been born in Munich in 1920 to parents of Austrian origin. Dick would discover that, having shown little interest in academic studies during her time at the St Anna Lyzeum, Erica had been withdrawn from the school by her father in response, she said, to the instruction to all pupils to join the *Bund Deutscher Mädel*, the League of German Girls: the female counterpart of the *Hitler-Jugend*. She had already been featured in the Berlin fashion magazine *Modenwelt*, a photographer combining her love of clothes with her equestrian skills in a spread for which she posed in a paddock, wearing jodhpurs and boots, with horses and a groom in the background. Her sister, aged twenty-four, was to be married in two weeks' time to an older man, Paul Heim, who had fought as a teenager in the Great War and was now the manager of the Daimler-Benz coachbuilding plant at Sindelfingen.

BMW had followed the Nazi instruction to German firms to dismiss their Jewish workers. But Franz Josef Popp did not entirely see eye to eye with the government, and a shadow was beginning to fall over his career. In the meantime his younger daughter, with an allowance amply covering her considerable wardrobe requirements and any form of entertainment that might take her fancy, was free to play in the sunshine with a new boyfriend of whom her family already thoroughly approved.

◆

There were two setbacks for German sport in the month of June 1938. After their humiliation by England, the country's footballers were quickly knocked out of the World Cup finals, losing to Switzerland in a first-round replay in Paris. In New York a few days later Joe Louis, the Brown Bomber, arrived at Yankee Stadium intent on avenging his unexpected defeat by Max Schmeling in the same ring in 1936, after which the poet Langston Hughes had walked down through Harlem and seen 'grown men weeping like children and women sitting on the kerbs with their heads in their hands'. But those who had mourned the fall of an African American hero at the hands of an Aryan superman could rejoice after the second meeting, for which 70,000 spectators bought a total of more than a million dollars' worth of tickets. What they saw was short, brutal and conclusive. In two minutes and four seconds of the opening round, Louis knocked Schmeling down three times, persuading the referee to halt the fight. On the drive back from the Bronx to his midtown hotel, Schmeling saw the streets of Harlem ablaze with celebration. As for himself, he knew that he was destined to be shunned by the very government officials who had previously fawned over him.

A measure of consolation for Germany came at the beginning of July. A convoy of lorries carrying three W154s, plus a spare, set off to compete in the French Grand Prix to be held on the long, fast *routes nationales* amid the cornfields outside Reims, in the Champagne region. Dick had been instructed to attend, and arrived with Laury Vermundt ('Dr Gläser's cutie', as he described her to Monkhouse), who had been staying in Garmisch, not far from Ambach. Her fiancé was due to arrive directly from the Nürburgring, where the Auto Union team had been testing. The Mercedes squad were making the most of the facilities offered by the Hôtel du Lion d'Or in the centre of the town. Neubauer, according to Dick in a letter to Monkhouse, was 'drinking half a bottle of Champagne for every meal and hopes to have tried most of the leading makes by the end of the week'. A lunch given by the Pommery marque had a special feature: 'Champagne on draught from a tap coming through the table in front of each guest. Neubauer wishes he'd taken a rubber tube!'

Three of the latest streamlined twelve-cylinder Auto Unions made their first appearance at Reims. Neither Alfa Corse nor the Maserati factory had entered, thanks to the Italian government's ban on its teams on competing in countries that had supported sanctions imposed by the League of Nations following Mussolini's invasion of Abyssinia. Dick was sent out in practice in the spare Mercedes, but was again excluded from the race by the new three-car limit, which seemed to be observed at the whim of the individual race organisers. When two of the Auto Unions crashed, H. P. Müller suffering an injury, the streamliners were withdrawn and hurriedly replaced by two of the previous year's cars, now with 3-litre engines, for Hasse and Kautz. Eventually the grid consisted of the five German cars ahead of a dismal quartet of French entries: a lone Bugatti, two sports Talbots and a SEFAC. What should have been a great spectacle on the high-speed circuit was ruined when both Auto Unions crashed on the opening lap. Three of the French cars retired and von Brauchitsch inherited the victory from Caracciola and Lang, both slowed by engine problems. The only other finisher was an old Talbot, nine laps behind the winner. As races go, Seaman said, 'it was quite one of the stupidest ever'.

He had not enjoyed sitting around watching the others race, and afterwards he entered into a tetchy correspondence with Neubauer over the bonuses paid for turning up without being required to race. 'I feel that it is as well to clear up about any possibility of misunderstanding over our agreement,' he wrote. 'I feel sure that after due consideration you will agree with my view of the matter.'

Since joining Mercedes, all he had to do was follow instructions to turn up at test sessions, race meetings and official functions. The rest of his time was his own, to be spent sailing, skiing, fishing, entertaining friends from England (Reggie Tongue and a couple of pals had paid a visit in the week before Reims), listening to his jazz records, visiting his mother when necessary, and – as the summer of 1938 progressed – to contemplate the entry of real romance into his life. But his ambition and motivation had not been dulled. His letter to Neubauer was a reminder to the management that he had not lost a sense of his own value as a racing driver, or the even more urgent desire for competition.

◆

For all those involved in European motor racing, the German Grand Prix on 24 July was the biggest event of the year. Mercedes planned to field four cars, giving Dick the hope of his first start of the season. Less than a fortnight before the race, however, the selection had yet to be decided. A memo from Neubauer to the board of directors and the senior management of the racing team on 13 July confirmed that three of the cars would be driven by Caracciola, von Brauchitsch and Lang. The choice of the driver of the fourth car, and that of a fifth to be used in practice, would be made between Seaman, Bäumer, Hartmann, Brendel and a new arrival, Erwin Bauer, a young Stuttgart driver who had made a modest reputation in a Bugatti, and was to be announced after the second practice session at the Nürburgring on 21 July. The competition may have been arranged by Neubauer to make the other reserves feel they were in with a chance; not surprisingly, given his record and experience, Dick won the verdict. Eight and a half months since he had finished the previous year's campaign in disappointing circumstances at Donington Park, a frustrating period of prolonged competitive inactivity was about to end.

For the public, the principal surprise in the Eifel mountains on the fourth weekend of July was the appearance of Tazio Nuvolari in an Auto Union. Rumoured to have retired after suffering burns to his legs in Pau, now he was back, hired to fill the gap left by Rosemeyer's death. Over several days of private practice at the Nürburgring, he had acclimatised himself to the rear-engined car. In his red leather helmet and bright blue trousers, with the four-ring badge stitched onto his yellow jersey alongside the tortoise that was his personal emblem, the little Mantuan seemed almost lost in the cavernous cockpit. But it was soon apparent that he had the measure of the machine, and that Auto Union's new Type D would be offering him, at the age of forty-five, the realistic hope of further victories.

In the latest of Neubauer's inspirations, the four Mercedes were colour-coded, using the drivers' wind helmets and the cars' radiator grilles for individual identification: white for Caracciola, red for von Brauchitsch, blue for Lang, green for Seaman. The team had brought no fewer than three complete reserve cars, one extra engine and one standby driver, Bäumer.

Neubauer was leaving nothing to chance; worried that a puncture early in the 14-mile-long circuit could force a driver to go so slowly that the plugs would oil up, on the first practice day he ordered Caracciola and von Brauchitsch to do a lap as gently as possible, to see what would happen. They drove around side by side, so slowly they were able to talk to each other.

Dick was driving the seventh of the ten W154s so far built by the factory. Its specification sheet, completed in the racing department on the day the convoy left Untertürkheim for the Eifel mountains, showed that it was fitted with engine No. 11, tested on the bench to produce 458bhp. Caracciola had the latest of the cars: chassis No. 10, engine No. 10. The team leader, however, was not feeling well. The cause was worms, according to Neubauer, although the press was told that he was suffering from indigestion. While Caracciola circulated without his usual zest, von Brauchitsch took the initiative, recording a time barely two seconds slower than the record set by Rosemeyer a year earlier under the old regulations, in a lighter car powered by a 6-litre engine. George Monkhouse, watching the red-helmeted driver hurl the car through the Pflanzgarten section in a series of hair-raising slides, called it 'one of the most exciting displays of broadside motoring I ever saw'. At the end of practice the Mercedes quartet headed the timing sheets: von Brauchitsch (9:48.4), Lang (9:54.1), Seaman (10:01.2), and Caracciola (10:03.1). Then came Nuvolari, followed by his teammates Hasse, Müller and Stuck, with the Alfas of Farina, Clemente Biondetti and Piero Taruffi leading the remaining dozen runners. The only other English driver was Arthur Hyde, the novice who had withdrawn his Maserati from the Donington race seven months earlier rather than get in the way of the German cars, but was now feeling confident enough to have a go on a circuit whose length meant that he would not be looking in his mirrors and moving aside the whole time.

On the morning of race day, the serenity of the Mercedes camp was disturbed when von Brauchitsch chose the wrong moment to aim one of his patronising remarks at Lang. The two men were squaring up when Dick stepped between them with a reminder of why they were there. Neubauer, who was not present, could only be thankful for the Englishman's cool head and willingness to intervene. Around the circuit, a crowd of 300,000 had gathered. In the main grandstand, a row of VIP seats was reserved for Daimler-Benz's guests, whose identities revealed the firm's close links with the civilian and military authorities. They included SS Obersturmbannführer Alfred Gutbrod, a leading figure in the publication of Nazi propaganda material; Gruppenführer Kurt Kaul, chief of the Waffen SS in the south-west; Dr Karl Strölin, a senior Nazi Party figure and the mayor of Stuttgart, who would later send 2,000 of the city's Jews to concentration camps; SA-Obergruppenführer Hanns Ludin, later the Third Reich's ambassador to Slovakia, responsible for deportations to Auschwitz; and Jakob Sprenger, the fiercely antisemitic Gauleiter of Hesse. Alongside them were the company's directors, including Werlin.

Observing the usual ceremony, the cars were rolled to the grid in line astern by white-overalled mechanics, supervised by Neubauer. German flags flew over the pits and grandstands but it was noticeable that the loudest applause from the public came when Nuvolari made his entrance, his charisma overriding national loyalties. Once again the starting system malfunctioned, the lights refusing to change from amber to green; the drivers took matters into their own hands and charged off on the first of the twenty-two laps as the traditional maroon – a signal rocket adapted from military use – went up with a bang in a cloud of white smoke. Immediately Nuvolari came through from the second row as Lang shot into the lead. Seaman overtook Nuvolari, a man old enough to be his father but the object of his unbounded reverence, for second place in the first corner, and by the time they came through the Karussell the Mercedes team occupied the first four places.

One of those W154s had been spraying oil onto Nuvolari's

goggles. Unable to see clearly, the Italian crashed at Brünnchen on the first time around. Although he managed to get the car back to the pits, its rear suspension was too badly damaged to allow him to continue. To Neubauer's astonishment, Obergruppenführer Erwin Kraus of the NSKK, Hühnlein's number two and the organisation's technical director, appeared in the Mercedes pit, demanding that since a leak from one of their cars had been the cause of the Auto Union leader's accident, they should all be brought in and checked over. Neubauer refused point-blank and the race went on.

Lang had opened an eleven-second gap to Seaman on the first lap, but soon Dick could hear the leader's engine losing its edge – 'going fluffy', in his phrase. He and von Brauchitsch quickly closed up, Seaman content to let his teammate take the initiative as they overtook their slowing colleague. Lang was called in, the plugs were changed and Bäumer took his place, simply to gain experience, before the two leading Mercedes came in to refuel and change tyres, resuming their respective positions after stops of forty-four seconds for von Brauchitsch and fifty-two seconds for Seaman. With von Brauchitsch so obviously hungry for the home win that would restore his standing in the eyes of the nation while putting Lang in his place, Seaman settled back and held station, acting the good team man, driving calmly but going fast enough to set the best lap time of the race while remaining at a discreet distance – ten seconds or so – behind the leader. When Caracciola came in for a second time, feeling thoroughly nauseous, Lang was ready to take over, but so much time had been lost that there was no question of mounting a challenge. Nuvolari was cheered when he also re-entered the race, at the wheel of Müller's car.

Since Lang's unpleasant experience with fuel-soaked overalls in Tripoli, thick towels had been draped around the drivers' necks and shoulders during refuelling stops to catch any spillage. Von Brauchitsch came in for his second and final stop for fuel and tyres at the end of the sixteenth lap, and to tell Neubauer that he felt Seaman was following too closely. The towel had just been removed and the engine restarted when an overspill of fuel ignited on the hot exhaust. The first sign of a conflagration was the agitated driver releasing the catch on his removable steering wheel, throwing himself out of the car and frantically trying to beat out the invisible flames of the burning alcohol-based mixture. Neubauer stepped smartly away and looked on aghast. Seaman, who had stopped immediately behind the other car, needing fuel but not tyres, saw what happened next in close-up as the rear of von Brauchitsch's machine was engulfed in a whoosh of fire. Very quickly three mechanics wielded extinguishers to douse the car with foam before the tank, full to the brim, could explode. Neubauer hesitated for a few seconds before dashing back and gesturing urgently for the engine of the number 26 car to be restarted and for the startled Seaman to get going again. Dick pulled out, steered deftly around the drama, straightened up and put his foot down.

Surprisingly, von Brauchitsch was not burnt by the flames. Once the foam and the scorch marks had been wiped from his car's bodywork, and Uhlenhaut had jumped into the cockpit to check that all the vital systems were working, he set off again, encouraged by Hühnlein and Neubauer. All hope of victory had been snatched away, however, and a crash at 120mph at the Flugplatz put a full stop on his race. He believed the steering wheel had come loose, and carried it back to the pits as if to prove his claim, with the crumpled car lying abandoned in a ditch. Later Erwin Kraus would accuse Neubauer of allowing von Brauchitsch to go back out into the race with burnt brake lines; a post-race inspection showed them to be undamaged.

At the front, with six laps of the Nordschleife – 84 miles, and around 850 corners – to go, Dick held a lead of two minutes over Caracciola's car, now driven by Lang. Despite considerable discomfort from the heat of the pedals – not an infrequent occurrence, since his height meant they were located 80mm (just over 3 inches) closer to the engine than those of his

Dick in a Mercedes W125 during the drivers' test at Monza supervised by Alfred Neubauer early in 1937. Inset: the times set by the five men competing for a permanent place in the team, clearly showing the Englishman's superior speed and consistency.

On board the *Bremen* with colleagues and rivals from the two German teams, en route to New York for the Vanderbilt Cup in July 1937.

Alfred Neubauer watches as Seaman takes the W125 out during practice for his only race in the United States, at Long Island's Roosevelt Raceway.

Caught out by a locking brake on the W125 in the hills above Pescara, Dick watches as the car is manhandled off the track during practice for the 1937 Coppa Acerbo.

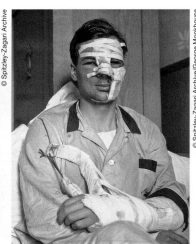

Disaster at the 1937 German Grand Prix: nudged by Ernst von Delius's Auto Union, Dick's Mercedes finishes in the undergrowth.

Both drivers are taken to hospital in Adenau, where von Delius dies from his injuries while Dick receives treatment to his battered face and broken arm.

The main office block at Untertürkheim, the Mercedes headquarters in a suburb of Stuttgart.

The dark blue diesel trucks of the Mercedes racing team, setting out on another expedition of conquest.

Dick on the Starnbergersee, giving his German neighbours their first sight of water-skiing.

Dick shakes hands with the former Edward VIII (with Lang between them) at the Mercedes factory on 21 October 1937, the day before the Duke's visit to Hitler in Berchtesgaden.

A raincoated Seaman at Berne in 1938 with his British pals (from left) Arthur Dobson, JoЎny Wakefield, Charlie Martin and Robert Fellowes.

Erica Popp, photographed for the magazine *Modenwelt* as a teenager in love with fashion and horses.

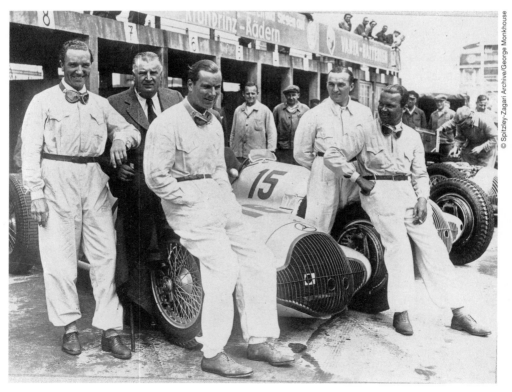

Dick perches on the W154 that will carry him to victory in the 1938 German Grand Prix, with (from left) Manfred von Brauchitsch, Alfred Neubauer, Hermann Lang and Rudolf Caracciola.

At the Nürburgring on the way to emulating Sir Henry Segrave, the hero of his schooldays, by winning a major continental Grand Prix. Inset: Mercedes artist Walter GotscÝe's poster celebrating the team's 1938 successes.

Dick accepts the victor's laurels on the balcony of the timekeepers' building at the Nürburgring while reluctantly observing protocol alongside the less inhibited Korpsführer Adolf HüÝlein (left) and the unlucky Manfred von Brauchitsch (right).

Emerging with Erica after a quiet register-office marriage ceremony at Caxton Hall in London on 7 December 1938.

A gift from Erica's father, Haus Buchenbichl in Untergrainau-bei-Garmisch gives the newly married couple a home beneath the Bavarian Alps.

In February 1939 Adolf Hitler greets the Mercedes drivers, lined up with their cars outside the Reich Chancellery before the Berlin Motor Show.

Captured by a photographer working on a spread for *Picture Post*, Dick and Erica finish their last meal together in Spa's Palace Hôtel des Bains, an hour or so before the start of the Belgian Grand Prix.

With a rain visor strapped around his helmet and a blanket over the bonnet of his Mercedes W154, Dick waits for the race to begin.

As the conditions worsen and great drivers like Caracciola and Nuvolari crash out of the race, Dick rounds the Stavelot hairpin.

Schorsch Meier had left his wrecked Auto Union and was walking back to the pits when he saw Seaman's car hit a tree and catch fire; he is making frantic attempts to extinguish the blaze.

Bearing Adolf Hitler's condolences, the wreath sent from Berlin to the funeral in Knightsbridge becomes the object of press curiosity and arouses mixed feelings among the mourners.

Two distraught women look on as the coffin is loaded into a hearse outside the Seaman family's London home. Erica and her father are just right of centre, while Lilian Seaman waits in the doorway.

teammates, and the mechanics often glued a protective layer of asbestos to the soles of his shoes – he was able to maintain his rapid but steady pace for the final hour. Seeing Neubauer's signals to slow down, he was chiefly worried that by doing so the plugs might start oiling up, but the engine continued to run perfectly. By the time the car with the green-painted radiator grille streaked past the chequered flag, with the British press corps rising to acclaim its green-helmeted driver, he had increased the gap to almost four and a half minutes – nearly half a lap – over the second Mercedes, with Stuck third, another four minutes back, in one of the two surviving Auto Unions. Dick had completed the race distance in three hours, 51 minutes and 46 seconds, at an average speed of just over 80mph, while using only two sets of tyres. His fastest lap – the fastest of the race – was timed at 10 minutes 9.1 seconds, an average of 83.76mph. It was the first victory for a British driver in a major continental Grand Prix since Henry Segrave, Dick's schoolboy hero, won the French race at Tours fifteen years earlier. As Dick returned to the pits, Neubauer was there to welcome him with a big kiss on the cheek. He released the catch on the steering wheel, eased himself out of the cockpit and borrowed a small comb from the team manager to tidy his sweat-matted hair before the ceremonies.

Some found his win harder to stomach. Hühnlein was not thrilled by the idea of an Englishman winning Germany's showpiece event when any one of the team's three German drivers might have taken the victory. And 'God Save the King' would have to be played alongside 'Deutschland über Alles'. To soften the blow to national honour, he quickly summoned von Brauchitsch, who, despite his disappointment, had been among the first to offer congratulations as his teammate rolled to a halt. Followed by Max Sailer, the two drivers walked together to the balcony of the timekeepers' office.

Then came the trickiest moment of all. Dick had accepted the *Preis des Führers* – a huge bronze trophy surmounted by an eagle with its wings outspread. Now, with the giant wreath of oak leaves on his shoulders, and a fringed red satin ribbon around his neck bearing the legend *Dem Sieger* (the winner) and a swastika in a white roundel, he saw the throng around him lifting their arms in the Nazi salute: '*Sieg heil! Sieg heil!*' Like England's footballers two months earlier, Dick had little option but to follow suit: as a convention, as a courtesy, and in his case as an acknowledgement of the organisation that had given him the opportunity of such a victory. Flanked by Hühnlein and von Brauchitsch, who – like the rest of the crowd – were making the salute in the approved straight-armed style, Dick raised his right hand, elbow bent, like a man flagging down a number 38 bus outside the Ritz. As captured in close-up by the camera of Robert Fellowes, this was a distinctly unemphatic version of the *Hitlergrüss*. But there it was, preserved for all time, the image of a young British sportsman wearing a swastika around his neck and joining the salute to a dictator who, with every passing day, was driving the world closer to catastrophe. Dick was standing to attention, it seemed, on the wrong side of history.

◆

As the public ceremony broke up, the winner was surrounded by his excited English friends: Dugdale, Fellowes, Walkerley and Monkhouse, who was remembering how Dick had told him during his year with the ERA that his ambition was to win the German Grand Prix. Seaman's first thought was to ask them for news of Arthur Hyde, who had crashed heavily on the fifteenth lap. He had seen the driver being treated at the side of the road, beside his overturned car. (Hyde had been taken to hospital in Adenau, where his survival was for some time in doubt.) Responding to Dugdale's congratulations, Dick thanked his old school friend and added, sotto voce, 'I only wish it had been in a British car.'

When the public fuss was over and he was able to sit down

with a cigarette and glass of champagne at an informal party in a room under the grandstand, the chair next to him was occupied by the 18-year-old girl he had met three weeks earlier. Ostensibly, she was there at the invitation of her friends Hans Frederick Wessels, a Mercedes-Benz dealer in Bremen, and his wife. Dick had wiped the oil and grime from his face but was still wearing his stained overalls, with his goggles around his neck. Erica was in a light summer frock, with white trim around the neck and shoulders, and a boater on the back of her head, framing her curls. Their smiles were a perfect match.

Dick's modest demeanour in victory was both appropriate to the circumstances and true to his nature. The writer of *Motor Sport*'s Continental Notes – probably either Fellowes or Walkerley, moonlighting under the byline 'Auslander' – commented: 'Seaman's behaviour after the race delighted everyone, because it fitted in so perfectly with the continental idea of how an Englishman would behave under such conditions. Although he was obviously gratified in the extreme at his success, he remained outwardly calm and without animation. It took von Brauchitsch's spontaneous congratulations to bring a smile to his face.' Hühnlein, meanwhile, was composing a difficult telegram to his ultimate superior: '*Mein Führer*, I report: the 11th Grand Prix of Germany for racing cars ended with a decisive German victory. From the start the German racing teams of Mercedes-Benz and Auto Union dominated the field. NSKK Sturmführer Manfred von Brauchitsch, leading from the beginning and giving admirable proof of his courage and ability, was deprived of victory by his car catching fire while refuelling. The winner and consequently the recipient of your proud prize, *mein Führer*, was Richard Seaman in a Mercedes, followed by NSKK *Hauptsturmführer* Hermann Lang, also in a Mercedes, Hans Stuck and Tazio Nuvolari in Auto Union cars. *Heil, mein Führer!*'

The Mercedes publicity department was already preparing a poster announcing the victory, based around a dramatic illustration by Walter Gotschke, a gifted 24-year-old former architecture student from Silesia employed at Untertürkheim to produce brochures, technical drawings and display material. He showed a W154 heroically speeding past the Nordschleife grandstand under a giant swastika flag. Below the headline *Doppel-Sieg!* (double win) the text gave equal weight to the first two finishers: '1. Richard B. Seaman* 2. H. Lang / R. Caracciola on Mercedes-Benz winning the great and gruelling test for cars and drivers on the Nürburgring in the face of the most severe international competition in a superior style.' The asterisk indicated that Seaman had also won the Führer's Prize. 'Both cars,' the text continued in smaller type, 'are equipped with Continental tyres, Bosch sparking plugs, Bosch ignition and EC Kolben pistons.' Translated into English, Italian, Spanish and French, the poster would be distributed to the company's dealers throughout Europe.

On his return to the Eifelerhof, Dick commandeered the hotel's only hot bath to ease the aches of the day's physical effort. Dugdale was allowed in for an informal interview, and noted that telegrams were already arriving: one from Ramponi, another from Birch reading just 'Good show!' and a longer one in German from Dr Kissel, whose message evidently pleased Seaman greatly. Reflecting on the afternoon, Dick said that the surface of the Nordschleife had been trickier than usual, thanks to a combination of dropped oil, rubber from the tyres and the heat of the day melting the asphalt. This, he said, was the reason the lap times were so much slower than they had been in practice.

'I was rather lucky, you know,' he told his old school friend, who picked up the huge, heavy trophy and asked: 'Is this all you get?' No, Seaman replied. Mercedes would certainly make him a replica – but, more important, he expected they would give him the special keepsake, a replica of the three-pointed star made in diamonds, presented only to drivers who had won a Grand Prix. 'The thought of possessing one appealed to Dick more than just about anything else,' Dugdale concluded. There was also, he noted, the matter of the winner's prize money: a cool RM 20,000, almost twice his annual retainer.

Emerging from his long bath, Dick got dressed in a dark suit, white shirt and tie, preparing to celebrate with the team. 'Auslander' recorded his evening: 'At the Mercedes dinner at the Eifelerhof in Adenau that same evening, he was given the place of honour, sitting with the Führer's enormous Prize in front of him and the charming daughter of the BMW managing director beside him – an enviable position indeed.'

24

In the country of 'Mr Smith'

Back in London from Pull Court that Sunday evening, Lilian Seaman heard the phone ring as she went through the front door of 3 Ennismore Gardens. It was Roland King-Farlow, calling in a state of great excitement to tell her of Dick's victory. The next day John Dugdale, who had just arrived home, telephoned to give her a detailed description of the race, the prize-giving ceremony and the celebrations afterwards. Delighted by her son's success in an event of such obvious significance, she sent a telegram of congratulations.

She would have been disappointed to see that three brief downpage paragraphs in the *Daily Mail* represented the only coverage of Dick's victory in a British national paper on the day after the race – and even that meagre story was headlined 'Racer's Escape', referring to von Brauchitsch's car catching fire. Otherwise the sports pages were preoccupied by England's progress in the Test match at Headingley, where Don Bradman's century was helping Australia to take a 1-0 lead in the Ashes series. Grand Prix racing was not high on Fleet Street's agenda. As her son had told her, the British press were only interested in the sport when there was a fatal accident to provide headlines and pictures.

In the specialist press, the significance of the result was fully understood. In his report for *The Motor*, Walkerley wrote: 'Seaman's win in the German Grand Prix is something to be proud of. It is the more opportune in that it had begun to look as though he was out of luck and merely a spare driver instead of a regular member of the team, all of which rumour is now thoroughly dispelled. This race proves Seaman to be the finest driver so far produced by this country. He is cool, really polished, doesn't whack his cars to death, uses less fuel than anyone in the Mercedes team, and at the Ring is as good as the best.' Bill Boddy's race report for *Motor Sport* contained the observation that 'Seaman's victory was due to the steady, unruffled style of driving which has made him famous'. The headline reflected his unbounded admiration of the German approach: 'Heil Seaman! Heil Mercedes!'

◆

During Dick's trip home in early June he had invited his mother to visit him in Germany. Her eager acceptance had been followed by weeks of planning. Her passport had to be renewed, first-class tickets booked on trains and ferries, and a German-speaking companion engaged for the whole of the trip. She needed new dresses and hats, even though Dick had told her not to bother bringing anything but simple clothes to the villa on the lakeshore. As late as the day before her departure, she was buying one last hat to add to her luggage.

That Wednesday, 27 July, she was driven to Liverpool Street station, where she met her companion, an Englishwoman of her own generation who had lived in Germany; together they took the train for Harwich, from where a ferry carried them overnight to the Hook of Holland. On a German train they headed straight to Munich, cancelling a planned overnight stop in Cologne. Arriving at their hotel a day earlier than planned, they went sightseeing in the Hofgarten and at the Residenz palace, where they saw a shrine to the men who had been killed protecting Hitler during the Beer Hall Putsch of 1923. Germans paying their respects at the sacred flame gave a Nazi salute while doing so. Lilian declined to follow their example.

Dick picked them up from their hotel the next morning in his Mercedes, followed by Monkhouse in his Bentley, with his father alongside. On the way to the Starnbergersee, Dick gave his mother two warnings. The first was that since butter was rationed in Germany, his English guests were having to be asked to restrain themselves when spreading it on their toast. The second was that if she ever felt like discussing Hitler in public while she was in Germany, she should refer to him as 'Mr Smith'. 'Otherwise,' Dick said, 'you might find yourself being tapped on the shoulder and carted off to a concentration camp.'

This did not spoil her admiration of the scenery en route – the ripening cornfields, the lush woods, the sunlight sparkling on the lake – and the victory wreath over the front door of the chalet, put up by the villagers of Ambach. She was delighted to meet Dick's other guests, Fellowes and his university friend Ben Plunket, a young diplomat at the British embassy in Washington, who impressed her by being the son of the Bishop of Meath and the brother of the Countess Fitzwilliam, a society beauty. It was Monkhouse, however, who had news for her, and they had barely sat down for lunch on the terrace when, with Dick occupied elsewhere, he could no longer restrain himself.

'Mrs Seaman,' George said, 'we have found a wife for Dick.' She smiled politely, as if he were making a joke. But he carried on. 'In fact,' he continued, 'the only possible wife for Dick. They are ideally suited.'

'If my son wanted a wife,' she told him, her blood starting to freeze, 'he would be quite capable of finding one for himself.' Monkhouse's father chimed in. 'Oh, but you haven't met Erica. She is the most beautiful girl in the world.' And he proceeded to list her assets: not just her beauty but her father's wealth and her interest in cooking and interior decoration and even needle-work. As he continued, she tried to persuade herself that this was just a middle-aged man acting, as she put it to herself, *en garçon*, indulging his own fantasies.

Lunch was finishing with coffee and cigarettes when the first of a new wave of guests arrived: a group of journalists and photographers with an appointment to interview the winner of the big race a week earlier. Lilian found herself in conversation with one of them, a handsome young man who assured her that Germany was very happy with the way Hitler was going about things. The next carful of guests was led by Herta Caracciola, Rudi's sister, who had been staying with friends on the Tegernsee and had brought them along. As the afternoon drew on, jazz records were played on a gramophone and Lilian, coming in from the terrace, found Dick and Herta dancing together.

After some of the guests had left, Monkhouse's father insisted that they all drive into Munich, where he would treat them to dinner. At the restaurant, he astonished her by raising the first glass of champagne and announcing, 'To Erica!' After dinner they strolled to the main Mercedes-Benz showroom, where a poster proclaiming Dick's victory took pride of place. Beside it was a full-sized portrait of the Führer, lit as if it were a religious icon, causing her again to wonder about the state of things in Germany.

Once Dick and his friends had set off back to Ambach, she went to the cinema to watch a newsreel of his triumph at the Nürburgring. For the first time she could see the events of that momentous day in her son's life unfold. The large audience was attentive and enthusiastic, breaking into applause at the end, when Dick's face was flanked by those of George VI and Adolf Hitler. 'There will be no war,' she thought. 'The Germans are a friendly nation. They don't want war.'

◆

On the next day she and her companion were due to move into the chalet. Again Dick picked them up, this time with their luggage. During a relaxed lunch she thought to herself that he seemed happy and at home in these surroundings. He was about to take her for a run across the lake in his motorboat when they heard the sound of wheels on the gravel drive. A car stopped and two girls emerged: Erica and her friend Annmarie.

In her memoir, Lilian wrote at length of her first impressions of the girl as she approached: tall, slim, with fine legs and ankles, a pure oval face, bright blue eyes, perfect teeth, flawless complexion ('the skin of lilies and roses'), soft fair hair, dignity, poise and grace all on show. Beautifully dressed, too, in a traditional dirndl made (so Lilian later discovered) with fabric imported from Liberty of Regent Street and sewn by her personal dressmaker in Munich. A vision of radiance, all told – and, it turned out, speaking English with a cultured accent while displaying a charming manner and a degree of sophistication that, Lilian decided, was a thing of wonder in a girl of eighteen.

Her loveliness was even more clearly revealed after she and Dick had gone to change into their bathing costumes. Erica re-emerged in a pale blue two-piece: a tiny bodice secured with a strap around the back and equally tiny shorts, all fitting like a glove, showing off her perfect proportions. Her toenails, Lilian noticed, were enamelled in carnation red, to match her fingernails. As they went off to swim in the lake – her handsome son and this breathtakingly gorgeous creature – under the admiring gaze of the villa's guests, all Lilian could think was that he would be too sensible to settle down with a German girl. An English bride and Pull Court were surely where his destiny lay.

◆

And so the afternoon went by. Dick demonstrated his waterskiing skills before he and Erica drove off in his car to collect some chickens he had been promised for the following day's lunch. On their return, Erica and her friend said their goodbyes. As the remainder of the party sat with a drink before dinner, another guest arrived: a fine-looking woman in her mid-thirties, introduced to Lilian as Laury Vermundt, the fiancée of Dr Gläser, staying at another chalet nearby.

Dick's mother would be struck by her son's closeness to this very elegant older woman. As they swam or talked together, the two seemed entirely at ease. But at dinner Laury shocked her by suddenly saying what was in every mind except that of Lilian Seaman: 'Well, Dick, and when are you going to announce your engagement to Erica?' Lilian hardly had time to register the question before Dick came back with his response: 'In September, in Munich.'

He was joking, she thought. It was his sharp sense of humour, very familiar to her. But she thought his answer had brought a wistful look into the eyes of his questioner, and she wondered if Laury Vermundt might not have waited until she saw Erica drive away before making her own entrance.

Lilian had trouble getting to sleep that night, not least because she had last glimpsed Dick, as she prepared to go to bed, stand-ing on the terrace, leaning against a pillar, staring out across the darkened lake towards Garmisch as a romantic tune played on the gramophone.

The days passed with visits and guests and swimming. The Aldingtons came to swim with their three children, and Dick took his mother up the Starnbergersee to look at Schloss Berg, where Ludwig II had died a mysterious death in 1886. Erica also returned, this time in a new white BMW 328 delivered that morning as her father's gift; she was wearing a grey and white striped jacket, a pale blue silk shirt and grey flannel trousers, all perfectly cut and making her look, Lilian thought, like a superb greyhound. She invited Dick's mother to pay a visit to her family's chalet the following Saturday.

Laury Vermundt was such a frequent visitor, and so clearly on good terms with Dick – one afternoon they changed into their bathing costumes and went out in the motorboat to swim together on the far side of the lake – that eventually Lilian found herself unable to hold her tongue. After dinner, when she and her companion were alone with her son, she warned him not to get involved in a flirtation with an older woman engaged to a man who might one day be in a position to save his life. He told her that while he and Laury were certainly great friends, he was equally friendly with Peter Gläser. As he laughed off her suggestion, she added, 'Don't say I didn't warn you.' He lit a cigarette and thought for a moment. 'And what would you say,' he responded, 'if I were going to marry Erica?'

Inwardly she was in turmoil. Once again, the sort of future she and her late husband had planned for Dick seemed to have been wrecked by his wilfulness. Now she was about to lose him, she feared, for good: to Germany, and to this girl who, she had been told by Ivy Aldington, was every bit as charming as she seemed but had grown up accustomed to being denied nothing. All she said, however, was something mild about her memories of the strain the Great War had placed on such Anglo–German households, and how difficult the life of a child of such a marriage might be.

Dick said nothing but got up and walked into the garden. His mother went upstairs. As she looked out, she saw him leaning once more against a tree, looking out across the water. Going back downstairs a little later, she discovered that he had taken his motorboat out for a run in the moonlight, alone with his thoughts.

◆

More guests were arriving at the chalet, and the plan was for Lilian and her companion to transfer to the Alpenhof Hotel in Garmisch, owned by a local hero: the bobsledder Hanns Kilian, an Olympic bronze medal winner. Dick ferried them in his Mercedes, taking a scenic route and stopping midway for a picnic lunch in a mountain forest. He and his housekeeper had packed the meal; his mother was impressed by the inclusion of a Thermos of hot coffee and a box of her favourite Turkish cigarettes. Later they drove to the Popp house above Grainau, a village outside Garmisch, where Erica greeted them with her usual warmth. Her parents and sister were not there, but her house guests that week included the Aldington family. She showed her impressed visitor around the features: the open log fire in the large living room, the modern kitchen, its cupboards fitted with sliding glass doors, the many gadgets unseen in a British domestic setting. What a pity, Lilian found herself thinking as she noted Erica's apparent pride in the house and its fittings and furnishings, that this girl is not English.

Later, as she watched Erica and Dick walk back from swimming in the Eibsee, arm in arm, heads touching, Lilian could not help but admire the girl's allure. 'She's got it all,' she told her companion. 'Yes,' the reply came, 'and she's got Dick, too. You'll never be able to get him away from her now.'

Two days later, Dick went off to join his Mercedes colleagues as they spent a day practising for the Grossglockner hill-climb, due to take place at the end of August. He took Erica with him on the 200-mile round trip across the Austrian border, stopping in Garmisch on the way back to see his mother. As they sat in the lounge, Lilian heard Erica address Dick for the first time as 'darling'. They discussed her plan to invite them and all their various house guests from Ambach and Grainau to the Alpenhof for dinner and dancing the following evening.

The Aldingtons were there, and the Monkhouses, father and son, and others, although Lilian had quietly asked Dick to exclude Laury Vermundt. There was a band playing, and while Dick was dancing with his mother after dinner he looked at her and said, 'Well, what *do* you think about it, Mother?' She reminded him of what she had said before, and asked him not to discuss it further that night but to enjoy the occasion. The drinking and dancing went on until long after midnight, when the guests departed and Dick drove away, with Erica alongside him.

◆

Lilian Seaman had seen enough. It was time to leave. The next day, she and her companion packed their suitcases for the journey home. They planned to stop en route in Nuremberg, Cologne and the Nürburgring, where she wanted to visit the scene of her son's recent triumph. As the train skirted the Starnbergersee, she looked towards Ambach. 'At that moment,' she wrote, 'I knew my son had gone from my life for ever.' Gone, she meant, in the sense that Ennismore Gardens and Pull Court would no longer represent his home.

At the station in Munich she bought copies of *The Times* and the *Daily Telegraph*, which carried stories about the deteriorating international situation. A command had gone out from the Reichstag that Jews must carry special identity cards, while the British government had placed an urgent order for a thousand Spitfire fighter planes. She thought of her discussions with Dick, in which he had said that the German government saw their British counterparts as, in effect, conscientious objectors: for men such as Lord Halifax, Chamberlain's recently appointed Foreign Secretary, first-hand memories of the Great War's carnage meant that they would go to almost any lengths to avoid a repeat of that nightmare. 'England should send some strong and determined characters out to Germany,' Lilian remembered Dick saying, 'who would open their eyes and let them see what we would do under intense provocation. England is literally asking for trouble, and it is going to get it.'

In Nuremberg she visited the recently restored medieval palace, the home of the painter Albrecht Dürer, and the shoe-maker's house featured in Wagner's *Die Meistersinger*, which she had seen at Covent Garden. While walking through the city's historic centre she turned into a cobbled square, to be confronted by an incongruous sight: a large building that appeared to have been part-destroyed, as if by artillery bombardment. As she watched, men were at work demolishing it with hammers and pickaxes. This, she was told, had been Nuremberg's main synagogue. Her informant added that the Jews had overrun

Germany, impoverishing its people in the process, and that this was the proper response. That night she discussed it over dinner with local friends of her companion. The woman who had accused a 'foreign Jewish syndicate' of interfering in the Ranelagh Club now heard things that astonished her about how Jewish doctors, lawyers and other professionals were being forced out of their jobs and made to forfeit their houses and savings.

She was urged to see the Luitpoldarena, where the annual Nazi Party rallies took place, in order to get an idea of what Hitler was up to. Climbing the steps to the podium from which he gave his speeches, she felt that she sensed something of the power with which he could sway his audience. She went away having concluded not only that Dick should never marry a German but that he should break his contract with Mercedes and return home as soon as possible.

They stayed the next night in Cologne and visited the Nürburgring the following day. She wanted to see the hospital in Adenau, where Dick had been patched up in 1937, and the Eifelerhof, where the victory banquet had been held a few weeks earlier. At the circuit itself an English chauffeur – a Great War veteran who had married a German woman – drove her around the Nordschleife before she mounted the steps to the terrace of the timekeepers' building, from which Dick had acknowledged the applause of the crowd in the grandstand opposite.

The following night she slept in her cabin on the ferry from the Hook of Holland to Harwich. She returned to London with her head full of decisions that, she believed, would brook no argument.

25

Picnic in the mountains

In between teaching Erica to waterski that summer, and dancing with her while favourites such as Fred Astaire's 'Cheek to
Cheek' and Al Bowlly's 'Did You Ever See a Dream Walking'
played on the gramophone at Ambach, he learnt more about
her family. Franz Josef Popp, born in Vienna in 1886, had
worked as a young man on electricity-powered locomotives.
During the war he had joined the Rapp aero-engine company
at their factory in Munich. In 1917 he replaced Karl Rapp, the
company's founder, as managing director and changed its name
to the Bayerische Motorenwerke, supervising the production
of a six-cylinder engine that, in the final weeks of the war,
replaced a less powerful Mercedes-Benz unit in the Fokker
D.VII fighter.

Four years after the war, with an eye on diversification, BMW
took over Automobilwerk Eisenach, a small company manufacturing the little Austin 7, built under licence and renamed
the Dixi. It was updated to become the first BMW passenger
car. Popp also negotiated with Pratt & Whitney to license the
American company's air-cooled radial aero engines, which his
own engineers developed throughout the 1930s. While Lilian
Seaman was making her visit to Germany, a Focke-Wulf Fw
200 airliner powered by four BMW engines was being prepared

for the first non-stop flight from Berlin to New York by a heavier-than-air craft.

Popp had joined the National Socialist Party soon after the 1933 elections, later claiming that it was a purely pragmatic decision, just as Enzo Ferrari had found it expedient to rub along with his local Fascist party officials after Mussolini came to power. Popp had certainly carried out the government's instructions to purge the company of its Jewish employees. Those removed even included a well-connected young trainee engineer called Louis Hagen, the grandson of a banker who had played a significant role in the merging of Automobilwerk Eisenach and BMW. Hagen, whose other grandfather had owned the Hotel Eden in Berlin, had been seized by Brownshirts after the family's maid reported him for writing an anti-Nazi joke on a postcard; he was taken to a camp where he was beaten and abused, along with communists and other Jews, before his release was secured by an influential family friend.

Erica's father had also been a member of the supervisory board of Daimler-Benz, just as Wilhelm Kissel had served on BMW's equivalent body, reflecting the two companies' collaboration on certain projects. But when Hitler and Göring put pressure on him to increase the military side of BMW's production (which included engines for the Focke-Wulf Fw 190 fighter) at the expense of building cars and motorbikes for sale to civilians, he resisted. It was his view that, were he to go along with their wishes, and were the predicted war not to happen, a sudden cut in demand could ruin the whole company. It may have been a commercial decision rather than a moral one, but it was also noticed that his family continued to be treated by a Jewish doctor. He was far from being the most ideologically committed of party members, and by the time his daughter fell in love with a young Englishman, he had begun to slip out of favour.

He had already become a rich man, however, with a big town house in Bogenhausen, a fashionable part of Munich, and a chalet in the mountains for his wife, Christine, and their two daughters. In childhood Erica had suffered from delicate health and spent three months of every winter in a hotel in Celerina, near St Moritz, where she learnt to skate and ski expertly. After leaving school she took courses in secretarial skills and cooking, but horses were her teenage obsession. Her close friends included Bimbo Haspel, born Gretel Schwab, the half-Jewish wife of Wilhelm 'Helmi' Haspel, a Daimler-Benz director who had also been a wartime comrade of Erica's new brother-in-law, Paul Heim. The Haspels were keen supporters of the Mercedes racing programme and had become friendly with Rudi and Alice Caracciola; their circle also included the Wessels, who had invited Erica to the Nürburgring. The girl had little interest in motor sport, but she did know who Richard John Beattie Seaman was; she and Eva had looked through a pamphlet in which Mercedes publicised their victories, and had giggled together when they read his full name.

It turned out that Lilian had been correct in her belief that something had gone on during that day trip to the Grossglockner. Dick had picked Erica up early in the morning of Tuesday 9 August in his Mercedes saloon, with a picnic hamper on the back. At the top of the mountain they stopped at a hotel, where they bumped into Hans and Paula Stuck, who invited the young couple to have lunch with them. To Erica's surprise, Dick declined. Instead they got back into the car and he drove to a quiet spot where he laid out the picnic.

He seemed preoccupied. Unusually, he wasn't interested in the food he had brought. Erica wondered if there was something wrong. But then, quite suddenly, he kissed her and said, 'Do you love me?' 'Yes,' she replied. 'Seriously, or only for a flirt?' 'Seriously.' 'Enough to marry me?' 'Yes.' And that was it. She was a little shocked to think that, at the age of eighteen, she had pledged herself to a man she had known for less than two months. When her sister had got married that June, just after she met Dick, she had told her father not to worry – she had no intention of following suit. But now she had no doubt about the decision.

Neither did their friends, it seemed. A delighted Bimbo Haspel offered to take on the job of breaking it to Erica's father, who was equally pleased by the news. To the circle of visitors who had met Erica in Ambach, it seemed an entirely natural development. But not a breath of the news could be allowed to reach Dick's mother, now safely back in England. That would take some preparation.

◆

Their summer idyll meant that Dick was a little less resentful of his status as Mercedes' reserve driver, which continued unchanged despite his win in the biggest race of the year. The team had left him at home while they went to Livorno for the Coppa Ciano on 7 August and on to Pescara for the Coppa Acerbo a week later. Caracciola looked like winning in Livorno, at the wheel of a new experimental lightweight W154, but he retired when a tread from a disintegrating rear tyre made a hole in his petrol tank. Von Brauchitsch took the chequered flag but was disqualified for having been push-started by spectators after sliding into the straw bales while trying to overtake Lang. So the victory was Lang's, his second of the year. In Pescara the engines of both von Brauchitsch's and Lang's cars blew up, with Lang lucky to escape when his W154 was completely incinerated, leaving Caracciola to cruise home as the first of only four finishers.

Dick was back on duty in Berne, where the Swiss Grand Prix was to be run over fifty laps of what had become, according to Monkhouse, his favourite circuit, on which he had won the voiturette race three years in a row. Mercedes entered four cars and took along Bäumer as a reserve. Caracciola and Lang both had the new experimental models, while Seaman was in his Nürburgring-winning car. In dry, bright conditions, Seaman dominated both practice sessions to show that the break had not affected his form, claiming his first pole position in a Grande Épreuve.

Rain arrived on race day, however, and would not relent. Most of the drivers wore visors instead of goggles, fastened with straps around their wind helmets. Dick got away to a brilliant start and pulled out a lead of ten seconds over the field, the Auto Union challenge collapsing through a variety of ailments as Caracciola worked his way through to second place and began to chase down his teammate. When the rain turned into a cloudburst, Seaman found himself stuck behind a couple of squabbling backmarkers; he opted for caution and waited for a clear opportunity to lap them, giving Caracciola the chance to catch up. Demonstrating his supreme skills in the wet, Rudi showed Dick the way by overtaking all three cars in a single manoeuvre. Thereafter Seaman settled back to finish a very good second, probably bearing in mind the sort of thought related by Monkhouse: 'Dick once observed that if he found himself travelling faster than Caracciola when the latter was on form and his car running well, then he, Seaman, was driving too fast and was heading for an accident.' He crossed the line just under half a minute behind the Rainmaster and a little more than that ahead of von Brauchitsch. Lang, who had opted to wear goggles, was battling through the field when he took a stone in a lens and pulled in to give up with a fragment of glass in his eye. Dick had the satisfaction of recording the fastest lap of the race, albeit thirteen seconds slower than his practice time, at an average of just over 95mph. In Monkhouse's view, it had been the greatest drive of his career, given the conditions. As Dick came to a halt and removed his sodden wind helmet, among the mechanics waiting for him was one carrying a raincoat, ready to put it over his drenched shoulders. Neubauer thought of most things.

◆

Five days later Dick flew back to London. A three-week gap before the next Grand Prix allowed him to take advantage of

Max Sailer's permission to drive for the works team of Frazer Nash-BMWs in the Tourist Trophy at Donington Park on 3 September. He would be missing one appointment on the Mercedes schedule, for reasons explained in a letter roughed out by Erica in her neat hand on Ambach notepaper. 'Thank you for your letter of the 12th, from which I gather than I'm expected to participate in the Grossglockner hill-climb,' he dictated to his fiancée, who translated his words into German. 'I had a look at the course last week and found it very poor and dangerous, and I will only drive it if you absolutely want to enter three cars. I found the course impossible. First, you can't get to know the road better using a private car since there is so much traffic, and second, if I can't get to know it well enough, it is indeed too dangerous to drive in a racing car, downhill and through tunnels. Therefore I would be very happy if I didn't need to drive.'

He dined with friends on the evening of his return. It was close to midnight when he opened the door of 3 Ennismore Gardens and found his mother waiting, ready to ask him about the rumour that had now reached her ears. They sat down in the drawing room and spent some time exchanging trivial news before she got to the point. Was it true, she asked, that he and Erica were engaged? He supposed it was, he said. Moreover, Erica and her parents would be coming to London to discuss it very soon. Dick's mother retorted that she would be very surprised if, once Herr Popp had listened to her views, permission for the marriage were not withdrawn. Curbing his anger, Dick went up to bed. Early the next morning he set off for Donington Park, leaving her to reflect that all the joy had gone out of their life as mother and son.

On arrival at the circuit he was told the strategy for the team of four white BMW 328s to be driven by Bira, Fane, Aldington and himself in the 100-lap race for unsupercharged sports and touring cars. The other three were to drive conservatively, observing a specified rev limit. Dick would be free to run at his own pace and push his car to the limit. Bira was not best pleased, but it was immaterial. After four and a half hours of racing, a variety of problems had relegated them in the overall standings to tenth (Aldington), eleventh (Fane), twenty-first (Seaman) and twenty-second (Bira). Dick had been hampered by brake and lubrication problems. This, as he may well have pointed out later to his prospective father-in-law, was the standard of preparation he had come to expect from ERA or Maserati, not while racing a German car.

Aldington had also provisionally entered him for the hill-climb at Shelsley Walsh the following Saturday, but there would be no return to the scene of his debut. His presence was required at Monza, where the Italian Grand Prix was to be held on 11 September and he had been included in the four-car team. Robert Fellowes turned up to support him. So did Erica, who arrived on the Saturday morning with the Haspels, having taken the overnight train from Munich. Dick met them at Milan's Stazione Centrale, still in his racing overalls from the early practice session. Despite Auto Union fielding the definitive version of their Type D for the first time, Mercedes dominated the practising. Lang, Caracciola and von Brauchitsch were the top three, with Seaman sixth, behind Müller and Nuvolari.

Dick was up to third in the opening stages of the race, but engine failure forced him out after a dozen laps – just one of a series of misfortunes for the team on the day, mostly caused by carburation problems. Lang's engine expired at half-distance. Caracciola spun, pushed his car out of the straw bales and restarted, but a leak from an exhaust pipe burnt one of his feet so badly that he handed over to von Brauchitsch, whose own machine had lasted barely longer than Seaman's. The combined effort resulted in third place, behind Nuvolari – whose victory, as well as being Auto Union's first since the death of Rosemeyer, sent the Italian crowd into ecstasies – and Farina's Alfa.

In a curious postscript, two weeks later a letter arrived from the Rome office of the Federazione Automobilistica Sportiva Italiana, addressed to the director of the Mercedes racing

team and headed '16th Italian Grand Prix'. It was signed by
Giuseppe Furmanik, a Swiss-born former racing driver of
Polish extraction and an ally of Mussolini, now president of the
FASI's sporting committee. Furmanik was demanding to know
whether Richard Seaman's racing licence had been issued by
the RAC in Britain or the ONS in Germany. 'I need this information about Mr Seaman's club,' he wrote, 'in order to inform
them of an incident that occurred at the above race, described
in a report from the Commander of the Red Cross, an incident
our committee greatly regrets. After Seaman had stopped his
car, which was about to catch fire, he kicked and hit a mili-
tiaman who had come to assist him. Perhaps this was because
he couldn't understand Italian. It would be appropriate for the
driver in question to show greater respect to the uniform of the
host country. I await your speedy response.' If he received one,
its content and the outcome were never made public and did
not survive. But whatever the nature of the altercation, it was a
reminder that Dick Seaman, like many top drivers, was capable
of a flash of temper when forced out of a race by circumstances
beyond his control. Confronted by an official whose actions
could have seemed obstructive, even a languid Englishman
might momentarily lose control. And he had, of course, studied
Italian in his first year at university.

Neubauer expressed his anger over the Mercedes debacle
by cancelling the planned banquet. Instead he took his wife
for a quiet meal at a favourite spot. But when drivers from
Mercedes, Auto Union and other teams began to arrive at
his chosen restaurant, he realised something was afoot. After
Chiron made a formal announcement of the Seaman–Popp
engagement, Neubauer took over, paying for a celebration that
was extended to incorporate Caracciola's coronation as the 1938
European champion.

Each of the season's four Grandes Épreuves – France,
Germany, Switzerland and Italy – had been won by a different
driver. But under an arcane scoring system Rudi's placings gave

him the title for the third time, twelve points ahead of Seaman. Despite having competed in only three of the races, Dick pipped von Brauchitsch by a single point. Two years after joining the team, and still without regular starts, he was now officially the second-best of the world's Grand Prix drivers.

Later that night, while a band played at the Hotel Ambasciatori, the engaged couple were once again the focus of attention on the dance floor. Among the witnesses was 'Auslander' of *Motor Sport*, who wrote: 'Milan highlight – Dick Seaman and Erica Popp giving a masterly display of the Lambeth Walk to a spell-bound audience.'

26

Home front

On the weekend Dick and Erica celebrated their engagement in Milan, Sir Nevile Henderson had been in Nuremberg, listening to one of Hitler's most impassioned speeches. Although the British ambassador was still willing to describe him as 'a constructive genius, a builder and no mere demagogue', he observed that the leader's megalomania might now have tipped over into insanity. The British Prime Minister had sent Lord Runciman, a Liberal Party politician, to Czechoslovakia to report on the situation of the 3 million ethnic Germans living in the Sudetenland, a territory on which Hitler had been casting covetous eyes. In June the Führer had approved a secret plan for an invasion to begin no later than 1 October. Runciman returned to London in early September with the recommendation that Germany be allowed to take over the region in exchange for a promise to extend its territorial ambitions no further.

On 14 September Dick phoned his mother to tell her that Erica's father had given his consent to the marriage and that the engagement had been officially announced. He and Erica were in Switzerland, on their way back from Monza; at Caracciola's suggestion, they were going to buy an engagement ring there, and Dick wanted his mother to get his bank to wire £500 (the equivalent of more than £30,000 today) from his account directly to a branch in Zurich, since he could not take any of his money out of Germany. Erica's parents, he added, would be flying to London soon to talk to her. Lilian told her son to go and buy the English newspapers, with their stories about the imminence of war between the two countries, and think again. The following day he would read of Neville Chamberlain flying to Germany. After a three-hour meeting with Hitler at Berchtesgaden, the Prime Minister returned to confer with his cabinet.

On 20 September Dick wrote to Monkhouse to inform him that the engagement of which he had so enthusiastically approved was now, thanks to Herr Popp's consent, absolutely official: 'Your carefully laid plans have come to fruition.' That day a notice appeared in *The Times* and the *Daily Telegraph*: 'The engagement is announced between Richard John (Dick Seaman), only son of the late William John Beattie-Seaman and of Mrs Beattie-Seaman, of 3, Ennismore Gardens, Prince's Gate, London SW7, and Pull Court, Worcestershire, and Erica, second daughter of Herr and Frau Popp, of Munich, Bavaria.' Five days later a determined Lilian was at Croydon to meet the flight from Munich. She had been driven there by Harold and Ivy Aldington, the Popps' friends; they lunched at Luigi's before setting off for the airport. When the passengers disembarked, there was no sign of Erica's parents. The uncertain political situation had persuaded them to remain at home.

Erica had insisted on travelling despite suffering from a heavy cold that had reduced her voice to a whisper. For one thing, she wanted to attend the lunch to be given in Dick's honour by the Royal Automobile Club on 27 September, in the week of the Donington Grand Prix. She left Croydon with the Aldingtons, having arranged to stay at Ambarrow Court, their Victorian manor house in Berkshire, while Dick returned home with his mother. There was little conversation on the journey. Crossing Westminster Bridge, they drove along Whitehall, through crowds waiting anxiously for news from Downing Street. The following day he made the 80-mile round trip to bring his fiancée back to London, where they posed in the drawing room and the gardens for a group of newspaper photographers, Dick in a business suit and Erica in a tailored outfit with fur trim by Molyneux and a brown felt hat. Lilian thought her son's fiancée looked 'very young and radiant, and very excited to be in London for the first time'.

Once the photographers had finished, the hard talking could begin. Dick told his mother that they wanted to apply for a special licence to get married in London as soon as possible, bearing in mind that war might break out any day. Once married, Erica's status as a British citizen would ensure that she could not be deported or interned as an enemy alien, and would make life easier were Dick to be called up into the armed forces. And a British marriage certificate might be useful if events forced them to scramble back from Germany to Dick's homeland. Lilian protested that surely Erica's parents would not allow her to risk being parted from them for the duration of any possible hostilities, and that, being under twenty-one, she could not marry without their permission. To Erica's straightforward riposte – 'But they've already given their consent' – she replied that she would certainly not be giving hers, even though the gesture would be meaningless since her son was over twenty-one. Nor, she said, did she approve of hasty marriages. Given that she had met her husband in November 1910 and married him the following June, this was not the most convincing line. During a pause in the argument, Lilian told them she was taking them to lunch at Claridge's. There, while they ate, friends who had seen the announcement came up to congratulate the couple.

That night, after Dick had returned from driving Erica back to Ambarrow Court, he tapped on his mother's bedroom door and went in to talk further. The discussion was calm, but she continued to warn him about the obvious dangers of bringing a German bride to England. And supposing he were killed in the war; how would she cope with a young widow and perhaps a grandchild? A German grandson – as she put it – would be 'anathema' to her. And perhaps to others, too. The conversation ended when Dick excused himself, saying he had to prepare the speech he would be expected to make at the RAC lunch. He also needed to get up early in order to go and book tickets for their flight back to Munich. She went to bed thinking she might have changed his mind.

Uncertainty was hanging over the Donington Grand Prix, scheduled for Sunday 1 October. The Auto Union team had arrived with a single car eight days earlier, all four drivers taking turns to practise on the course. The Mercedes convoy arrived the following day, while the remaining Auto Unions joined them on the Monday. The Mercedes management and drivers, among the ninety or so guests invited to the lunch in Dick's honour, arrived in London and stayed overnight at the Rubens Hotel, close to Buckingham Palace. They saw large quantities of sandbags being delivered to the palace and anti-aircraft batteries being erected in Hyde Park. In Berlin that afternoon Hitler had received a letter from Chamberlain, asking him not to resort to force in Czechoslovakia. Hitler responded by threatening mobilisation in forty-eight hours if his demands were not met.

In the early hours of the next morning, alerted by telegrams, the German teams' technical personnel left their quarters in Donington Hall and began packing up the cars and equipment in preparation for a swift return home. After dawn, the two convoys set off for Harwich. Within an hour of their departure, however, communications between Hühnlein in Berlin and the team managers, Neubauer and Dr Feuereissen, resulted in a change of plan: the British police were asked to intercept the lorries as they passed through Leicestershire and send them back to Castle Donington.

Meanwhile Neubauer, von Brauchitsch, Lang and Uhlenhaut presented themselves at the RAC for the celebratory lunch in the club's Great Gallery. Caracciola had remained at home in

Switzerland, his wife sending a letter of apology to explain that his burnt foot had prevented him from making the trip. Among the British guests were Lord Howe, Sir Malcolm Campbell, Prince Bira, and the recently naturalised Whitney Straight, who met Lilian with a military salute and a joke about how he was now eligible for the call-up. Erica arrived with the Aldingtons and greeted Dick's mother before sitting next to her fiancé for a meal that began with Whitstable oysters or smoked salmon, continued with *délices de sole florentine*, reached a climax with *suprême de volaille Maryland* and concluded with a *bombe glacée orientale friandise*, all accompanied by white and red wines from Bordeaux, a 1927 Château Carbonnieux and a 1924 Pontet Canet, and – for a toast to the King – a 1923 Heidsieck Monopole dry champagne.

Then they listened as Dick was eulogised by Lt-Col James Sealy-Clarke, the chairman of the RAC, who proposed a toast to the guest of honour and presented him with a blue leather box containing a pair of gold cufflinks inscribed with his initials. He was also awarded a BRDC Gold Star in further recognition of his deeds as a representative of British motor sport. In response, Dick made a speech that started with a welcome 'for our German friends – we wish they would come as often as they can'. He made a gracious acknowledgement that fortune had given him – rather than his friend Manfred, seated nearby – the win in Germany. Von Brauchitsch, he said, had endured 'the worst possible luck, which he accepted with a degree of good sportsmanship that did him as much credit as if he had won the race'. Dick had often been asked, he said, why he chose to drive for a German team. 'I love motor racing,' he said, 'and after my successful season in 1936, when I was invited to join the Mercedes team, I naturally accepted. If there had been a British Grand Prix team, it would have been different. There is no such team now.' He also spoke about adapting his technique to these powerful machines, describing how he had learnt how to line the car up well in advance of a corner, developing a precision that included a 'tactful' use of the accelerator pedal on the exit. He concluded by returning to a more general theme: 'Motor racing knows no frontiers, no political animosities, no international rivalries – only a sincere friendship and a love of sport.' He had jotted his notes for the speech in pencil on the back of the printed menu; afterwards he signed it and gave it to Monkhouse as a keepsake.

Out in the streets, newspaper billboards were full of dire warnings. In the banqueting room, conversation alternated between the prospects for the race at the weekend and the near-certainty of war. As the lunch broke up, there was speculation over whether the Mercedes drivers would continue with their journey up to Donington. John Dugdale caught the strange atmosphere. 'It was, of course, unfortunate that a function which could have done much to promote international friend-liness should have been overshadowed by the political situation,' he wrote. 'It is some evidence of the essential sanity still remain-ing to humanity that expressions of friendliness on both sides were made by English and German drivers.'

Dick and his colleagues went on to a reception at the German embassy, where the staff were receiving a growing stream of worried compatriots. Back at Ennismore Gardens, Lilian was fully expecting to say farewell to Erica as Dick took her back to Munich, perhaps for good. But after the couple had returned and spent some time talking quietly together, she was aston-ished to hear Dick announce that he was taking his fiancée up to Donington Park. The Aldingtons were present as the couple departed, Ivy Aldington reminding Lilian of something she had said when they were all together in Dick's chalet at Ambach: 'Erica always has her own way.'

◆

Around midnight Dick called his mother from the Black Boy in Nottingham, where the Mercedes party were staying, to say they had arrived. With Hitler's order to mobilise seemingly only hours away, the situation was fluid. The German embassy was telling travellers that there was no cause for alarm, but some German nationals with jobs in London were already making their way to Harwich. The next morning, with heavy rain falling outside, Neubauer stayed in the hotel, trying to make telephone calls, some of them to Dr Feuereissen, who had stayed in London to liaise directly with the embassy. Calls to Germany were next to impossible, with the lines constantly jammed. He noted the presence of Dick and Erica in a corner seat of the hotel lounge, holding hands and looking preoccupied. The other drivers came and went, sharing scraps of gossip. Lang told Neubauer that German radio was playing nothing but martial music.

At around noon Neubauer took another call from Feuereissen, who told him: 'We have been instructed to leave.' Once again the two sets of mechanics repacked their cars and equipment into the transporters while frantic efforts were under way to book places for the crossing from Harwich. Lang remembered a fierce knock on his door and a frantic Neubauer saying, 'Things are getting serious – pack immediately, we leave at dawn tomorrow. The private cars will form one column, and the lorries another. The embassy has told us to leave for home, even if the cars have to be left behind.' Back in Stuttgart, perhaps Max Sailer was remembering August 1914, when a Mercedes Grand Prix car – one of the team that had just swept the board in the French Grand Prix – was sent for display in the company's London showroom, only to be seized by the British authorities on the outbreak of hostilities; its mechanical secrets had been examined and certain features incorporated into the design of the Rolls-Royce Eagle, a military aircraft engine. This time all of them – the cars, too – made it back to the Hook of Holland, and thence to Germany. All except Dick and Erica. Neubauer had asked Erica if she intended to travel back to Germany with them. 'No,' she told him. 'Whatever happens, I'm staying with Dick.'

The worst did not happen, at least not for a while. In Berlin, Mussolini persuaded Hitler to back away from his plan for immediate mobilisation. Chamberlain told the House of Commons that he would be flying to Munich the following day for a meeting with the leaders of Germany, Italy and France. By that time, however, there was no chance of recalling the German teams once again. In a fraught telephone call, Dick told his mother of Erica's decision and asked if she could stay with them at Ennismore Gardens. She would have been welcomed back by the Aldingtons, but the time involved in travelling to and from Ambarrow Court made it inconvenient. At first Lilian flatly refused. 'It would be unwise to have a German girl here at this time,' she said. 'She would be most unwelcome.' Dick pleaded and, as usual, prevailed to the extent that his mother agreed that Erica could stay 'for a night or two'.

They returned the next day. Lilian had been taking her jewellery and important papers to be lodged in a safe-deposit box at her bank; in the afternoon she went to a local school to pick up her government-issued gas mask. When she greeted Dick and Erica that evening, she was surprised by their high spirits. They told her the news they had just heard on the car radio: the four leaders had reached an agreement in Munich under which Hitler would be allowed to annexe the Sudetenland, on the promise of going no further. That night Dick and Erica dined together at Luigi's and then went dancing. Lilian was still awake when they returned home at two o'clock.

Before they went out, she had asked them if they wanted breakfast in their bedrooms. No, they replied, they would come down. She ordered it for nine o'clock. It was a quarter to eleven before Dick appeared, followed some time later by Erica, both looking exhausted. Lilian noted that Erica was wearing 'a deep pink chiffon negligée loosely tied with a crimson velvet ribbon over a pale pink nightdress, her feet thrust into pink satin sandals', and was wanting nothing more than a small cup of black coffee. Her hostess wondered why she had bothered ordering breakfast, and was even less impressed when she complained that the house was chilly. Nor did Lilian approve when Erica left the house without a hat as the couple announced they were walking down to Knightsbridge to do some shopping. They returned with Marjorie Martin, whose husband, Charlie, arrived for tea and cocktails. After listening together to Pope Pius XI's plea for peace on the radio ('While millions are still anxious about the impending danger of war and the threat of destruction and massacres without precedent . . .'), the two couples went off to the cinema.

Late that night Dick again visited his mother's room to tell her that he and Erica had found the perfect flat, just off Belgrave Square. Clearly there had been something more than shopping on their itinerary when they strolled down to Knightsbridge. He told her the amount of the rent, which he considered to be reasonable, bearing in mind the location. She thought it was exorbitant. Given that he would not come into his inheritance until he was twenty-seven, he needed her to sign the lease and guarantee payment. And he wanted her to do it the next morning, so that they could get on with buying furniture and choosing curtains. He had brought some colour samples for her approval. She refused. She would do no such thing, she said, until she had spoken to Erica's father. Dick did not take it well. After he went away, Lilian could hear him having a whispered conversation with Erica outside her bedroom door. The girl, she concluded, had wrapped her son around her little finger.

On 30 September, Neville Chamberlain landed at Heston on a flight from Munich and descended the steps of his aeroplane waving a piece of paper that he claimed guaranteed 'peace for our time' before proceeding to Buckingham Palace, where his appearance on the balcony, at the King's invitation, was greeted by cheering crowds. Almost simultaneously, an announcement came from Donington that the Grand Prix had been cancelled.

After Lilian had scanned the following morning's newspaper headlines proclaiming Chamberlain's diplomatic triumph, she took a call from the Aldingtons. They told her that, in the changed circumstances, Erica's parents were now prepared to fly to London to meet her. They would arrive on 5 October. In the meantime, however, her opinion of her house guest was changing fast. After Dick had announced one morning that they would be going up to Yorkshire to spend a few days shooting with Tony Cliff, they went out shopping. When they had gone, one of the housemaids approached her employer and asked her to take a look inside Erica's bedroom and bathroom. There, to her horror, Lilian found quantities of fine underclothes and expensive dresses and silk stockings strewn around as if a hurricane had passed through. 'The dressing table,' she noted, 'was a jungle of toilet apparatus.' She thought of her late husband, who was in the habit of describing the way things should be kept as 'yacht finish'.

It set another bee buzzing in her bonnet. 'Like most other residents of London houses,' she wrote, 'I had been forced to fall back on morning housemaids, women who come from the purlieus of Hammersmith and the backstreets of Battersea from 7.30 in the morning and stay until one o'clock, with large families, and mostly a husband out of work and on the dole. They are highly paid and glad to come and earn the money. Erica knew the type of woman I was forced to employ to get any workers at all. And I thought, where was Erica's common sense to ask and expect this type of woman to act as a professional ladies' maid?'

They returned as she was mulling this over. While Dick walked round to the mews to fetch the car for their journey, she noticed that Erica appeared to be in a bad mood and asked what was the matter. The reply, which came as a surprise, was that she didn't want to go to Crayke because she disliked the country in general and shooting in particular. Dick had bought her a mackintosh and some sensible shoes, and she had no intention of wearing them. Further enquiry elicited the information that among other things she detested were cooking and housekeeping, which she believed in leaving to the servants.

While Dick took his fiancée off to Yorkshire, where it turned out that Erica enjoyed herself enormously, Lilian headed for Pull Court. They reconvened in London after only a couple of days in order to drive down to Croydon, where Franz Josef and Christine Popp would also be met by the Aldingtons, with whom they would stay at Ambarrow Court. It was Wednesday 5 October. As they waited, Hitler's troops were marching across the Czechoslovakian border, where they were met by the euphoria of the Sudeten Germans and the fearful resentment of the Czechoslovaks.

When the plane from Munich landed, Erica's mother emerged alone. Her husband, she said, was not feeling well but hoped to arrive later. Lilian's first impression of Christine Popp was of a woman of youthful appearance, great animation and fashionable wardrobe: not unlike her younger daughter, in fact. Soon Lilian would come to the conclusion that Christine was not a woman with whom to discuss a matter of any gravity, be it the prospect of war or the future of their children.

The next day Lilian hosted a lunch for her at the Ritz. Having seen Erica go off to spend the morning choosing furniture for their new flat, she told Dick that no such acquisitions should be made until she had talked to Herr Popp. Over lunch she listened to Christine Popp, who spoke good English, expressing happiness about the prospect of the marriage, while enquiring about the status of Pull Court: did the house belong to Dick, she wondered, or would he have to wait until his mother's death to inherit it? 'Pull Court was purchased for my son,' Lilian replied, 'but I retain full control of it.'

Another lunch was arranged for the following day, this time at Claridge's, and Lilian was distinctly unimpressed when Frau Popp arrived an hour late, claiming to have been delayed while having her hair and nails done. Afterwards she suggested that they should go together to meet Dick and Erica at the flat off Belgrave Square, something clearly prearranged. Lilian inspected it without commenting, and on the drive back to

Ennismore Gardens she was surprised to hear Frau Popp suddenly confess that she had experienced three great love affairs
during her marriage, and that a man had recently shot himself
for love of her. Lilian was not inclined to pursue the subject,
but later at Ennismore Gardens she made her feelings absolutely
plain when Erica requested that the money should be paid to
secure the flat without delay. Apart from refusing to take any
action until she had spoken to the girl's father, Lilian pointed
out that this was not the way things were done. When would
they use the flat, when they already had homes in Germany,
and Dick would be spending so much time away at the races?
Who would pay for servants to maintain it during their long
absences? To Erica's heated response that they would need a
pied-à-terre in London, she replied that if that was what they
required, surely a hotel would do. The angry stand-off was
ended when the Aldingtons arrived to take Frau Popp back
to Berkshire – issuing an invitation to a party to celebrate the
engagement at Ambarrow Court on the Saturday night – and
Fane and his wife, Evelyn, turned up to take Dick and Erica
out dining and dancing.

The strained atmosphere continued the next day, when Lilian
again took Frau Popp for lunch, this time at the Berkeley. While
they were waiting for the main course, Christine Popp suddenly
began crying and confessed that she planned to divorce her
husband, whom she knew to be having an affair with the young
wife of a man who was a director both of his own firm and of
Mercedes-Benz. Lilian, having told her to eat her food before
it got cold, advised her strongly against taking such a step. She
was coming to dislike Frau Popp, and to imagine that she saw
in her the sort of woman Erica might become.

On the Saturday afternoon Dick escaped the family imbro-
glio by accepting an invitation to present the prizes during
the Imperial Trophy meeting at Crystal Palace. That evening's
engagement party at Ambarrow Court was a success, despite
the emotions roiling beneath the surface. The next morning

the young couple did not emerge from their rooms until one
o'clock. This, Lilian believed, showed a change from the Dick
she believed she had known: the one who looked after himself
in order to be at his best in the pursuit of his ambition. Erica,
she thought, seemed to exist on not much more than cigarettes,
cocktails and black coffee.

Late that night, after returning with Erica from an evening
out, he came to his mother's bedroom, sat down, and told her
that, given his age, she no longer had the right to interfere in
his affairs. She expressed surprise that Herr Popp had not yet
found the time to come and see her, but added that even if he
did, she would never consent to the marriage. 'The engagement
will have to be broken off,' she said. Dick exploded, telling her
how much he loved Erica and demanding an explanation for
such intransigence. Having repeated her arguments, she chose to
tell him what she had learnt about the marriage of Erica's parents and of Christine Popp's intention to divorce her husband.
'That's nothing to do with us,' Dick said. 'We have no divorces
in our family,' his mother replied.

When that clearly failed to sway him, and he had repeated
Erica's demand that money be produced for the flat and its
furnishings, Lilian played her last card. 'You had better let her
know,' she said, 'that if you sign the lease on the flat and order
the furniture, I shall stop your allowance.' Infuriated by the
threat, he then had to listen to her claim that she could see his
future clearly enough to know that the marriage would wreck
his life and his career. 'What Erica says is true,' he responded. 'It's
always the goddamned mothers who go and upset everything.'

She was appalled. Erica could speak like that about her own
mother, she replied, but she would not have her son saying
such a thing. She told him to leave her room. As he did so, she
announced she would be going up to Pull Court in the morning and by the time she returned to Ennismore Gardens she
expected to find no trace of Erica or her mother. Nor would
they ever be welcome to return.

He was up in time to see her before she left at nine o'clock to catch her train, but his attempt to apologise for his hurtful words foundered on her refusal to reopen the matter. All she would say was that while she was still perfectly prepared to present her arguments to Herr Popp, she wanted to see no more of his wife and daughter. When Dick attempted to continue the conversation, she swept past him and out of the house. Two days later she returned from Pull Court to learn from her London housekeeper that Frau Popp had spent the day helping Erica to pack her scattered possessions, after which Dick had driven them to the Mayfair Hotel, where he had booked rooms. He, too, had spent his last night under his mother's roof.

◆

He made a brief return two days later to pick up his mail, and Lilian went through her arguments again, emphasising the financial penalty that he would pay if he went ahead with the marriage. She stressed how diligent and sensible she had been in protecting the wealth his father had left behind, pointing out the risk he was taking by marrying a girl she now characterised as 'a shallow, neurotic butterfly'.

On 15 October Dick flew back to Munich with Frau Popp and Erica. Two days later he returned alone for the rearranged Donington Grand Prix, now to be held on 22 October with all the original participants. He stopped off briefly at Ennismore Gardens to pick up his clothes. He told his mother that Herr Popp, having learnt of the vehemence of her objections, no longer planned to come to London but had reaffirmed his consent to the engagement and indicated his approval of Dick's financial position, even in the absence of her support. She asked what exactly had been said about his finances. He replied that he had informed his prospective father-in-law that, as well as his Mercedes salary and bonuses, he benefited from the proceeds of one trust fund of £100,000 and another smaller one, and that on turning twenty-seven he would receive half of his late father's estate. She asked if he had mentioned that, if he were to come into that inheritance, he would need his mother's consent, as one of the three executors and trustees of her late husband's will. They argued about his understanding of how to handle money; when he told her that she had more money than she could possibly spend herself, she retorted that the combination of his extravagance and Erica's shopping habits would lead to disaster.

They parted acrimoniously, Dick pointing out that this was hardly the right preparation for competing in a Grand Prix, and his mother noting the signs of strain in his face. After he had driven away, she sat down to write a letter to Franz Josef Popp in which she outlined all the points she would have made in person, including the warning that if war broke out, his daughter would find life in England intolerable. She sent it by registered post, awaiting a reply that never came.

27

A quiet wedding

Dick was late arriving at Castle Donington on the first day of practice. According to one observer, there were words with Neubauer when he failed to join his colleagues for lunch. He was in time, however, for a tea party at Donington Hall given for the drivers by the meeting's organisers. In between practice sessions, the drivers amused themselves by playing football and clock golf on the hall's lawns. Caracciola's place was taken by Bäumer, but the team was otherwise complete. Once more the convoy of Mercedes transporters had rolled through England, this time from Dover, bringing with them twenty-five mechanics and 1,100 gallons of their specially mixed fuel.

One sight would not astonish the spectators in the way it had a year earlier. The top of the rise after Melbourne Corner had been smoothed out, and the suspension of the W154 was softer than that of its predecessor, meaning the cars no longer left the ground with all four wheels as they went over the bump at full throttle. But those who observed the training sessions still marvelled at the sensation of the silver cars coming out of the woods 'like bombs', in one witness's words, and of Seaman power-sliding elegantly through Red Gate Corner. Nuvolari had gone out on the Monday, setting fast times but killing a deer – one of several hundred living in the park – that emerged from the trees onto the track, cracking a rib as his chest banged into the steering wheel. Once Mercedes got going, von Brauchitsch narrowly missed another wandering stag. The Auto Union engineers had discovered a problem with their superchargers; lacking the equipment to make the necessary modification, they requested help from the Rolls-Royce factory in Derby, a dozen miles away, where skilled men worked overnight to complete the job. Lang set the fastest lap in 2 minutes 11.0 seconds, half a second slower than von Brauchitsch's pole time in the 5.6-litre W125 a year earlier. Nuvolari lined up next to him, with von Brauchitsch – nursing a little finger broken when he fell from the running board of Dick's Mercedes saloon while being given a lift across a stretch of parkland at an unwise speed – and Seaman completing the front row. Dick's time of 2 minutes 12.2 seconds was more than three seconds faster than his best practice lap in the W125 in 1937, an indication of how much more comfortable he was with the power-curve and handling of the new 3-litre car.

An estimated 60,000 spectators made their way to the circuit through the morning mist on race day, at least 10,000 up on the previous year's attendance. They included the staff from Mercedes-Benz's London depot on Grosvenor Road in Pimlico, who had been given the day off and a coach-ride to the race; they could watch their drivers, bareheaded, bring the cars down from Coppice Farm to the start. They also saw Dick drive the Duke of Kent, the president of the British Racing Drivers' Club, twice around the circuit in a Lagonda V12 saloon, the first lap at touring pace and the second rather faster. In Germany the *Völkischer Beobachter* had made much of the anticipated presence of the younger brother of Edward VIII and George VI: 'This is not only proof of the sportsmanlike attitude of the British Royal Family but also a particularly friendly gesture towards the German drivers, who came to England as the best messengers of peace in order to build the stable bridge of friendship between sportsmen.' The more knowledgeable spectators would also have spotted, in a Bentley following the Lagonda, the visiting Adolf Hühnlein. Dressed – as always outside Germany – in civilian clothes, he had chosen tweeds for the English autumn. Accompanied by his wife and one of his daughters, the Korpsführer was introduced to the Duke, whom he greeted with a raised right arm.

A year and a day after helping to give the Duke of Windsor a guided tour of the Mercedes factory, Dick showed his brother around the Donington grid, introducing him to the drivers, many of them wearing coats over their overalls against the late-October chill, and to Neubauer and Dr Feuereissen. Of the nineteen machines lined up in front of the grandstand, the cars of the two German teams occupied the first eight places. Luigi Villoresi, whose works-entered Maserati had arrived late from Bologna, was the best of the rest. The fastest of the British entries, Arthur Dobson's ERA, was thirteen seconds slower than Lang around the 3.1-mile course. The second quickest of the seven ERAs was driven by Ian Connell, a contemporary and friend of Seaman from their days in the Cambridge University Auto Club and now the co-proprietor – with Peter Monkhouse, George's cousin – of the Monaco garage in Watford. Dick's old R1B was alongside Connell in the fourth row, driven by its new owner, Billy Cotton. The prizes on offer included £250 for the winner, £50 for the leader at half-distance, £100 for the fastest race lap and a similar sum for the first British finisher. The German, Italian and French entries had received starting money, and the Germans were also paid travelling and accommodation expenses.

At noon the Duke lowered the flag to signal the start of the eighty-lap, 250-mile Grand Prix. Nuvolari raced into the lead, with his teammate H. P. Müller coming through from the second row. Behind the Auto Union pair came von Brauchitsch, Seaman and Lang, whose engine had bogged down when he let in the clutch ('Like a beginner!' he said to himself). The first quarter of the race saw the retirement of the Maserati and Kautz's Auto Union, which had rammed a bank with its throttle stuck open. A pit stop to change a plug cost Nuvolari the lead, and Seaman excited the crowd when he overtook von Brauchitsch for second place, behind Müller. But the complexion of the race changed on the twenty-fifth lap when the engine of Robin Hanson's Alta blew up, spreading oil on the track between Holly Wood and the Old Hairpin. Nuvolari was the first to come upon it, managing to retain control despite a series of slides that had the spectators gasping. Von Brauchitsch spun round twice and carried on. Then came Rudi Hasse, who went through a fence and hit the bank, leaving his Auto Union a crumpled mess. Seaman, arriving at high speed, also spun off. Having stalled his engine, he was pushed back into the race by the marshals and dropped to sixth, behind Bäumer.

While Dick lost more time with a plug change in the mid-race pit stops, Lang had taken the lead from Müller. He was pulling away when, at around half-distance, a stone thrown up by another car broke his aeroscreen. The discomfort caused by air blowing on his unprotected face slowed Lang by three seconds a lap, putting him in the sights of Nuvolari, who had passed Müller. Only three weeks from his forty-sixth birthday, the little Mantuan was thrilling the spectators as he broke the lap record several times. The gap was twenty seconds with twenty laps to go, and he needed only seven of them to take a lead that, to the crowd's delight, he held to the end. Seaman had climbed to fifth place after Bäumer's car caught fire during a refuelling stop, and he moved up to fourth by passing von Brauchitsch. Driving, in Rodney Walkerley's view, 'better than any German on the circuit', although still a lap behind the leader, he snatched third place from Müller in the closing stages. A wind-battered Lang held on to second, collapsing when he climbed out of his car. Dobson was sixth, the first finisher in a non-German car.

In a gesture to the visitors, the cups were presented to Nuvolari and Dobson by Hühnlein and his wife. As the German anthem was played over the Tannoy to salute the winning team, followed by 'Giovinezza', the official anthem of the Italian Fascist Party, for the victorious driver, *Motor Sport* noted that 'our biggest motor racing crowd, now rapidly invading the course, stood most impressively to attention'. Nuvolari left the circuit carrying the stag's head, which had been stuffed and mounted as a gift from the organisers. In Derby that evening he and the other competitors attended a banquet at the Friary Hotel. More awards were presented, and there were speeches from Dr Feuereissen, Neubauer, Nuvolari and Seaman, who repeated the Italian's tongue-in-cheek suggestion, received with laughter even by the joke's victims, that 'Mercedes would win some races if they made cars that went properly'. Meanwhile Fred Craner was already telling reporters that the next Donington Grand Prix had definitely been arranged for 30 September 1939.

Nuvolari departed for Italy the following day, but this time the Germans – their season over and the prospect of war apparently averted – were in no desperate rush to get home. The convoys of transporters set off promptly for the ports, but the drivers headed for London, where the BRDC held a party for them on the Monday night at the Rembrandt Hotel, across the road from the Victoria and Albert Museum in South Kensington. The managers and drivers of both teams were present, along with many of the leading figures of British motor racing. Dick, wearing his new Gold Star, was among friends.

He had visited Ennismore Gardens earlier in the day to pick up his post. He had chosen not to stay there; from now on, when he was in London, he would lodge at the RAC, giving 89 Pall Mall, London SW1 as his address when completing documents. In an effort to heal the rift between mother and son, Aldy Aldington paid a visit to Ennismore Gardens. He listened as Lilian gave him a full account of her misgivings about the marriage, and he promised to convey them to Erica's father on an imminent visit to Munich. Ten years older than Dick, Aldington had played a part in introducing him to his fiancée,

was a witness to their short courtship, and felt entirely sympathetic to the couple. He was also both a business partner and a
friend of Franz Josef Popp. Nevertheless Lilian had convinced
herself, by the time he left her company, that he would argue
her case with the bride's father.

But when Aldington returned from Germany and paid
another visit to Ennismore Gardens, he brought bad news. Herr
Popp, he said, had left their meeting at BMW's headquarters
immediately after their formal business had been concluded;
there had been no chance to discuss personal matters. Lilian
was devastated, the more so when Dick arrived to tell her that
he was going to Munich to make arrangements for the wedding
and to make a will in Erica's favour. She reminded him that she
fully intended to stop him inheriting his share of the family
estate. Be that as it may, he retorted, she could do nothing to
stop him receiving the proceeds from the two trust funds his
father had set up in his name. When she asked what he thought
he would do if war broke out and they returned to England
deprived of his Mercedes salary, he answered, 'I don't know.'

In her bitterness, she had strengthened her resolve by recalling
her late husband's low opinion of the German character. As she
went off to spend the weekend at Pull Court, she reflected that
it would have horrified William Seaman to know that his son
intended to marry a German girl, and that his fortune would
pass into what she insisted on thinking of as the German hands
of their children.

On the night of 9 November broken glass littered the streets
across Germany as Jewish homes, schools and hospitals were
destroyed and looted, 267 synagogues were attacked, several
hundred Jews were killed, and 30,000 men were captured and
taken away to concentration camps. The Brownshirts were
carrying out the pogrom that became known as *Kristallnacht*,
ostensibly in revenge for the murder in Paris of a German diplomat by a Jewish teenager who had been born in Germany
and brought up in Poland. In London the next day, under the

headline 'A Black Day for Germany', *The Times* carried a story reporting that 'No foreign propagandist bent upon blackening Germany before the world could outdo the tale of burnings and beatings, of blackguardly assaults on defenceless and innocent people, which disgraced that country yesterday'.

◆

Dick returned to England in the second week of November, in time for a visit to the Midland Motor Club, where he was due to give a talk and Monkhouse would show his recent colour films. On the way he again collected his mail at Ennismore Gardens, and there was a last confrontation in which he told his mother that the marriage was definitely taking place. When she asked where and when, he replied, 'In Munich, I suppose, in December.' She put her hands on both of his shoulders and, looking him in the eyes, asked if he wished to kill her with sorrow. She pleaded for him to reconsider a plan bound to lead to such unhappiness that he would be unable to concentrate properly on driving a racing car. There was no response. And then she spoke what she remembered as her final words to him: 'Dear boy, I would rather see you lying dead in your coffin than that you should contract this disastrous marriage.'

She was still looking into his eyes as he removed her hands from his shoulders, stepped back, turned around and walked out of her study and across the hall to the front door. As she stood, transfixed, she heard him say, 'Goodbye.'

He had wanted to slam the door behind him, he told Erica, but instead closed it quietly. He was leaving the house from which, as a small boy wearing a new red cap, he had been taken to his first school. It was where, in the mews garage, his ambitions had been incubated and the rebuilt Delage had burst into glorious life. Here his friends had so often arrived for cocktails and laughter before trips to the cinema, a restaurant or a night club. This, for most of his young life, had been his home. But no longer.

◆

On 18 November the BRDC held a dinner at the Savoy to celebrate the international success of a quartet of British motor sport heroes: the record breakers George Eyston, 'Goldie' Gardner and John Cobb, and the youngest of them (in fact the only one born in the twentieth century), Richard Seaman. In his speech of thanks, Dick appealed for an effort to start a proper British Grand Prix team, pointing out that two totalitarian countries, Germany and Italy, were using the sport to enhance their international prestige at Britain's expense. His words were supported by an article on the same subject in the latest edition of *Motor Sport*. Under the headline 'The Case for Grand Prix Racing', the anonymous author called for the British motor industry to put its collective effort behind ERA's desire to compete at the top level. A writer for *The Motor* went further, estimating the cost of such a project at £1 million, spread over a five-year programme. This, it was suggested, was 'equivalent to only twenty bombing aeroplanes or one 5,000-ton naval vessel. As to drivers, everyone would wish Dick Seaman and Arthur Dobson to be in the team.'

But the season was over, and the forthcoming wedding – not in Munich, but in London – was now Dick's priority. Since it seemed that war had only been postponed, they wanted the ceremony to take place as quickly as possible, which ruled out a church wedding with the drawn-out process of having the banns read. On 29 November, Aldington returned to Ennismore Gardens to break the news to Mrs Seaman and to ask her to attend the register-office ceremony, for her son's sake. The date, he told her, would be Wednesday 7 December – barely a week away. She refused to countenance the possibility. At Pull Court that weekend she received a telegram from Monkhouse, asking if he could visit her as a matter of urgency. He arrived at Ennismore Gardens late on the Sunday night, repeating Aldington's plea. She had always liked George, but now she told him that he had misjudged her: she was not one of those women who resisted and resisted before eventually giving in. Her son had been given an ultimatum. Nothing would change, she told his representative. George passed on the message, and no more efforts would be made from that direction.

◆

Dick and Erica were married on the morning of 7 December at Caxton Hall, an ornate red-brick and pink-sandstone edifice built sixty years earlier as Westminster Town Hall. It had become a register office in 1933, its location ensuring its popularity as the venue for fashionable people wanting a civil marriage or barred by divorce from a religious one. The haste and other factors meant that it was a small, quiet affair, very far from the sort of event the groom's mother had envisaged when she imagined him marrying a suitable English girl. Erica was late. Dick had sent a limousine to pick her up without specifying the destination, but eventually the driver worked it out. Eva Heim, Erica's sister, was one of the witnesses. Tony Cliff, who had met Dick when they were still in short trousers, was the other. On the marriage certificate, Dick gave his occupation as 'mechanical engineer' and his address as the Royal Automobile Club, while Erica ('Erica otherwise Erika Elfriede Popp') left the space for her occupation blank and gave her address as the Rembrandt Hotel. Two registrars, J. S. Clare and Joseph P. Bond, officiated. As the couple emerged from the register office, photographers captured their smiles and youthful elegance: the bride in a tailored pale coat with a fur neck, a fur-trimmed hat and a bouquet of carnations, and the groom in a double-breasted coat over a pin-striped suit and a stiff-collared shirt, holding a bowler hat. On the Social Events page of *The Bystander* the following week, their photograph appeared alongside those of the Countess of Enniskillen attending a performance of Verdi's *Don Carlos* at Sadler's Wells and the American shipbroker Ernest Simpson — the former husband of the Duchess of Windsor — with his new wife at a London cocktail party.

The bride and groom and their witnesses went straight from Caxton Hall to the Rembrandt Hotel, where the wedding breakfast was held in a private room. H. J. and Ivy Aldington, Charlie and Marjorie Martin, A. F. P. and Evelyn Fane, and George Monkhouse were also present, along with Dick Wilkins, a wealthy young stockjobber in the City of London and Brooklands habitué, another friend of Seaman's from his Cambridge days. The cake was made to resemble a racing car, a reasonable facsimile of a Mercedes. The bride's father paid for the celebration, via the Aldingtons.

Looking for a distraction, the bridegroom's mother had arranged a lunch with a friend who came up from the country, after which they went to a matinee at the theatre. Having seen her friend onto the train home at Charing Cross station, Lilian walked across to a newspaper kiosk and bought the late editions of all three London evening papers. On page thirteen of the *Evening Standard* she found a single-column picture of a smiling, fur-hatted Erica outside Caxton Hall, under the headline 'Racing Motorist Weds German Bride' and a short paragraph of text: 'Fraulein Erica Popp of Munich on her way to Caxton Hall today, where she became the bride of Mr R. J. B. Seaman, one of the foremost racing drivers.' The *Star* had no picture, just two short sentences in the middle of a busy broadsheet front page, practically lost between 'Quakers To Plead For Jews In Berlin' and a story about a man falling from a train outside Chelmsford: 'Mr Richard John Beattie Seaman – Dick Seaman, the racing motorist, who won the German Grand Prix last July – was married today at Caxton Hall Register Office to Miss Erica Eldriede [sic] Popp, an 18-year-old German, seven years the bridegroom's junior. The couple are spending a motoring honeymoon in Switzerland.' And the detestable headline: 'Racing Motorist Weds German'. She looked through the *Evening News*, finding neither photograph nor story. She handed the papers back to the vendor. 'Sell them again,' she told him, and turned for home.

◆

They had planned to spend their honeymoon in Davos, but since snow had not yet arrived in decent quantities, they made for Stuttgart. At the factory Dick sat down alone with Neubauer to discuss the future and was delighted to accept the offer of a new contract based on a much higher retainer. The annual reckoning showed that in 1938, in addition to the RM 1,000 per month, he had earned RM 20,400 for winning the German Grand Prix, RM 4,968.60 for finishing second in Switzerland, RM 2,231.25 for third at Donington Park and RM 2,000 for taking part at Monza. Adding up to RM 41,599.85, this was increased through appearance bonuses calculated under a new and more complex system, lifting the total to match that of the previous year, more or less. Lang and von Brauchitsch had both earned more than RM 70,000 in the year, both having started (and, in Lang's case, won) more races; the highest earner, Caracciola, would have made more than RM 100,000. But there was no doubt that Mercedes valued Dick's presence in the team. All he needed now was proof that they no longer saw him as a reserve to be held back for emergencies and special occasions.

He and Erica drove across to Munich to spend a day with Helmi and Bimbo Haspel at their hunting lodge before they all returned to Untertürkheim for a formal reception hosted by Dr Kissel, who made a speech extolling the couple's qualities and presented them with a silver salver. Erica was given a bouquet of roses and the champagne flowed. This was the first time, someone told Seaman, that flowers and a female had been seen in the Daimler–Benz boardroom, where the table was decorated for the occasion with swastika flags and Union Jacks.

28

A moveable feast

Haus Buchenbichl was a low, single-storey building with a whitewashed chimney and a tiled roof. Given to them by the bride's father, it was hidden away up a winding drive through the beech spinneys from which it took its name, just outside the village of Untergrainau. In the grounds was a cottage occupied by the gardener and his family, while Erica had a live-in maid to fold her stockings and iron her dresses. There was room for house-party guests; the other permanent residents were a pair of cocker spaniel puppies named Whisky and Soda, a wedding present from an English friend, Dick Shuttleworth, a racing driver and aviator known to his chums as 'Mad Jack'. A stream at the bottom of the garden, the Krepbach, fed water from the mountains into the nearby Loisach river, running alongside the road to Garmisch.

The Bavarian Alps were now all around: not glimpsed in the far distance, as at Ambach, but practically on their doorstep. Turning right out of the drive would take them to Garmisch; turning left would lead them through Untergrainau to the Eibsee, a couple of kilometres from the house. A much smaller lake than the one Dick had been living next to for the past two years, it was prettier in a picture-postcard way, with the terrace of a lakefront hotel making a pleasant place for lunch or a drink at dusk. And directly above the Eibsee reared the almost vertical north face of the Zugspitze, at 2,962m the highest peak in Germany, marking the border with Austria and beckoning skiers to the sun-filled open snowfields. A cog railway running from the Eibsee through a tunnel to the summit had been opened in 1930, in time for the arrival of hundreds of thousands of visitors to the seven-hour Passion play presented every ten years by the villagers of nearby Oberammergau.

Dick and Erica returned to Munich to spend Christmas with the Popps before heading for Davos, where they joined the Martins, Dick Shuttleworth and other friends. The snow was still not abundant, so they spent a day in St Moritz, where they bumped into Rudi and Alice Caracciola and a friend from England, Eddie Hall, who had finished second in the Tourist Trophy three years in a row in a Bentley bought with the proceeds of his family's Yorkshire textile business; he was in St Moritz for the bobsledding. On their return to Davos they were able to toast the New Year in good company at the Hotel Parsenn.

Dick had been invited by Lagonda to drive one of their cars in the 24 Hours of Le Mans in June, a repeat of his outing with the team at Spa three years earlier. Monkhouse reminded him of Pat Fairfield's fatal accident, one of many throughout the race's history caused by mixing drivers of diverse competence and experience – including what George described, with typically forthright disdain, as 'idiots' – in cars of varied performance. Dick said he knew the idea was stupid and dangerous, but added: 'I feel I ought to drive an English car when the opportunity *does* present itself, apart from the fact that I like the Lagonda people and think they should be encouraged.' To Monkhouse's relief, permission was denied in a letter from Max Sailer. 'We have to point out that in June we shall be in the midst of the racing season which is extremely rich of events this year,' the sporting director wrote, 'so that we think we are to have all of our forces at our disposal at any time. Plenty of examples have

shown, by the way, that in consequence of many private drivers
participating with various kinds of types at Le Mans, this race
is very dangerous and we, therefore, don't wish you to go to Le
Mans. We hope you will appreciate our point of view.'

At the end of January a different sort of letter arrived from
Untertürkheim. Given the problems over transferring money,
Dick was using the Mercedes accounts department as a sort of
bank; they held his salary and bonuses, from which he could
draw when necessary, and from which they deducted his
advances. Now, thinking about his financial affairs in the light
of his mother's declarations, he had asked the management for
details of the money they were holding for him. 'We enclose
an account statement as per 31.12.38,' they replied, 'concluding
with a balance of RM 21,650.70 in your favour.' At the 1939
rate of exchange, that would amount to £1,882 (the equivalent
of about £120,000 today).

He and Erica went to Garmisch to watch a downhill race on
the Olympic piste. It was, he told Monkhouse, 'the Nürburgring
and Masaryk of ski courses'. The winner was Willi Walch, an
Austrian ace who now competed in the colours of Germany,
becoming the national champion (and who, after being
drafted into the Wehrmacht, would be killed in Russia in the
summer of 1941 on the very first day of Operation Barbarossa).
Dick, reaching for the highest compliment he could think of,
described him as 'the Caracciola of ski-racers'.

Thanking Monkhouse for attempting to intercede with his
mother, he indicated in a letter in January that he had not given
up hope of a rapprochement. 'I think the fact that she has not
already told you to —— off and has sent you a Xmas card is a
very good sign,' he wrote, 'and may possibly mean that she is
toying with the idea of eventually magnanimously giving way,
and therefore does not want to brush off every means of recon-
ciliation. I should not however rush her too much, but allow
time to help too.'

Dick had listened with approval to a speech made by Neville

Chamberlain in Birmingham a few days after returning from Rome, where the Pope had told the Prime Minister that democracies must resist dangerous regimes that pursued policies based on racial discrimination. Three days after that meeting, the German government had banned Jews from being dentists, vets or pharmacists and from driving and going to cinemas, theatres and concerts. At the end of the month, Hitler made a speech in the Reichstag promising that if 'Jewish financiers' started a war, it would lead to the extermination of the race throughout Europe.

◆

On 4 February, they celebrated Dick's twenty-sixth birthday. Two weeks later they set off for Berlin, the Eden Hotel and the motor show. Since the *Rennabteilung* was hard at work finishing the updated W154s for the new season, a quartet of 2-year-old W125s was polished up and aligned for Hitler's inspection in the courtyard of the Reich Chancellery. Puddles from a recent shower lay on the ground as, one after another, Caracciola, von Brauchitsch, Lang and Seaman – each standing by his car and wearing his complete all-white racing outfit – stepped forward to greet the Führer. They were watched over by Neubauer, while the mechanics arrayed behind them gave the salute. Then the engines were started, the drivers got into their cars, and the quartet roared away, past Hitler, Göring, Hühnlein and Werlin – wearing his SS uniform, as he sometimes did – and through the Tiergarten towards the landmark of the soaring Funkturm.

Later, assembled in a room at the front of the exhibition hall, they listened as Hitler spoke. 'Unable as I was to understand it,' Dick told George, 'I found him a most electrifying orator.' When it ended, vast curtains parted to reveal the main hall, with a trumpet fanfare ('I doubt that Cecil B. DeMille could have done it better'). Pride of place, under a drape emblazoned with a giant swastika, was taken by an assortment of streamlined

Rekordwagen and open-wheeled Grand Prix cars. There followed an NSKK gathering, at which Hühnlein introduced a
film made over the previous two years, showing the German
teams in action; it had been directed by Erich Stoll. The motor
show pulled in a record 825,000 visitors during its three-week
run, with the long-awaited appearance of Dr Porsche's little
KdF-Wagen as the main attraction. British journalists were
among those permitted to test-drive this prototype of the
People's Car.

Many years later, in an interview with Chris Nixon, Erica
would recall a conversation with Dick on the eve of their
departure for Berlin, one that suggested a profound change in
his attitude to the German government. Since he was due to
come face to face with Hitler, he told his young wife, perhaps he
should phone the British government and say, 'If I kill him, will
you give me a million pounds?' She had almost been inclined
to take him seriously.

◆

They were back in Bavaria in time to celebrate Erica's nineteenth birthday on 7 March. They had been married three
months to the day, and spring was coming. A week later they
were at the Principe e Savoia in Milan, for pre-season training
at Monza. They sent Monkhouse a cheerful postcard from the
hotel, signed by both of them, along with Lang, Uhlenhaut and
Hanns Geier.

For several months Dick and George had been engaging in
banter about the rumours that Mercedes had started work on a
car for the new Grand Prix formula, restricted to supercharged
1.5-litre cars, scheduled to come into effect in 1940. The formula – in effect, the upgrading of the voiturette category to full
Grand Prix status – had been devised at a meeting of the sport's
governing body in 1936, with the barely disguised intention of
promoting a category in which the Italians, the French and even
the British had more experience than the Germans. Mercedes

and Auto Union had begun to think about it, but in September 1938 the matter took on a new urgency when it was announced that all the major races on Italian territory in 1939 would be restricted to cars conforming to the new formula, starting with the Tripoli Grand Prix in the first week of May. Knowing that it normally took eighteen months to get a racing car from drawing board to track, the Italians clearly believed they had caught out the Germans, who had no 1.5-litre single-seater.

Within a week of the Italian announcement, however, the directors at Untertürkheim, mindful not just of prestige but of the substantial prize money collected from their North African victories in 1935, 1937 and 1938, had given their approval for a new machine to be built. Work went ahead, under Uhlenhaut's supervision, at great speed – with special bonus payments for the extra hours involved at the factory – and in absolute secrecy. Inevitably stories were soon circulating in the racing world, sometimes drawing amusing responses. 'Neubauer thanks you for your letter about the 1.5-litre car but knows nothing about it,' Dick wrote to Monkhouse, who had been seeking information. 'Dr Kissel is himself going to send you all the blueprints of the new 750cc 24-cylinder 2-stroke Mercedes.' Uhlenhaut scribbled a postscript in the margin: 'You had better come over and give us your very special advice on our new 750cc.'

Meanwhile there was the latest version of the W154 to be tested at Monza. The car for the new Grand Prix season had been restyled, the hulking ferocity of the previous year's model giving way to a more streamlined look. It was also around 100kg lighter than the 1938 model, as Dick told George ('in confidence'). The week, he wrote, had been 'quite interesting, apart from the unusual interminable waits while the machines were mended or altered'. But when Lang knocked five seconds off the Monza lap record, they knew the car was going to be quick.

Dick and Erica got home to discover that snow had finally fallen in significant quantities in the Bavarian Alps, and Dick was able to lay out a slalom course and a ski jump in his new garden. He was also looking forward to exchanging his 2-year-old 2.3-litre Mercedes saloon – 'on its last legs' – for a special-bodied 3.4-litre model inherited from Caracciola. Erica, too, was awaiting delivery of a new car: a BMW 327, like the one her father had previously given her, but with a more potent overhead-valve engine. 'I anticipate being able to attend to the Garmisch–Munich record,' Dick wrote to Monkhouse.

On 22 March he went to the British consulate in Munich to sign his will, which had been drawn up in London. He appointed two trustees. One was his wife. The other was Carl Hermann Windschuegl of North Cray Cottage, Sidcup, Kent. An importer of pharmaceutical chemicals with a City of London office in Leadenhall Street, Windschuegl had been born in Nuremberg in 1865, arrived in England at the age of thirty, and was the second husband of Lilian Seaman's older sister, Madge. Dick's instructions stipulated that all his possessions should pass to his wife – or, had she predeceased him, to any children of theirs, once they had passed the age of twenty-one. The income from the trust funds set up by his father in 1921 and 1930 were to go to the same beneficiaries. Should they have no children, and should his wife die before him, on his death all the proceeds and properties would be divided between the daughter of his mother's first marriage, Vahlia Graham Pearce, who would receive one half, and the three children of his father's daughter by his first marriage, Valence, Catherine and Doreen Maclaren, sharing the other half equally between them. This was signed by Dick, giving his address as the RAC in Pall Mall, and witnessed by two officials of the British consulate.

◆

Throughout the month of March, Europe edged closer to the precipice. After his troops had occupied the rest of Czechoslovakia, Hitler arrived in Prague as a conqueror, again claiming that his territorial ambitions were now at an end. He and his army were badly received there, while Chamberlain pointed out in the House of Commons that for the first time Hitler had taken territory not inhabited by Germans. Aware that events were pressing in, on 27 March Dick wrote from Untergrainau to Lord Howe, making it clear that he was preoccupied by the question of whether he should continue to drive for a team representing a state with which, in all likelihood, his own country would soon be at war.

'Anglo–German relations having reached the stage they have,' he wrote, 'and with the future outlook not at all rosy, I am, as you can probably imagine, being forced to reconsider very seriously whether I ought to give up racing with Mercedes.' His reasons for not already doing so were twofold: first, a reluctance to mix sport and politics, and second, his good relationship with the team. But perhaps the time had come to set those considerations aside. 'In considering this rather difficult matter, I should naturally very much appreciate your advice.'

Howe responded by saying that he would like to consult more widely before offering an opinion. Those consultations – which he described as including 'a cabinet minister, two or three highly placed officers in the Navy, and one or two MPs' – informed the view he took in his letter of 5 May: 'The general consensus of opinion seems to be that if you can stick it, it would be very much better for you to stay where you are, and continue to drive for Mercedes. If things become unpleasant, which I do not gather that they are, it might be another matter. You might feel that things were really so difficult that you could not carry on ... As to this you must be the judge, but I do not suppose you want to stay in a concentration camp for the duration any more than I would. It really is a terribly difficult situation, and I do sympathise with you enormously in it ...'

In his reply, Dick expressed relief. 'I am very glad that your advice takes the form it does,' he wrote, 'for I have always thought it would be better for me to remain with Mercedes in spite of the political difficulties.' To do so would require turning a blind eye to certain features of life in Germany that could no longer be entirely avoided, even from the vantage point of a village in the Bavarian Alps. The opposite course of action would require a decision to leave two families – the *Rennabteilung* and the Popps – who had enthusiastically and affectionately adopted him, in favour of returning to a country where his sport had no great public profile and his surviving parent had cut him off from his inheritance, declaring that she no longer wanted anything to do with him.

But he was prepared for the moment when he would need to get out fast, and he knew that his wife would be with him. When that moment came, there would be no time for packing up the contents of their home. They would just have to go, the two of them, with a car and a couple of suitcases and their two dogs, heading back to England, the country where they had been married six months earlier, accepting whatever destiny lay ahead.

◆

At the end of March Dick and Erica were in south-western France for the Grand Prix around the streets of Pau. Staying at the Hôtel de France, they explored the pretty town in the foothills of the Pyrenees. But sightseeing was no compensation for the unwelcome discovery that once again he had been entered as a reserve; the time occupied in making the new 1.5-litre cars so quickly meant that Mercedes did not have the resources to field a four-car team that weekend, he was told. Allowed out on the second of the two practice days, he set the fastest lap of the day, equalling von Brauchitsch's time from the day before.

With the Italian authorities forbidding their teams and drivers from racing on French soil, and Auto Union also giving the race a miss because the participation of Nuvolari, their number one, would not be permitted, the Mercedes trio had virtually no opposition. Fifty thousand turned up to watch Caracciola take the lead before losing time when a broken oil pipe had to be repaired. By half-distance von Brauchitsch and Lang had lapped the rest of the field, but the former's famous jinx struck again when his engine stuttered briefly. Thinking he had run out of fuel, von Brauchitsch came in for a top-up, handing the first victory of the season to the team's former mechanic. Later, when his car was examined, he was infuriated to be told that there had been plenty of fuel in the tanks.

Seaman was interested to watch the reaction of the French crowd to the German drivers. 'A little incipient booing as the boys gave the Nazi salute during the hymn [anthem] was quickly drowned by applause, which was repeated *forte* when they saluted again during the "Marseillaise",' he observed, adding that four communists who had paraded around the town on the Saturday with anti-German banners had been locked up for the duration of the meeting.

Dick's exasperated reaction to his treatment by the team, as Uhlenhaut remembered, had taken him into dangerous territory before the race. 'He was very angry to be only the reserve driver and made some bad remarks about Mercedes and Hitler, saying that the company had promised him a car but it didn't keep its word, just like Hitler, who also lied. I told him to shut up, or he might be heard by the wrong people.' Neubauer repeated the warning, but Dick was still seething when he and Erica left Pau for Paris. They stayed at the Plaza Athénée, she visited her favourite clothes shops, and they dined well. It was at the Tour d'Argent in the Latin Quarter – mentioned by Proust in *À la recherche du temps perdu* and by Hemingway in *A Moveable Feast* – that they bumped into Neubauer, enjoying a menu whose celebrated highlight was pressed duck in a sauce containing cognac and Madeira wine. The initial frostiness of the chance encounter soon thawed in the warmth of the team manager's habitual good humour in the presence of haute cuisine.

But in his overall disappointment, Dick had begun talking to Erica about the possibility of giving up his career as a driver and going back to London to start a business. She had never tried to dissuade her husband from risking his life, but she would be happy for him to stop. She liked London, and she did not like the Nazis. Dick and George Monkhouse already had talked about embarking on a partnership. He was convinced that Mercedes would grant them a dealership, and he thought that they could branch out into race preparation; perhaps they could persuade Ramponi to join them. Thanks to the currency regulations, Dick would not be allowed to take his accumulated income from Mercedes out of Germany, but in a few months' time he would reach the age at which, under the terms of his father's will, he was due to come into his full inheritance, but only with his mother's consent, which she had vowed to withhold.

In the meantime he was still a professional racing driver, one whose main ambition was to go racing, and in early April his frustration drove him to take his complaint to the very top. Dr Kissel's response was immediate and emollient: 'My dear and most honourable Herr Seaman! I have received your valued letter, from which I conclude that you have concerns and that you believe you have not always been treated fairly by us. I ask you therefore first of all to take note of the fact that to us you are not only "the racing driver Seaman" but that all of us regard you as a friend of this house. I am also firmly of the opinion that you will race for us not only now or temporarily, but that you should feel bound to the company and us here for all time, just like the rest of the drivers, such as Herr Caracciola. I ask you, therefore, to try to accept that everything that happens is considered and determined from this point of view: we regard you as a friend and expect you to feel like a friend to us and accordingly to accept our decisions in a spirit of friendship. Please be reassured that we always treat you fairly.' He concluded by requesting a personal meeting with Dick in Stuttgart after Easter.

These were encouraging words, and perhaps Kissel did indeed view Seaman in the same light as men such as Sailer and Geier, whose working relationship with the company had extended far beyond their years as racing drivers. In the meantime he was required to make the 250-mile journey from Untergrainau to the autodrome at Hockenheim, where the secret tests of the new 1.5-litre car were taking place. Caracciola and Lang were to be the drivers in the Tripoli GP; they were impressed by what they found when they took the V8-engined W165 out for its first laps, but not unduly optimistic about the chances of success for a car prepared in such haste.

29

The upstarts

Despite Dr Kissel's assurances, there was no place for Dick in the squad that embarked for Tripoli, with Caracciola and Lang chosen to drive the new cars and von Brauchitsch travelling as the reserve. Instead he and Erica were taking a short holiday on the French Riviera when the team arrived on the other side of the Mediterranean, where the new Silver Arrows faced a wall of red: a starting grid containing no fewer than twenty-two Maseratis and six Alfa Romeos, making up the field of thirty necessary to fulfil the conditions for holding the lottery.

From the start of the week there was tension between Caracciola and Lang, initially arising over the differing specifications of the two W165s. Both drivers wanted the car that had been fitted with lower gear ratios and quicker steering. When Neubauer decided in favour of the senior man, outlining a strategy aimed at helping Caracciola win the race, Lang's annoyance increased. His appointed task was to go out as fast as possible, even at the risk of blowing his engine, setting a pace that would break the opposition as they tried to keep up; his tyres would certainly be destroyed in the process, whereas Caracciola would take it slightly easier and go the whole distance with only a short stop to refuel.

The friction was increased during the final practice session by an apparent misunderstanding. After Luigi Villoresi had set the fastest time to date in the new Maserati, Caracciola was sent out to beat it. As the team leader returned to the pits, Lang was sent out to scrub a set of tyres for the race. On the assumption that he had set the fastest time, Caracciola was furious that his team-mate had been given the chance to do better. In fact Caracciola had not beaten the Maserati's time, and neither did Lang, so his complaint was unjustified. Nevertheless he stormed off in a rage. When Lang, too, disappeared, Neubauer went looking for him; he found him sitting with his wife under a palm tree behind the pits. A weeping Lydia Lang told the team manager that they had endured enough of Caracciola's jealousy, and she had advised her husband not to race. It took the persuasive powers of Max Sailer to get Lang back into the car. But resentments continued to boil on both sides, and there was another outburst when Caracciola demanded scrubbed tyres for the race, only to be told there were none available to him because his tantrum had cost him the chance to prepare a set.

In 40-degree heat, Lang stole a march on the field by reacting to the starting lights, which changed to green a fraction of a second ahead of the fall of Marshal Balbo's tricolour. As the Maseratis and Alfas succumbed under the pressure of trying to keep up, Lang held on to his lead, destroying neither his engine nor his tyres and leading Caracciola home to secure a stunning one-two victory for Mercedes. In trying to remove the threat of the German teams, the Italians had succeeded only in highlighting their supremacy in every aspect of motor racing. Several drivers of the Italian cars complained afterwards of the effects of the fumes from the exhausts of the German cars: dizziness, nausea, and even hallucinations. The dizziest Italian of all, however, would have been a man in Busto Arsizio, north of Milan, who had drawn Lang in the final lottery selection and collected 3 million lire for the winning ticket. While he enjoyed the proceeds, history would ensure that the W165s – eight months in the making from start to finish, with an unblemished triumph to show for it – were never seen in competition again.

◆

When the team reconvened at the Nürburgring for the Eifelrennen on 21 May, Dick was called up for his first appearance of the season. Lang told him (he had no English, but Seaman's German was now fluent enough for conversation) all about the trouble Caracciola had made in Tripoli, while the two older drivers griped together about the young upstarts. For this race, Uhlenhaut had produced a car with a new two-stage supercharger. Since there was only one, it was offered first to Caracciola, who turned it down, then to von Brauchitsch, who did likewise, and then to Lang, who accepted it and put in a practice lap three seconds faster than Nuvolari and Caracciola, with whom he shared the front row. Dick and von Brauchitsch, together on the second row, were both a further second slower.

Suspecting that the Auto Unions were planning to run the whole of the relatively short ten-lap Eifel GP without changing tyres, Neubauer gave his drivers a staggered schedule of fuel and tyre stops: Lang on the fourth lap, von Brauchitsch on the fifth, Caracciola on the sixth and Seaman on the seventh. Hans-Hugo Hartmann, whose father was the head salesman in Mercedes' Dortmund showroom, had also been entered in a fifth car. The team manager told them all to go flat-out.

Before the race, Lang and Caracciola entertained the crowd with a parade lap in the Tripoli cars. When the flag dropped, von Brauchitsch and Seaman both made excellent starts but damaged their clutches in the process. Dick was forced to retire immediately, to his great disappointment, while von Brauchitsch struggled on to the finish with severe clutch-slip. (Back at the factory after the meeting, Uhlenhaut took the hint and ordered a change on all the cars from cast-iron to steel clutch plates, which solved the problem.) The race soon developed into a battle between Lang, Nuvolari and Caracciola, who finished in that order after the Italian, worried about the wear on his unchanged tyres, had backed off in the closing stages.

Lang had won his third race in a row, and afterwards Seaman wrote to Monkhouse about the team's increasingly turbulent internal politics: 'Rudi of course did a terrific sulk, saying (a) Lang was given the fastest car (quite forgetting he himself had declined the offer of driving it). (b) His engine was cold at the start. (c) The mechanics bungled his pit stop (though actually they did it very well considering he overshot the mark and they had to run backwards and forward to get the new wheels). He was ably assisted by Manfred, who I must say has been behaving extremely childishly the whole year, and is practically back to his 1936 form in this respect. Their whole wrath is of course directed at poor Lang, with whom they are now starting to include Seaman, apparently for the sole reason that we are younger and have our own share of success.'

At the victory banquet, Max Sailer made a speech that began with amusing anecdotes about his own racing career but developed into what Dick described as a 'peroration': 'He declaimed that people are saying motor racing is no longer interesting because Mercedes–Benz always win. But we cannot help them. Mercedes-Benz have been winning races for forty years and we don't propose to stop now.' He was received, Dick reported, with thunderous cheers. The letter to Monkhouse ended with a lighter postscript: 'Have you got [Benny] Goodman's "Opus ½"? I like it.'

Both German teams stayed on after the race for two days of filming and a day's testing. Dick was given a lap in the W165, which he found light and easy to handle but not as interesting to drive as the more powerful 3-litre car. He had asked Mercedes to enter the new cars for the Nuffield Trophy, a scratch race for voiturettes, at Donington on 10 June. Sailer liked the idea, but Neubauer pointed out that they had only intended to race the W165s once in 1939, and that they did not want to spoil the public's anticipation of the 1940 season by a further demonstration of their continuing ability, despite the change of formula, to humiliate the opposition.

The clutch of his Grand Prix car repaired, Dick took part in the filming. Again the director was Erich Stoll, this time shooting footage of both German teams with aerial and car-mounted cameras. Mercedes had also brought a two-seater W125, built a couple of years earlier to allow Uhlenhaut to examine the behaviour of the rear suspension at close quarters and subsequently used for film projects. The drivers were invited to take their wives for a lap of the Nordschleife – Erica, still a fearless teenager, was particularly delighted by the experience – while Caracciola went out with the portly Neubauer squeezed into the passenger seat. Stoll's previous experience as a cinematographer included Leni Riefenstahl's *Triumph of the Will*, the film of the 1934 Nuremberg Rally. His next job would be as a cameraman on a propaganda film called *Der Ewige Jude* (*The Eternal Jew*), a depiction of the threat to western civilisation allegedly posed by the Jewish presence, ending with the speech in which Hitler promised their annihilation.

With time on their hands until the Belgian Grand Prix at the end of June, for which Dick had been promised a start, the Seamans joined the Mercedes party in Vienna for a round of the European hill-climb championship. 'All Vienna seemed to have gone to the Kahlenberg,' Lang remembered. 'Not a square yard of grass was to be seen, and everywhere the gay colours of summer dresses.' Dick was appalled by the organisation of the event, which was being run by local NSKK officials. Spectators were allowed to wander across the road, and at the finish, situated just before a bend, there were several crashes in practice, including a fatal accident to a competitor in the motorcycle event, before the line was moved further back down the hill. Lang's win seemed inevitable, given the form he was in.

The trip offered an opportunity to see Erica's friends in the city of her parents' birth and to accept Neubauer's invitation to dine in some of its best restaurants. They were also taken to inspect the course for the Grand Prix of Vienna, scheduled for mid-September and laid out in a city park. 'The straight was three kilometres long, which made Uhlenhaut's knees tremble considerably,' Dick reported to Monkhouse, 'while the rest consisted of *colossally* fast continuous bends on a badly cambered (and in the wet suicidal) road, rather narrow and bordered by an avenue of decorative but very uncompromising chestnut trees.' After discussions between the racers and the organisers, it was agreed to shorten the course, halving the length of the straight.

From Vienna they made for Stuttgart, where Dr Kissel marked the Tripoli triumph by hosting a celebratory lunch lasting from 12.30 p.m. to five o'clock. Noting that the Caracciolas seemed subdued, Dick was told that Rudi had made such a fuss after the Eifel race, even threatening to quit the team on the spot, that Kissel had called him in and given him a dressing-down. 'Apparently he objects to being no longer considered the best and only driver in the team,' Dick observed.

◆

In early June, a long letter from Monkhouse arrived at Untergrainau. It included news of a visit to a six-day cycle race in London, an enthusiastic account of his adventures as a trout fisherman in Somerset and elsewhere, and praise for a recent win in the Naples GP by Johnny Wakefield, a very promising young Englishman whose Cumbrian family had made a fortune from gunpowder. In mentioning the two-seater Mercedes, George continued the use of surnames that characterised their correspondence over the years, marking them both out as public schoolboys who had not entirely grown out of their old social habits: 'I must say Monkhouse would like a ride in this piloted by Seaman! Do you think there would be any object in my dropping a little line to Uhlenhaut and asking if he would have it there for the GP?'

Also mentioned was a specially made amplifier for Dick's gramophone, which Monkhouse – a confirmed radio ham who enjoyed fiddling about with electrical bits and pieces — was hoping to deliver personally. He was planning a summer visit to Germany, and the idea had been to bring it with him to Untergrainau in the Bentley. In the circumstances, however, it seemed prudent to reconsider. 'It would be a pity to leave it behind,' he wrote, meaning to abandon it in Germany when war broke out. The possibility of Dick and Erica needing to make a quick exit from the country had clearly been discussed. But Monkhouse, like most of their circle, still believed that a solution might be found. 'Do you think it might be better,' he asked, 'to leave it for a little while and see how things work out?'

Dick was also pursuing a new interest in fishing in nearby lakes and trout streams with rods presented to him by his father-in-law, and looked forward to Monkhouse joining him in July. The Chris-Craft had been overhauled, with a new berth in a yacht club at Tutzing on the Starnbergersee; the dinghy was to be sold and replaced by a larger sailing boat on which his eye had fallen, a 16-foot Bermuda rig of a class called Olympiajolle, created in Germany and introduced at the 1936 Summer Games.

With two weeks of freedom before they were due to set off for Belgium, he and Erica could enjoy a quiet time at home. This was the first relationship to which he had given any serious commitment, and he found — to Erica's delight — that he was enjoying being married. When they entertained the Aldington family at Haus Buchenbichl, she noticed that he was happy to play with the three small children. He had told her, she remembered, that when he was in the London Clinic for surgery on his nose, he had liked wandering along to the maternity ward to admire the new babies. They had made no plans in that regard, but it seemed inevitable that children would come along, perhaps when his racing career was over and they had, in all probability, returned to England. Dick would finally come into his inheritance and he could settle down to run the business he had discussed with Monkhouse, putting to good use the commercial skills he had acquired in his partnership with Straight and while running his own team. Perhaps there would also be a way, through the RAC or the BRDC, for him to help drive the development of British motor racing, so that his successors would find it easier to realise their ambitions and compete with the world's best. And if he could reach some sort of rapprochement with his mother, Pull Court was waiting for them. Erica was contented and confident about the future – if one could ignore for a moment the state of the world around them – and so was he.

30

In the high fens

Telegraph poles, high earth banks, deep ditches, pole-and-wire fences keeping cattle off the road, loose verges, low stone walls, sharp changes of elevation, the occasional farmhouse abutting the track, and trees, trees, trees, so many trees bordering the fastest curves: the high-speed circuit of Spa-Francorchamps was, from its inception, one of a handful of Grand Prix racing's great theatres, echoing with drama and danger.

The circuit was in the Hautes Fagnes – the high fens – on the edge of the ancient forests of the Ardennes. Its outline had been sketched by three men who sat down shortly after the end of the Great War at the Hôtel des Bruyères in Francorchamps: Jules de Thier, owner of the daily newspaper *La Meuse*, Baron Joseph de Crawhez, the burgomaster of Spa, and the racing driver Henri Langlois van Ophem. Together they identified a triangle of public roads – routes 32, 23 and 440 – measuring 9 miles, over which the races would be run in a clockwise direction. The right-handers at Burnenville, Stavelot and La Source would be linked by long stretches of fast road, in a combination designed to test every element of a racing car: acceleration, top speed, stability in high-speed curves, heavy braking. Even at a time when most circuits made use of public roads, few tracks exploited and responded to their surroundings as organically as this one. In 1922 the first Belgian Grand Prix was won by Baron de Tornaco-Bruyère in an Impéria-Abadal. Three years later, after the addition of a scoreboard, a timing booth and a press stand, the winner was Antonio Ascari in an Alfa Romeo, the great Italian's last success before his death at Montlhéry. In the 1930s the winners included Chiron, Nuvolari, Dreyfus, Caracciola and Hasse.

For 1939, one important modification had been made to the circuit. Soon after the start, which took place on a downhill stretch of road beneath the hairpin at La Source, the cars had always turned sharp left towards the Virage de l'Ancienne Douane, a right-handed hairpin named after an old customs post: a reminder that, before the Great War, the frontier between Belgium and Germany had cut across this piece of land. Now, intending to raise the average speed in order to compete for the informal status accorded to the fastest circuit on the Grand Prix calendar, the organisers cut out that hairpin, redrawing the track so that the cars plunged down from the start into a snaking high-speed left-right at the bottom of the hill before howling up a 17 per cent gradient, rising 134 feet in altitude to a brow at which they briefly left the ground. Daunting for the drivers, mesmerising for those merely watching, the fast left-right was known as Eau Rouge, the name coming from a stream passing under the road, tinted red by iron oxide deposits. In the days of the Roman empire it had marked an administrative border. The crest at the end of the rise was called Raidillon, and hid a blind left turn. Other features of the circuit were almost as impressive: the flat-out challenges of the Burnenville and Blanchimont curves and the kink halfway along the Masta Straight, the long hairpin at Stavelot and the tighter one at La Source, which brought the cars down almost to walking pace before they opened up again in the charge for the finish line.

A western extension of the Eifel mountains, this was the coldest and wettest part of Belgium, its weather regularly affecting the Grand Prix, even at the height of the European summer.

Spa was a resort, but its attraction was its mineral water rather than its climate. The healing benefits of its springs had been celebrated in the first century AD by Pliny the Elder, a colonial administrator as well as a writer. Charles II of England visited Spa in 1654, Peter the Great of Russia followed in 1717, and the name was adopted by English-speakers as a generic term. The town acquired a Boulevard des Anglais, and the introduction of a casino in the eighteenth century increased its popularity. Dick and Erica were staying with the rest of the Mercedes team at the 150-room Palace Hôtel des Bains, a four-storey belle époque building in the tree-shaded Place Royale.

◆

For the first Grande Épreuve of the season, Mercedes had entered four W154s. Dick's car left Stuttgart with the convoy on the Tuesday, in a truck crewed by two of his mechanics, Fischer and Braun. The machines and their technicians were quartered close to the circuit at the Hôtel les Bruyères, which Mercedes block-booked each year, and where the old stables served as garages. There were four D-type Auto Unions, for Nuvolari, Müller, Hasse and a new recruit to replace von Delius: Georg 'Schorsch' Meier, a motorbike ace who had come straight from the Isle of Man, where he had won the Senior TT for BMW a few days earlier. The only serious competition to the German cars was offered by Nino Farina in a new works V16 Alfa with curious bodywork, representing the Italian team's final attempt to make a mark on the 3-litre formula. The remaining four starters in the thirteen-car field were Raymond Sommer in his own Alfa, the private Delahayes of Louis Gérard and Robert Mazaud, and Adolfo Mandirola's Maserati. The drabness of the opposition testified to the German hegemony.

As so often at Spa, the weather was changeable throughout the practice sessions on Wednesday, Thursday and Friday. On such a long circuit, the track could be inundated at one end and bone-dry at the other as the rain clouds moved around the mountains. Since the grid positions were to be decided not by practice times but in the old-fashioned way, by drawing lots, the practice times were not as significant as usual. Nevertheless, on the second day Lang emphasised his magnificent form by taking advantage of a dry spell to record the fastest lap in 5 minutes 3.2 seconds, a second quicker than his best in the last Belgian GP, two years earlier.

Saturday was a rest day, and while Erica went shopping with Rudi and Edith Uhlenhaut, Dick spent some time with Robert Fellowes, who arrived in the company of a couple of Brooklands types, Mort Morris-Goodall and George Harvey-Noble. The pair had begun the journey to Belgium in Morris-Goodall's Aston Martin, which ran its bearings on the way. As a courtesy to two compatriots he hardly knew, Dick arranged for a Mercedes mechanic to make a repair over the weekend and for a team car to ferry them around. They had arrived on Friday night without reservations, but managed to get a single room to share in a small hotel near the final hairpin at La Source.

In the days before the race, too, a lunch was given for the teams, including the drivers and their wives, by the president of the Royal Automobile Club of Belgium. It was, Erica would remember, 'the last lovely thing that happened to me for a long time'.

◆

When Dick woke up in his room at the Palace hotel on the morning of Sunday 25 June, he was greeted by a knock at the door. At lunch the previous day he had been approached by a photographer working for a Belgian agency called Reflect, inviting him to collaborate on a feature for the popular British weekly magazine *Picture Post*, which was running a series of photo essays on a day in the life of people in different occupations. At first he politely demurred, suggesting that it might be better to approach someone more famous, such as Caracciola or Nuvolari. But the photographer pointed out that since *Picture*

Post was British, the magazine might be more interested in spot-lighting an Englishman representing his country at the pinnacle of an international sport.

Dick gave his consent, and at eleven o'clock the next morn-ing – only two and a half hours before the start of the race – he was photographed in bed, wearing his pyjamas and reading a copy of *The Motor*. Erica was nowhere to be seen, although the other half of the pushed-together twin beds had clearly been occupied. At 11.15, according to the photographer's timing of the morning's events, Dick got up to open the curtains and check the weather. At 11.30, now in a jazzy zigzag-striped dressing gown, he was photographed in the bathroom, framed in the large mirror, honing his cut-throat razor on a leather strop attached to a hook on the door, his face already lathered. At 12.30 he and Erica were photographed at a table in the hotel restaurant, the remains of a late breakfast in front of them.

'He has eaten little, his wife nothing,' the photographer's cap-tion records. Both have unlit cigarettes in their mouths, taken from a packet lying on the table. They resemble innumerable young couples on their travels, preparing for a day in a foreign town. But not exactly: he is dressed for the coming race, with a trenchcoat buttoned and belted over his white overalls, and his goggles around his neck. She wears a light double-breasted coat with peaked lapels, finely tailored, over a white blouse with a double row of smocking beneath the small rounded collar. His hair looks freshly barbered and is, as always, neatly brushed down. Hers is arranged in soft curls. Both look serious, even preoccupied, perhaps a little older than their years, as they turn towards each other, his head slightly lowered to light his cig-arette from the flaring match she is holding out towards him.

◆

An hour later he is on the starting grid, looking down the hill towards Eau Rouge, feeling the car shudder as he blips the throttle. The racing numbers painted on the four Mercedes indicate the drivers' status within the team: 20 for Caracciola, 22 for Lang, 24 for von Brauchitsch, 26 for Seaman. Dick's car is chassis No. 5, the one he had used at the Eifelrennen. Built for the 1938 season, it had been driven that year by Lang in Pau and by von Brauchitsch at Reims, the Nürburgring and Pescara. Rebodied in the 1939 style, it returned to Pau, again in von Brauchitsch's hands. Now its engine – No. 14 in the series – has already been warmed up by a mechanic, working to a set procedure in a range between 2,200 and 4,000rpm. Dick has lined up on the second row of the grid, with Müller, Lang and Farina ahead and Nuvolari – one of the two drivers he admires most in the world – alongside him. The other, Caracciola, is behind them, flanked by the Auto Unions of Meier and Hasse. Von Brauchitsch is on the fourth row, alongside Sommer. Each W154 has a small handbrake to the left of the cockpit, but the drivers have enough to do at the start without being required to think about using it. Neubauer has adopted an idea originally used by Alfa Romeo in 1925, wedging lumps of chalk under the rear wheels to hold the cars stationary against the downslope. The chalk will disintegrate harmlessly as soon as the surge of power is fed from the engine to the wheels.

Fellowes has taken a couple of pictures on the grid, including one of Dick with a tarpaulin over the car's bonnet to keep the rain off the engine's electrical systems. (Running short of film, he had asked Dick to bring some for him, without success, so he has to limit himself to very few frames.) Another grid visitor has been the Eton-educated, 37-year-old King Leopold III of the Belgians, whose cup will go to the winner. Now he has taken his place in the royal box to await the start.

The rain eases a little, but the woods above the valley are veiled in mist. Like most of the drivers, Dick is wearing a lightweight waterproof windbreaker on top of his overalls. A visor is fastened around his white leather helmet. In front of him is a steering wheel with four alloy spokes and a lam-inated wooden rim. He has a small glass aeroscreen with a round rear-view mirror in a domed alloy casing on either side. Reflecting Uhlenhaut's belief that a driver should not be distracted by superfluous information, there are only three dials in front of him: the largest, the rev counter, runs up to 9,000rpm. The others, on either side, are for water and oil temperature. There is a magneto switch on the left-hand side, and a small knurled knob allowing the driver to adjust the firmness of the hydraulic rear dampers to compensate for the changing fuel load. On either side of his upholstered seat run large-diameter flexible metal hoses, connecting the fuel tank mounted above his knees – the 'saddle tank', holding 40 gallons – with the tank in the tail of the car, holding 52 gallons. The intention is that as the fuel is consumed, the weight balance between the two tanks should remain as equal as possible. And with 92 gallons on board, the W154s should be able to complete the race distance – thirty-five laps, satisfying the 500km minimum distance of a Grande Épreuve – with only a single stop.

Now it is half past one and the lights are about to turn green. The immediately identifiable figure of Neubauer stands on the verge of the track, opposite the pits, where his drivers can see him, with his hand raised, counting off the final seconds. The cars of Lang and Müller jerk forwards by a foot or two, anticipating the signal, then hesitate. Inside them, Farina has judged it more precisely and jumps away, with a clear lead as the thirteen cars stream under a footbridge before plunging down into the left-right of Eau Rouge. The Alfa is a length ahead as they start up the steep ramp of Raidillon, but the power of the German engines is too much for the Italian car, and both Müller and Lang have gone past by the time they reach the crest. Behind them come Caracciola and Nuvolari, with Seaman a few lengths back, then Hasse, von Brauchitsch, Sommer and Meier.

Lang tries for four laps to grab the lead from Müller, but the spray from the Auto Union's wheels makes it impossible for him to attempt a pass; impossible, too, for Müller to see in his mirrors that Lang is shaking his fist at him. Meanwhile Caracciola and Seaman are working their way past first Farina and then Nuvolari. Neubauer is trying to persuade an official to wave a blue flag at Müller, but Lang decides to let his teammates have a go and waves them through. At the end of the eighth lap, Caracciola is trying to accelerate past the Auto Union as they exit La Source, but applies too much throttle and the car spins, ending up in a shallow ditch. From their vantage point at the hairpin, Morris-Goodall and Harvey-Noble witness this rare misstep by the man long famous for his mastery of wet conditions. Unable to push the car out of the ditch, Caracciola is left helpless only a couple of hundred yards from the pits, where Neubauer, realising that his team leader is out, tells a mechanic, Karl Bunz, to run up the hill to him with his coat, his cigarettes and instructions to stay with the car. Two laps later, when Müller dives into the pits for a fuel stop, Seaman crosses the line to start the eleventh lap in the lead, followed at a safe distance by a cautious Lang. Müller resumes in third place but his engine has lost power and he falls back before crashing out of the race on lap fourteen. The conditions also catch out Meier, the Grand Prix debutant, who is unable to restart after leaving the road at Blanchimont while trying to lap Mandirola's Maserati.

On lap seventeen, Dick stops for fuel and new tyres. He cuts the engine 100 yards from his pit, in order to prevent the plugs oiling, and glides silently to a halt. Three mechanics surround his car. Two lift it up on a jack and change the wheels; a wheel-nut proves momentarily awkward. The third mechanic wipes the driver's visor and the aeroscreen with a chamois leather, and then runs to the front to connect the electric starter unit and turn the motor over. The car with the green-painted radiator grille is away after thirty seconds. When Lang comes in for the same procedure, his stop is five seconds faster, but he is still more than twenty seconds behind the leader when he rejoins, and about twice that in front of the third-placed Nuvolari. Aware that his skill in the rain does not match Seaman's, Lang is content to hold his position. The gap goes out to half a minute, and then contracts again when the rain eases. Lang is speeding up on the instruction of Neubauer, who has been told by his timekeepers that Nuvolari is starting to catch the second-placed Mercedes. Dick speeds up, too. The rain comes down harder again, spray hanging in the air.

Schorsch Meier has left his stranded car at Blanchimont. He is walking back to the pits in the rain, following the direction of the circuit, when the Mercedes with the red number 26 on its tail swooshes past him on the way to La Source, with thirteen and a bit laps to go. Surface water plumes off its tyres as it shapes to take Club House Corner at around 140mph, the line of the left-hand bend marked by a row of fir trees bordering what will revert, when the racing is over, to being the public road to Verviers. From about 300 yards away, Meier sees what happens next: the silver car abruptly leaves its normal trajectory, spinning out of control. The world seems to speed up as the car whirls around as if on ice, 910kg of unguided kinetic energy looking to spend itself, veering over the verge on the outside of the track and glancing off one tree, shearing off its left rear wheel, before cannoning into another, just past the Club House gates. It strikes this tree broadside, bending itself around the trunk, against which it comes to an abrupt halt. Meier begins to run towards the scene.

Further ahead, Morris-Goodall and Harvey-Noble watch as the Mercedes travels towards them, leaving the road and smashing into first one tree, then another. To their horror, they see yellow flames. Stretched by the second impact, the flexible metal hose on the left side of the cockpit has broken loose. Fuel gushes out from the almost-full tanks and catches fire immediately on the hot exhaust pipe running along the outside of the bodywork.

Lang arrives at the scene twenty seconds after the accident. A yellow warning flag is being waved and he slows as he passes the wrecked car. He sees the number 26 on its bodywork. He sees the fire. He glimpses the driver, motionless in the blazing cockpit.

Dick is unconscious. At some point during the double impact he has been knocked out by a blow to the head, against which his leather wind helmet has offered no protection. His right arm has been broken. Insensible, unable to release the steering wheel and escape from the cockpit, he is helpless as the flames rise around him and begin to burn his cotton clothing and exposed skin.

There are no marshals stationed at this spot. The first man on the scene is a soldier, Lieutenant Pierre Hauman of Belgium's 1st Regiment of Lancers. Twenty-seven years old, born in Romania, Hauman is a graduate of the École Royale Militaire. Garrisoned in Spa, he and his regiment are manning frontier observation posts at a time of rising tensions with Germany. He has recently led the regimental motocross team to victory in an international competition against German, French and Italian rivals, and was happy to be offered the chance to help steward the track and watch some of the heroes of the age at close quarters. Now he tries to reach Dick through the flames, but is beaten back. Two marshals sprint up the side of the track from the hairpin to join him: a Monsieur Orban and a Monsieur Cokaiko, both from Liège. Meier has also arrived to give help. Lacking fire-fighting equipment, they attempt to smother the blaze with soil from the verge. Eventually someone with a pair of shears cuts through the spokes of the steering wheel, allowing the rim to be removed and making room for Dick to be dragged from the cockpit and laid on the ground.

The little group is joined by Karl Bunz, the Mercedes mechanic; he has been alerted by a shocked Lang, who has stopped by Caracciola's stationary car to tell them what he has seen and then carried on down the hill to the Mercedes pit. Lang wants to give up, but Neubauer tells him to stay calm, go back out and win the race. Back at the scene of the accident, Bunz, who has run and climbed fences to get there, looks at the driver lying on the verge, much of his clothing burnt away, now semi-conscious. Finally someone has an extinguisher and is putting out the fire. Bunz helps to carry Seaman through the gates and up the drive to the villa; he looks at Dick's charred face and hears him calling out in German, asking for a doctor.

Within a few minutes Peter Gläser arrives from the pits, carrying his medical bag. To dull the excruciating pain, he injects Dick with morphine. They wait for the circuit's ambulance; the race is still going on, and the emergency vehicle is having trouble getting through.

Lang races on, sickened by what he has glimpsed. Nuvolari has retired after spinning off. The leading Mercedes is now two minutes ahead of Hasse's Auto Union, but on the penultimate lap, 2 miles from the pits, Lang's engine starts cutting out. Thinking he must be running out of fuel, he makes it back to the pits for a refill. He comes out still ahead of Hasse, but after 100 yards the engine stutters again and cuts out completely. With the car coasting silently through Eau Rouge, he keeps it in gear and engages the clutch. Nothing happens. He does it again. Nothing. Again. Finally the engine fires. Hasse is still a handful of seconds behind and Lang can complete the lap to take the victory. Just past the finish line, he turns the car round and drives back up the hill to the pits to receive the laurel wreath and the King's trophy, but the smiles are brief and strained.

Erica has been watching the race from the pits. She knows very quickly that Dick has been involved in an accident. She has seen Lang stop and speak to Neubauer. She has seen Peter Gläser rushing into action. At this stage she has no idea of her husband's condition, but soon it becomes apparent that this is a bad one. Her friends gather round. Lydia Lang, Laury Vermundt and Baby Caracciola provide immediate support for this 19-year-old girl to whom life has, until this moment, brought nothing but happiness and the promise of security. A priest comes to talk to her.

The ambulance takes Dick out of the circuit and threads its way through the race traffic, on a 5-mile journey along the road that passes by the village of Francorchamps and climbs to a plateau before descending towards Spa, past a small aerodrome. The Institut Médico-Chirurgical de la Croix Rouge is on the Rue de la Sauvetière, a few hundred yards from his hotel. It is a whitewashed building shaped like a blunted wedge, with a four-sided slate spire and a glass conservatory where convalescent patients can sit. He is taken to room thirty-nine, where his clothes are cut away and he is bandaged from head to foot.

In the hours that follow, visitors come and go. The doctors withdraw, leaving the nurses to care for him. There are differing accounts of what happens in those hours. He speaks in English. He speaks in German. When Erica arrives, driven from the circuit in an official car commandeered by Hanns Geier, Dick apologises for being unable to take her to the cinema. Bewildered and distraught, she is led away by the Caracciolas. Dick tells Neubauer, in the presence of Uhlenhaut, that the accident was his fault; he had been going too fast for the conditions. He asks Dr Gläser to get him a beer. Fellowes turns up, and is greeted with the words 'I wondered if you'd be coming along'. Morris-Goodall and Harvey-Noble arrive, having been given a lift from the circuit by Nuvolari; horrified by what they see in room thirty-nine, and feeling they have intruded, they leave quickly.

Erica is back at the hotel, being comforted by her friends as the hours pass, crying herself to sleep in Alice Caracciola's arms. Gläser and Fellowes stay with Dick, but neither they nor the nurses can do anything as the severity of the burns slowly takes effect and his systems start to shut down. The doctor, who has helped so many injured men, knows there is no hope. His major organs failing, Dick lapses into a coma. Shortly before midnight, about eight hours after the accident took place, he dies.

31

Nunc Dimittis

The news went out over the wires in time to catch the final editions of the London papers. There was a paragraph in *The Times*, and the *Daily Telegraph* carried a four-paragraph story under the headline 'Famous Driver Killed'. Someone, almost certainly Fellowes, would have phoned Monkhouse or Aldington during the night. One of them would have taken on the responsibility of dialling KENsington 5400 early the next morning and breaking the news to Dick's mother before she could read it in the paper or hear it on the radio.

There were tears in the Mercedes team that night, not least from Alfred Neubauer. The team manager acted swiftly to arrange a small memorial service the next day at Spa's English church. Dedicated to St Peter and St Paul, this was a red-brick Gothic Revival building erected in the 1870s by the members of the town's sizeable expatriate community on the Rue Brixhe, halfway up the hill above the town centre. Sitting in the dark wooden pews as Neubauer made a moving address, the congregation included the German ambassador and the president of the Belgian Royal Automobile Club.

In Unterfürkheim, the Mercedes press office composed an In Memoriam notice, published prominently in the next day's German papers, set inside a black box rule, with a translation sent to the English newspapers and magazines. 'A great driver and a real man has gone from us for ever,' it said. 'We have lost in Richard Seaman a remarkable fighter, full of promise, and a great friend. Loyally we shall always retain for him an honoured place in our hearts and our memory.'

Later, while Erica was taken back to her family in Munich, it was Fellowes who volunteered for the sombre duty of escorting Dick's body home, via Ostend, where representatives of the Belgian club saw him off. Carrying a copy of the death certificate, signed by the British consul in Liège, he arrived at Dover to discover that there was no one to meet him, either from the RAC or the British Racing Drivers' Club, on whose committee Dick had served. 'In Germany and Belgium a Grand Prix driver is regarded as a sportsman of the highest importance, and this, I suppose, is a point of view that will never be properly understood in Great Britain,' he wrote later. 'Perhaps it is best to leave it at that.'

◆

Had Dick crashed through taking needless risks, given that he was winning the race and the conditions were so dangerous? Uhlenhaut, who liked and admired him, was unequivocal: 'He drove unnecessarily hard and unnecessarily fast, and that contributed to his relatively frequent accidents in our cars, and also – I am afraid – to his fatal accident at Spa in the rain, where he was leading very comfortably and there was no need to keep pressure on so hard.'

This contrasted with the opinions of others who had observed him at work earlier in his career. After seeing him win the JCC 200 at Donington in 1936, T. P. Cholmondeley-Tapper had described Dick driving in 'his usual sound, unostentatious fashion'. Monkhouse described going to watch the cars through a demanding sequence of fast downhill bends at Berne in 1938, and comparing the drivers' techniques. 'In my opinion,' he wrote, 'Caracciola and Seaman were infinitely more polished than anyone else.' Both of those rainmasters had crashed that day at Spa, as had Nuvolari. Until he lost it, Dick had driven impeccably, as he had in similar conditions when coming second to Caracciola at Bremgarten – another fast, tree-lined circuit – the previous August. But no one was invulnerable on a wet track.

What could not be ignored was that there had been crashes earlier in his career. The first had been in the Eifelrennen at the Nürburgring in 1936, when the Delage left the track in the rain. The second was a week later, at Péronne, when he was feeling ill and misjudged his braking at the end of the long straight. Until he joined Mercedes, those were the only blemishes on his safety record. The more powerful cars of the German team clearly required acclimatisation. In his first season there were four incidents. He crashed heavily at Monza during testing, injuring a knee and destroying a car. At Pescara a locked brake sent him into the side of a house, without damage to himself. At the Nürburgring during the German Grand Prix he badly injured his face and his car was wrecked in the accident – for which he was blameless – that cost von Delius his life. And at Donington Park it was Müller who had shunted the rear of his Mercedes. All these 1937 accidents – only two of them Seaman's fault – were in the 750kg W125, with its 5.7-litre engine. After the switch in 1938 to the 3-litre W154, there were no incidents in three Grand Prix starts before the one that killed him.

To the charge sheet might be added two indiscretions away from the track. In the first, as a 20-year-old, he wrote off his Bugatti in a collision with a bus outside Victoria station. In the second, four years later, he lost control of Monkhouse's borrowed Mercedes in the rain and crashed into a fruit market in a small town in the Alps. Those incidents suggest a certain youthful recklessness, but it was a fallibility that he had perhaps already grown out of.

There was also the question of his refusal to wear a hard–shell crash helmet. Had he not been knocked out, he might have been able to release the steering wheel and escape before the fire took hold. 'It is queer, when you come to think about it, that none of the Grand Prix drivers wear them,' *Motor Sport* observed. Not one of the front-line drivers against whom Dick raced in Grands Prix during his last three seasons chose that form of head protection. To them, it would have been like a matador entering the ring in a suit of armour: an affront to the ethos of their sport, something for amateurs.

◆

In the following days, the British newspapers gave Dick's death far more space than they had given his achievements in life. 'Briton dies after race crash in blazing car' was the *Daily Express*'s headline, its story describing how his German-born wife, having been told there was no hope, had sat for hours by his bedside 'silently weeping, speaking to no one, refusing to eat'. 'Speed Ace Dies – Wife At Bed' was the *Daily Mirror*'s headline, above a story containing what purported to be a quote given by Erica to the newspaper on the phone from the hospital: 'I did not see the accident, although I was at the races. Somebody told me about it – it was a dreadful shock.' Under a wedding photograph of Dick and Erica, the *Daily Herald* carried an appreciation by Tommy Wisdom. 'A likeable personality, friend of all the leading racing drivers, Seaman told me that motor racing was his very life,' he wrote. 'He hated driving a German car, but since Britain did not build what he regarded as "real" racing cars, he had no choice.' Whitney Straight was quoted in the *Evening Standard*'s story: 'Some people, because he married a German girl last year and spent most of his time in Germany, might have imagined that he was pro-German. He was not. He raced German cars because they were fastest and best, and his love of the sport forced him to drive their cars.' *The Times*'s sober single-column obituary concluded: 'To Richard Seaman, motor racing was not a sport to be undertaken lightly. He regarded it with a seriousness that doubtless contributed much to his success. This, combined with exceptional driving skill, habitual coolness, and great powers of endurance, made him the ideal racing motorist. He can ill be spared by Britain, the German team for which he raced with such distinction, and the sport of motor racing generally.'

The RAC circulated a telegram sent by Korpsführer Hühnlein on behalf of the NSKK: 'German motor sport stands at the bier of its young English sports comrade, who, as a member of a German racing team, was particularly close to them. In the two years of his membership of the Mercedes-Benz racing team, Seaman had by the chivalry of his nature, by his cheery enterprise, and his outstanding sporting achievements, which contributed so much to the increasing of the fame of the German colours, won our affection and respect to a high degree. We will never forget him.'

At Untertürkheim, messages of condolence were arriving in a flood from the company's dealerships around the world, from rivals (including Stuck and Kautz), national automobile clubs, equipment suppliers, other manufacturers, from newspapers and magazines, and private citizens. Perhaps the most touching of them was sent to Neubauer from Paris: '+ TRES TOUCHES PAR DECES SEAMAN VOUS ADRESSONS SINCERES CONDOLENCES EQUIPE BUGATTI BENOIST WIMILLE VEYRON +'

John Dugdale, Dick's old schoolmate, was preparing his appreciation for *The Autocar*. 'Seaman was a man of determination,' he wrote, 'and whatever he set his mind to do, he carried out thoroughly and efficiently. One can but regret that he has not lived longer to mould his fine qualities even deeper in our memories.' Drawing on similar emotions in an obituary for *The Motor*, Rodney Walkerley wrote of Dick as a man who 'loved life and the joy of living with a schoolboyish zest which he never lost. His great modesty and shyness never left him, even when the whole motor racing world hailed him as the coming man. We have lost not only the finest of British drivers and one of the great drivers of Europe, but a loveable personality, a true friend, and a splendid sportsman.'

◆

A notice in *The Times* on Thursday 29 June announced that the funeral service would be held the following day at 2.30 p.m. at All Saints Church, Ennismore Gardens, 100 yards from his old home, followed an hour later by a burial at Putney Vale cemetery. Floral tributes could be sent to 3 Ennismore Gardens.

When they arrived, one dwarfed the rest. Six feet tall, the wreath of white Madonna lilies required two men to deliver it and to hold it upright for the press photographers, who were keen to capture the ribbon imprinted with the eagle and swastika motif and the name of the sender: Adolf Hitler. It was not taken to the cemetery; after the service it was quietly returned to German hands and discreetly taken away. In the window of the Mercedes showroom on Park Lane, all the cars had been removed and replaced by a single large portrait photograph of the dead hero.

It would be hard to imagine the tension in the church and at the graveside between two heartbroken women, Erica Seaman and her estranged mother-in-law. Erica arrived with her father, her sister, Eva, and Eva's husband, Paul Heim. Her friends Helmi and Bimbo Haspel were in attendance, the former also acting as one of Mercedes' official representatives. The task of supporting Dick's mother fell to Monkhouse and Fellowes, and to her daughter, Vahlia. Also by Lilian's side as they took their places at the front of the church were her sister, Madge, and her German-born brother-in-law, Carl Windschuegl, whom Dick had nominated as one of his trustees.

Inside All Saints, Mercedes were represented by a second director, Carl Schippert, with Neubauer, Caracciola, von Brauchitsch and Lang. From Auto Union, Dr Feuereissen and Hasse came to pay tribute to a fallen opponent. Representatives of the British racing world — many of them members of the

Brooklands crowd – included the Lords Howe, Selsdon, Waleran and Cottenham, Sir George Hastings, Sir Algernon Guinness (representing the RAC) and Lady Guinness, Lt-Col John Moore-Brabazon MP, the record breakers Eyston, Gardner and Cobb, Fred Craner of Donington, Percy Bradley and Hugh McConnell of Brooklands, Humphrey Cook of ERA, Cecil Kimber of MG, the Princes Chula and Bira, Johnny Wakefield, Kay Petre (who had been on the boat to South Africa in 1936), Arthur Dobson, Desmond Scammell, Charles Follett, John Eason Gibson, Kenneth and Denis Evans of Bellevue Garages, Charles Dodson, Ian Nichols, Bill Esplen, R. J. W. Appleton, the motorbike racers Reuben Harveyson and Rex Tanner, the journalist Harold Nockolds, and Mort Morris-Goodall and George Harvey-Noble, the last British witnesses to the deceased's racing career. The German ambassador was represented by Baron Edward von Selzam. Capitaine-Commandant Léon Hemeleers-Schenley, an assistant military attaché at the Belgian embassy in London, represented the Belgian Royal Automobile Club. Others, including Tony Cliff and Ray Lewthwaite, the Aldingtons, the Martins, the Fanes, Ramponi and Reggie Tongue, escaped the attention of the recording angels of *The Times* and the *Telegraph*.

As they entered, the mourners were handed an order of service: a folded single sheet of white card with blue text, containing only the words of the three hymns – 'Onward Christian Soldiers', 'The Church's One Foundation' and 'O God, Our Help in Ages Past' – and the Nunc Dimittis: 'Lord, now lettest Thou Thy servant depart in peace . . .' The service was conducted by the Rev Dr H. Maurice Relton, the vicar of All Saints, a prominent theologian whose residence was a few doors away from the Seamans' house, at 10 Ennismore Gardens. Afterwards the mourners gathered outside number 3. Many of the men, including Neubauer and Caracciola, wore full mourning dress, including top hats.

A number of them would also make the 7-mile journey

through south-west London to the committal. Putney Vale cemetery lay between Wimbledon Common and Richmond Park, on what had once been farmland. Opened in 1891, it soon became the resting place of notable figures, including, a few weeks earlier, Howard Carter, the celebrated Egyptologist who had discovered the tomb of Tutankhamen in 1922. Gathering around the reopened Seaman grave, the mourners heard prayers from Dr Relton and a short address from Dr Schippert before Dick was lowered into the earth. As they made their way out of the cemetery, just over two months of peace remained between England and Germany.

A new stone, commemorating father and son, would mark the grave. Below Dick's name there were two inscriptions. The first was from Laurence Binyon's Great War poem, 'For the Fallen', already familiar from Armistice Day ceremonies and slightly misremembered but still with a special poignancy when applied to one who, had he lived just a little longer, would have played a role of some sort in the next conflict: 'At the going down of the sun and in the morning / We shall remember them.' And beneath those lines, as if to lay a special claim, the last word: 'My beloved son to you eternal peace & rest in our hearts and memories always – Mother'.

EPILOGUE

A week after the funeral, Erica wrote to Monkhouse from Untergrainau about his plan, made before Dick's death, to return to Germany for the Grand Prix. 'My dear George,' she wrote on black-bordered notepaper, 'Though I am not a good writer and in English it is so difficult, I am trying to do so, please do not laugh too much. I want to thank you for everything you did [for] Dick. I know what a great friend you have been to him and all the happy times you had together ... You can't imagine how much I am looking forward to see [sic] you. I definitely need you, you help me such a lot ... All my love, Erica.'

A few days later her mother-in-law wrote to Untertürkheim. In a letter mixing deep pain, gratitude and confused impressions of what had taken place, Lilian expressed thanks:

For the great kindness and consideration ever shown to my son
by the directors and personnel of the Daimler-Benz company,
and the help and encouragement he always received at your
hands, my son on his side being devoted to the company and
everyone connected with it. In fact he loved Germany and the
German nation, and the years he spent there were without
doubt the happiest of his life ... The way in which the German
government brought Richard Seaman home, to be laid to rest in
his own country, and the honour and esteem shown by them at

his funeral, has evoked high praise and deep gratitude in every British heart. His Excellency Herr Hitler's noble tribute and message of sympathy has touched everyone in this country and it has received world-wide comment . . . As for myself, the death of my dearly loved son has been the gravest blow of my life, and has caused me intolerable anguish. It is going to be very difficult for me to face the future without him.

◆

Müller's Auto Union won at Reims, Caracciola struck back for Mercedes at the Nürburgring, and Lang triumphed at Bremgarten in the final Grande Épreuve before Britain and Germany went to war. Just one more Grand Prix remained, in Belgrade on 3 September. The race started two hours after Chamberlain's formal announcement in London, with only five competitors. Von Brauchitsch led, but his wild driving sent a stone from a verge smashing into Lang's goggles. Nuvolari won while Dr Gläser was extracting fragments of glass from both of Lang's eyes. When the Mercedes convoy arrived back at Untertürkheim, after using the last of their petrol on a long journey via Croatia, Slovenia and Austria, the army had already taken over the factory, and all their trucks and cars were immediately confiscated. Their golden age was over.

◆

As if to demonstrate that her sympathies had never been with the Nazis, Erica returned to England shortly before the declaration of war. She would not see Germany again for fourteen years. At first she stayed with the Martins in Surrey, with Fellowes in Sussex, with Ivo Peters – another member of the Brooklands set, and a friend of Reggie Tongue – and his wife Cynthia in Bristol, and with Ray Lewthwaite's family in Cumbria. She spent some weeks in Devon by herself. Since Dick's own funds could not be transferred from Germany, seemingly the only capital sum available was the £1,448 2s. 7d. left to her after Dick's will had passed through probate: hardly a fortune, but still amounting to seven times the national average annual salary in 1939. As his widow, she would also have received the income from his two trust funds. Everything else was controlled by his mother, whose refusal to have anything to do with her never wavered.

To say the least, life could not have been easy for a 19-year-old German widow in Britain during the first year of the war. She needed shelter, and in March 1940 her engagement to Reggie Tongue was formally announced in *The Times* and the *Daily Telegraph*. A photograph of the couple strolling in a garden was published, but the marriage would never take place. Tongue had been accepted by the RAF as an acting pilot officer the month after the engagement and, despite the British nationality conferred by her marriage to Dick, Erica must have felt threatened by the detention of increasing numbers of 'enemy aliens'. They included Germans and Italians with legitimate citizenship rights who had become the victims of false and malicious denunciations, stirred up by certain newspapers. Most of Dick's other racing friends, too, were now in the forces.

In November 1940, helped by a business friend of her father, she sailed for America. She would find her way from New York to Los Angeles, where she worked at Saks Fifth Avenue, a clothes shop in Beverly Hills. She did not have an easy time once the US had entered the war; the research of the historian Richard Armstrong shows that she was even interned for a while. Her adventures in America included a marriage in 1951 to an American colleague, James Glenn Stewart, but in 1953 she was divorced and back in Germany. At some point she would have received the money held by Mercedes since 1939 on Dick's behalf, mentioned in a letter from Wilhelm Haspel to Franz Josef Popp dated 19 June 1941 and describing a meeting between Erica's father and Wilhelm Kissel at which the matter had been discussed. This was six months before the United States entered the war, and presumably Popp was trying to see if the money could be sent to his daughter in California. Haspel informed Popp that the sums involved were RM 29,433.30 in residual earnings plus RM 100,000 in insurance. Thanks to the currency-exchange regulations and Germany's law on the treatment of hostile property, the money could not be moved. There was also, Haspel mentioned, the question of a Ford saloon belonging to Seaman, with a value estimated at RM 870 (about £80). Mercedes would apply for special permission to sell the car and add the sum received to the balance being held.

Erica retained her links to the company, meeting the Caracciolas again at a drivers' reunion soon after her return to Germany. Now she also had two nieces and a nephew, her sister Eva's children. Paul Heim had become a director of Daimler-Benz after the war but had died in 1951. Franz Josef Popp, cleared by the denazification process, had attempted to regain his position at BMW, without success, and died in 1954. That was also the year Erica married her third husband: the newspaper publisher Curt Schwab, the brother of her old friend Bimbo Haspel. They lived near Stuttgart and had a son, Stefan, who died of cancer at the age of sixteen. In retirement the Schwabs moved to Florida, where Curt died in 1973, followed by Erica in 1990 – on 4 February, Dick's birthday. Since Dick's death, she had continued to wear the engagement ring he had bought her in Zurich.

◆

On 25 June each year from 1940 to 1947, Lilian Beattie-Seaman placed a notice in *The Times*: 'Beattie-Seaman / In remembrance of my beloved son, Richard John Beattie-Seaman (Dick Seaman), who was killed in the Belgian Grand Prix Motor Race, July 25, 1939, aged 26. "They shall not grow old, as we that are left grow old; / Age shall not weary them, nor the years condemn. / At the going down of the sun and in the morning we will remember them" – MOTHER.' Once again she had quoted from the Binyon poem, this time accurately.

Two tasks now occupied her. The first was to create a room

at Pull Court dedicated to his memory, displaying the possessions he had left behind in England with, in a place of honour,
a favourite photograph of her son taken by Monkhouse in the
mountains when Dick was recovering from the Nürburgring
crash. The second task was to set down her memories of his
life. When Prince Chula came to write a biography of her son,
published in 1941, he was the first to make use of her manuscript. Lilian Beattie-Seaman continued to live in both London
and Worcestershire, no longer employing staff in the numbers
to which she had become accustomed. Now, when travelling
to Pull Court, she rang the local garage for a car to pick her up
at Tewkesbury station. By 1946 she was making efforts to sell
the country estate.

On 9 April 1948, alerted by her solicitors, who had been
unable to make contact with her, the police gained entry to 3
Ennismore Gardens and found her body. She had last been seen
alive a week earlier and had been dead, the pathologist believed,
for three days; perhaps a morning housemaid had arrived from
Hammersmith or Battersea at half past seven one morning,
received no answer to her knock, and assumed that Mrs Beattie-
Seaman was at Pull Court. The coroner recorded her death,
at the age of seventy, as due to heart failure. She was buried at
Putney Vale, in a grave immediately behind that of her husband
and her son. Vahlia, her daughter, specified the inscription on
the stone, choosing words from 'Hymn of a Virgin of Delphi,
at the Tomb of Her Mother', by the nineteenth-century poet
Thomas Moore: 'Fond soother of my infant tears / Fond sharer
of my infant joy / Is not thy shade still lingering here?' Lilian
left an estate valued at £286,784 (the equivalent of around £9
million today). Her country house and its contents were sold by
her executors at auction over six days in September 1948. Her
will, which she had rewritten a week after Dick's death, divided
her wealth equally between Vahlia and her late husband's three
granddaughters.

After her half-brother's death Vahlia had returned to France, where in 1941 she married Victor Hugo Duras, twenty-one years her senior, a well-connected American diplomat who had served in Belgium, Bulgaria and Russia, where he was arrested as a spy in Petrograd in 1916, and whose family owned a château in the Lot. Later that year Duras returned, apparently alone, to Washington DC, where he died in 1943. Vahlia died of heart failure in 1970 at her home in Chelsea. She was sixty-nine, and had chosen to live under the name Vahlia Ravenhill, using her father's middle name; it is believed that she may have spent some of her later years as a nun. The summary of her will stated: 'The deceased was at the date of her death (and had been for some years) a patient of the Court of Protection and her personal effects and belongings (other than jewellery retained at the bank) were, at her own insistence, of the most meagre kind and of poor quality; she lived at 12 Lawrence Street, London SW3 with a companion/housekeeper.' On her death she left £160,420 to be distributed between her half-sister's three daughters. Dorothy Maclaren died in 1977, aged eighty-five, and was buried in Glasgow with her mother, Annabella, William Seaman's first wife.

◆

Tony Cliff wanted to join the RAF. As a farmer, however, he was in a reserved occupation, and had to settle for the Home Guard. ('He could never watch *Dad's Army* after the first episode,' his son, Peter Cliff, said. 'He said it was too much like how it had really been.') He continued to ski, played a great deal of golf, and, having served on his local authority's police and education committees, received the MBE for public service before his death in 1995, aged eighty-two. Ray Lewthwaite won a Military Cross with the Scots Guards in Tunisia in 1943, having directed his anti-tank batteries against Rommel's Panzer divisions before being severely wounded. In 1945, after a spell on Field Marshal Montgomery's staff during the Normandy landings, for which he was made a member of the Légion d'Honneur, he returned to his regiment and fought up through Italy. He retired from the army in 1968 as a defence attaché with the British embassy in Paris and became the head of protocol in Hong Kong. Brigadier Sir Rainald Lewthwaite, 4th Bt., the last survivor of the Three Musketeers, died at Broadgate House in 2003, aged eighty-nine.

Whitney Straight joined the RAF and was badly wounded in Norway in 1940 but recovered to lead a squadron of Hurricanes in the Battle of Britain. Shot down over France in 1941, he escaped from a POW camp and made his way back to Britain, where he was promoted to air commodore. In 1947 he became managing director of BOAC. Much decorated, he died in 1979, aged sixty-six. His brother Michael piloted a Flying Fortress bomber in the war before becoming a magazine publisher; in 1963 his testimony during a US government background check set off the chain of events leading to the exposure of Anthony Blunt as a Soviet spy. He died in 2004, aged eighty-seven.

George Cosmo Monkhouse became Kodak's chief engineer in the UK. He met his wife, Connie, after the war, while she was working as Whitney Straight's secretary. When they had a son, they called him Richard. George published further books of his motor racing photographs and died in 1993, aged eighty-five. Richard Bickford, who had introduced Dick to George, joined the RAF in 1936 and was killed five years later – aged thirty and a squadron leader, already the recipient of the DFC – when the Halifax bomber he was piloting crashed in Yorkshire while returning from a raid on Frankfurt.

John Dugdale and Robert Fellowes bumped into each other in Tobruk in 1942. Dugdale was captured and held at various camps; freed in April 1945, he was awarded the Military Cross. He returned to *The Autocar* before moving to New York to work in the motor industry and came back to the UK to run British Leyland's publicity department. He died in 2000, aged eighty-six. Fellowes was severely wounded at El Alamein in 1942, losing a leg when his Jeep was blown up. From inhaling sand during the explosion, he contracted the silicosis that killed him in 1945, aged thirty-four.

Giulio Ramponi had become a British citizen in the 1930s, but was interned on the Isle of Man from 1941 to 1945. After the war he and Bill Rockall ran an Alfa dealership in west London, and he became a consultant to the motor and aircraft industries. In 1968 he retired to South Africa, where he died in 1986, aged eighty-four. Frank 'Lofty' England served as a bomber pilot and instructor during the war, after which he managed Jaguar's highly successful sports-car team. He was appointed chairman and chief executive of the company in 1972 and died in 1995, aged eighty-three.

The two Siamese princes spent the war in Cornwall, where Chula, the author of thirteen books, died of cancer in 1963, aged fifty-five. Bira continued to race cars after the war and competed in four Olympic Games as a yachtsman. He was married six times, on the second and sixth occasions to the same woman, and died of a heart attack at Barons Court tube station in London in 1983, aged seventy-one.

Ann Hunter, who disappeared from Dick's life after travelling with him to South Africa in 1936, joined the WAAF on the outbreak of war, serving in a senior role in the east of England. She married Peter Legg, a navigator from a Canadian bomber squadron, in 1942. Five years later she divorced him in order to marry Colin Kerr, a bank manager, in Cairo. They lived for many years in Kenya's Happy Valley before returning to England, where – now known as Anna – she died in 2009, aged ninety-two.

Of the two men who introduced Dick to Erica, H. J. Aldington died in 1976, aged seventy-three, having set up a successful Porsche dealership in London, while A. F. P. Fane was killed in 1942, aged thirty, while trying to land his Spitfire in bad weather at RAF Duxford after an aborted photo-reconnaissance mission to the U-boat yards on the Baltic Sea. Charlie Martin ferried agents and weapons to France on gunboats; afterwards he gave up motor sport for sailing, and died in Chelsea in 1998, aged eighty-four. Reggie Tongue flew Spitfires in the Battle of Britain, was active in the post-war motor trade, and developed an interest in sailing. He died in 1992, aged seventy-nine.

Lieutenant Pierre Hauman, the first man at the scene of Dick's fatal accident, served with the 1st Lancers in the Hautes Fagnes until they were overwhelmed by dive-bombers on the second day after the declaration of war between Belgium and Germany in May 1940. In France that summer he created a clandestine network, codenamed Tégal, to convey Allied airmen back to England via Lisbon. He died in 1961, aged forty-nine.

◆

By April 1945, when Allied troops arrived at the Mercedes offices and factory at Untertürkheim, where up to 15,000 people – including around 3,000 slaves brought from occupied territories – had worked during the war on military projects, more than 90 per cent of the buildings had been obliterated by Allied bombs. Many of the key personnel, however, had survived. One who did not was Wilhelm Kissel, who died of a heart attack, aged fifty-six, in 1942, and was succeeded as chairman by Wilhelm Haspel. When Himmler, knowing the new chairman had a part-Jewish wife, made efforts to remove him, Haspel was saved by the intercession of Göring and Hitler, possibly at the behest of Jakob Werlin. He supervised the post-war rebuilding of the company until his death, aged fifty-nine, in 1952. His wife, Bimbo, died the following year.

Alfred Neubauer remained at Untertürkheim until 1942, when he took charge of a military vehicle repair workshop in Berlin. He returned to Mercedes, overseeing a victory at Le Mans in 1952 and the full-scale comeback of 1954 and 1955, in which Juan Manuel Fangio won two Formula One world championships and his number two, Stirling Moss, won the Mille Miglia, all overshadowed in the public mind by the deaths of more than eighty people at Le Mans in 1955, killed by one of the team's cars. Moss was the Mercedes Grand Prix team's second British driver (in 2013, Lewis Hamilton would become the third). Neubauer died in 1980, aged eighty-nine.

Rudolf Uhlenhaut worked on tanks and aero engines during the war; as it neared its end, he helped Neubauer arrange for the dispersal of several Grand Prix cars at various secret sites. Two W154s were hidden in Lower Silesia, where Uhlenhaut had been sent to work. After escaping capture by the Russians, he made his way back to Bavaria. Through a pre-war contact, he spent two years with the Royal Engineers in a maintenance plant in the Ruhr before rejoining Mercedes in 1948. He resumed his old role, supervising the design of the post-war generation of racing and sports cars whose dominance echoed that of their predecessors. He died in Stuttgart in 1989, aged eighty-two.

Rudolf Caracciola saw out the war with his wife at their villa in Switzerland. He remained close to Mercedes, Kissel awarding him a monthly salary until Göring objected and payments were stopped in 1942. There were attempts at a post-war comeback, but he retired from racing after a couple of bad crashes. He died in 1959, aged fifty-eight. Hermann Lang continued to work for Mercedes throughout the war; in 1945 he was interned by the Allies for almost a year. Returning to Mercedes, he won at Le Mans in 1952 and had a single outing with the team on their return to the Grand Prix circuits in 1954, spinning off at the Nürburgring. He died at Bad Cannstatt in 1987, aged seventy-eight. Manfred von Brauchitsch worked throughout the war as a private secretary to a senior army officer in Berlin and then spent a short time in Argentina. Back in Germany, his secret contacts with the DDR led to a six-month jail term for treason before he fled to the East in 1955 while on bail, leaving a wife, Gisela, who committed suicide. He worked for the East German sports ministry, presiding over the movement to uphold the Olympic ideal – which the DDR did so much to betray – as well as the country's motor sports activities. He married again and returned to the West at Mercedes' invitation to drive a W125 at the opening of the new Nürburgring in 1984. The *Pechvogel* died in 2003, aged ninety-seven, the last surviving member of the pre-war Silver Arrows squads.

◆

Of the places Dick lived during his twenty-six years, Aldingbourne House, where he was born, still stands in its fine grounds off the road from Arundel to Chichester, now divided into eighteen luxury apartments. Kentwell Hall has been restored by its present owner and is open to the public. No. 3 Ennismore Gardens is divided into five apartments (the mews garage, where the black Delage was prepared, is now a private house). Weald Hall, damaged by wartime army use and subsequently by a fire, was demolished in 1950; its grounds are now a country park. Pull Court became a prep school and now, under the name Bredon School, specialises in educating pupils with dyslexia and dyspraxia. Haus 12 in Ambach exists under a different name, overlooking the Starnbergersee behind security fences and closed-circuit cameras. Haus Buchenbichl was knocked down and rebuilt in a similar style, much enlarged but still sitting amid the beech spinneys off the winding road between the Eibsee and Garmisch.

◆

A memorial was erected at Spa opposite the site of Dick's fatal crash, commissioned from a local stonemason by a group of friends, including Robert Fellowes and Rodney Walkerley; it was removed when the circuit was extensively modified in the 1970s, taken to the museum at Stavelot, never reinstalled, and is now said to be lost. Other forms of commemoration survive: each year the British Racing Drivers' Club awards the Richard Seaman Trophy to the British driver outside Formula One with the highest points total in the annual Gold Star competition, and

the Vintage Sports Car Club awards two trophies in his name
annually to the winners of races for vintage and historic cars.

As the years went by, myths began to accumulate around
Dick's memory, starting with the rumour that the coffin buried
in Putney Vale cemetery had been far too short for a man well
over 6 feet tall, and that perhaps, therefore, he had not died at
all. Those intrigued by this possibility tended also to believe –
in the light of his association with a German company also
engaged in military projects, and given his encounters with
various left-leaning Apostles at Cambridge – that he must have
been a spy. But if so, for which side? It would be easiest to
imagine, perhaps, that the British government had shown an
interest in his knowledge of one of Germany's most advanced
factories, and in his reading of the nation's mood. In eighty
years, however, not a shred of evidence has emerged.

How deep did his affection for Germany run? He loved the
lakes and mountains, he had been prepared to do his bit by shaking hands with Hitler and the Duke of Windsor, and he would
have been saddened had war parted him from the companionship of Uhlenhaut, Lang and others. But did Lilian Seaman
really keep the windows of Pull Court blazing with light during
the wartime blackout in order to help guide German bombers
to their targets, and stock an attic room with provisions for
Luftwaffe airmen who were shot down? Was Dick in fact buried
in the grounds of the house, sitting upright in the remains of
the W154 in which he had crashed at Spa, after it had been
transported to England in boxes? Some of those who find such
nonsense appealing – and perhaps inspired by the true story of
Neubauer stashing Grand Prix cars away in caves and cellars
during the war – have wandered the 84 acres of its grounds with
metal detectors, without success. The staff at Bredon School
still repeat handed-down tales of Dick testing his Silver Arrow
on the estate roads and flying swastika flags from the roof. The
most persistent story of all is the belief that Mercedes-Benz continue to look after Dick's grave; some, with apparent seriousness,

have called it Hitler's last extant order. The suggestion has always been denied by the company and is contradicted by the experience of the racing driver Alain de Cadenet and this author when, quite separately, they visited the cemetery in the 1970s and found the grave to be definitely untended, a state of affairs subsequently rectified by various hands.

◆

In his autobiography, Hermann Lang elegantly expressed a German teammate's view of Richard John Beattie Seaman. 'I will always remember him,' Lang wrote. 'He was kind-hearted, cool and fair as a sportsman, just as I had always pictured Englishmen to be.' Much of that was assuredly true. Dick Seaman was also ambitious and determined, but the occasional use of the word 'ruthless' seems unfair. When he was thwarted by the incompetence of others or their inability to keep their side of a bargain, he took swift and decisive action. When he felt he was being treated unfairly, he voiced his complaints with polite firmness. The £30,000 his mother estimated she had spent on funding his racing career was probably not much more than the outlay required in those days to qualify as a barrister or to subsidise a career as a Member of Parliament, the destinies his parents had in mind. And it was certainly not wasted or frittered away.

For George Monkhouse, the pain of loss was still fresh when, in a coda to Chula's 1941 biography of Seaman, he wrote: 'Of one thing I am convinced and that is that Dick died as he would have wished, doing what he liked best with victory in sight.' A thought with which to comfort those left behind, perhaps, and there was a certain solace for the bereaved in the image of Seaman meeting his end at the wheel of the finest racing car of the day, at the peak of his abilities on the kind of track where he always felt most stimulated. But he would certainly not have chosen death, and the evidence suggests that he was already looking ahead to a different sort of life.

In the summer of 1939 no one could have predicted the future with any certainty. Even had there been no war, he might have taken his wife back to England and re-entered the business world to which Straight had introduced him and from which he had turned aside only in pursuit of his immediate personal ambitions. In seven months' time, too, he would have come into his very substantial inheritance. A few months later he would in all probability have been leading a squadron of Spitfires or Hurricanes, exercising his skill and courage in aerial combat against Luftwaffe planes whose engines were built by his old employer and the company his father-in-law had founded. Back at home, a young German wife would have been waiting for news of his safe return. The odds on even medium-term survival would not have been favourable.

As for his achievements, the total of thirteen wins he amassed over the span of his career – including nine in international voiturette races and one in a classic Grande Épreuve, at a time when the calendar contained far fewer events – may look unimpressive when compared with the statistics compiled by later generations. Yet when racing resumed after 1945, it was to the short but glorious career of Dick Seaman that a new generation of heroes – Stirling Moss, Peter Collins, Mike Hawthorn and Tony Brooks among them – could turn as they sought an example of a British driver challenging the world's best. Moss in particular followed Seaman's example of professional preparation, expecting commensurate rewards in return; having raced with success for the Mercedes and Maserati factories, he strove to fulfil Dick's ambition of winning Grands Prix in a British car. In 1958, at the wheel of an Acton-built Vanwall, he missed the world championship by a mere point, thanks to a chivalrous gesture that his predecessor would have applauded; there was some consolation when the team became the first winners of the constructors' championship, thus realising the Seaman dream of a world-beating Grand Prix car made in Britain.

Racing had changed radically after the war, particularly in

Britain, where a sudden surplus of redundant airfields allowed enthusiasts to organise race meetings on closed circuits and to build the machinery that suited those conditions. Smooth asphalt surfaces encouraged the development of the lightweight cars that would shape the future of racing design, soon to be dominated by independent British teams. On this platform were erected the careers of the British champions of later years, from Graham Hill, Jim Clark, John Surtees and Jackie Stewart to James Hunt, Nigel Mansell, Damon Hill, Jenson Button and Lewis Hamilton, whose Silver Arrows – the direct descendants of the W125s and W154s that Dick drove – are designed and built in England.

Some of Seaman's successors were well aware of his exploits; others would be largely oblivious to their significance. For the general public, six years of cataclysmic war, following so soon after his death, blurred and finally obscured the memory of a man whose decision to race for a German team had added a layer of ambivalence to his image, at least in the minds of those who neither knew him nor understood the grounds on which he had made his choice.

Had he carried on to win the race that day in Spa, his reputation would have received another boost – enough, perhaps, to lift him permanently out of the ranks of Mercedes' reserve drivers, with several years of his prime left in which to confirm his standing among the greatest of his era. In any case, however, events would have overtaken him. 'I should rather die doing something I love than be killed doing something I loathe,' Pat Fairfield had told his family a few months before his fatal crash. Although Dick would no doubt have shared his friend's distaste for the business of killing other men, the onset of war would have offered him, like many others of his background, a chance to repay the debt to privilege. Spared that opportunity, he was denied much else.

ACKNOWLEDGEMENTS

The great motor racing historian Doug Nye offered vital support throughout the writing of this book, never too busy to entertain a question about the colour of Dick Seaman's racing overalls or the layout of a W154 cockpit, and in general to share so generously his vast store of knowledge. Adam Ferrington, editor of the ERA Club's newsletter, went in search of the documents that, inter alia, led me to the truth about Lilian Seaman's background and to the identity of the girl who sailed to South Africa with Dick Seaman in 1936. The wisdom and enthusiasm of both these men was invaluable.

Dennis Heck welcomed me to the Mercedes–Benz Classic archive in Stuttgart, granting access to a wealth of extraordinary documentation of the interwar period. At Beaulieu, Patrick Collins opened the National Motor Museum's boxes of relevant documents and correspondence. Andrew Lewis allowed me to browse in the Brooklands Museum. I am also grateful to staff at the British Library, the Richmond upon Thames library and Putney Vale cemetery.

Background to Dick's years at school and university came from Stephen Ball of Broadstairs Books, a former pupil of Hildersham House; Dr Jonathan Smith, archivist at Rugby School, and the staff of the school library; Tim Day, housemaster of Michell House (formerly Molony's) at Rugby, and the boys who entertained me to lunch at 3 Hillmorton Road; and a second archivist named Jonathan Smith, this one at Trinity College, Cambridge.

Visits to Dick's various homes were assisted by Patrick Phillips at Kentwell Hall, Rachel Carter and Chris Iddles at Bredon School (Pull Court), Silvia Schutz in Ambach, Frau Nass in Münsing, and Josef Bader in Untergrainau-bei-Garmisch. In Spa, I was helped by Anne Piloy and Pascale Bronfort at the Office du Tourisme, Marie-Christine Schils at the Musée de la Ville d'Eaux, Herman Maudoux of the Musée du Circuit de Spa-Francorchamps at the Abbaye de Stavelot, and Pastor Heike Sonnen and Sandrine Peeters at the Église Protestante de Spa.

Peter Cliff in Crayke and Diana Lewthwaite at Broadgate House talked to me about their father and father-in-law, respectively. Charles Tongue gave me a copy of his father's autobiography. Mike Dodds helped confirm the identity of his aunt, Ann Hunter. Richard Armstrong permitted me to read the manuscript that brings together his research into the later life of Erica Seaman, and Simon Davis shared some of the findings for his forthcoming biography of Rudolf Caracciola. Neil Corner showed me his collection of Seaman memorabilia and talked about the experience of owning and restoring pre-war Silver Arrows.

Other valuable assistance came from Jackie Sullivan, archivist at Roedean School; Rose Wild, archive editor of *The Times*; Christopher Maume, assistant obituaries editor of the *Daily Telegraph*; Kevin Wood, archive manager at Motorsport Images; Adrian Fisher, archive manager at PA Images; Stephanie Sykes-Dugmore, BRDC archivist; Wayne Fortune, archives assistant at the Lambeth Palace Library; and Caroline Hagen Hall, who sent me her late father's unpublished autobiography.

Nigel Cullen provided advice on the finer points of William Seaman's will; the rowing historian Chris Dodd checked the Henley Regatta records; Ian Jack shared his knowledge of Glasgow and steam yachts; Ben Macintyre kindly considered (and rejected) the notion that Dick Seaman might have been a spy; and Belinda Scott helped with translation. Others who gave various forms of encouragement and information include Pierre de Coninck at the FIA, Richard Wiseman, David Weguelin, Eric Dymock, Anne de Courcy, Andrew Swift, Bernhard Völker, Alain de Cadenet, Hugo Vickers, Michael Watts, George Taylor and Melanie McFadyean.

My agent, Clare Alexander, guided me to Simon & Schuster, where Ian Chapman and Ian Marshall showed an immediate enthusiasm for the project. I am grateful to them, and to Melissa Bond and Bea Joubert, for enabling me to tackle a subject close to my heart. The copy-editing skills of Charlotte Atyeo were invaluable.

Thanks are due to the late Hans Koningsberger for the title, adapted from that of his novel, *A Walk with Love and Death*, published in 1961.

BIBLIOGRAPHY

Four volumes, one of them unpublished, offered vital source material for *A Race with Love and Death*. Prince Chula's biography, written soon after Dick Seaman's death, had the benefit of first-hand observation and acquaintance. Chris Nixon's handsomely illustrated book contained testimony gathered from important witnesses, such as Tony Cliff, Ray Lewthwaite, Charlie Martin and, most notably, Erica Seaman. Doug Nye and Geoff Goddard scrupulously compiled the correspondence between Dick and George Monkhouse, adding wonderful photographs. Above all there is Lilian Beattie-Seaman's memoir, a document that, with its wealth of circumstantial detail and reconstruction of events both dramatic and mundane, needs to be read with a constant awareness that a grieving mother is seeing the past through a veil of mourning. By testing, where possible, her statement of facts against the historical record (such as those of her own family history), I hoped to acquire a feeling for when she was allowing the intensity of her emotions to influence the accuracy of her recall and thus falling into exaggeration or distortion. This is a story, after all, that requires nothing more or less dramatic than the truth.

Beattie-Seaman, Lilian: *Richard Seaman: His Life and Death* (private manuscript)

Chakrabongse, Prince Chula: *Dick Seaman: Racing Motorist* (G. T. Foulis, 1945)

Nixon, Chris: *Shooting Star* (Transport Bookman, 2000)

Nye, Doug and Geoffrey Goddard: *Dick & George: The Seaman–Monkhouse Letters 1936–1939* (Palawan Press, 2002)

The following volumes were also helpful:

Bellon, Bernard P.: *Mercedes in Peace and War* (Columbia University Press, 1990)

Bentley, John: *The Devil Behind Them* (Angus & Robertson, 1959)

Birkin, Sir Henry: *Full Throttle* (G. T. Foulis, 1945)

Bouverie, Tim: *Appeasing Hitler* (The Bodley Head, 2019)

Boyd, Julia: *Travellers in the Third Reich* (Elliott & Thompson, 2017)

Brauchitsch, Manfred von: *Ohne Kampf Kein Sieg* (Verlag der Nation, 1964)

Brown, Jane: *Angel Dorothy* (Unbound, 2019)

Cabart, Daniel and Christophe Pund: *Delage: Champion du Monde* (Orep Editions, 2017)

Caracciola, Alice: *Memories of a Racing Driver's Wife* (Automobile Quarterly, Vol VII, No 1, 1968)

Caracciola, Rudolf: *An Autobiography* (G. T. Foulis, 1955)

Carter, Miranda: *Anthony Blunt: His Lives* (Macmillan, 2001)

Chakrabongse, Prince Chula: *Road Racing 1936* (G. T. Foulis, 1937/1946)

Chakrabongse, Prince Chula: *Blue and Yellow* (G. T. Foulis, 1947)

Cholmondeley-Tapper, T. P.: *Amateur Racing Driver* (G. T. Foulis, 1953)

Court, William: *Power and Glory: History of Grand Prix Motor Racing 1906–1951* (Macdonald, 1966)

Crabtree, Reginald: *The Luxury Yacht from Steam to Diesel* (David & Charles, 1973)

Davis, S. C. H.: *Racing Motorist* (Iliffe & Sons, 1949)

Downing, David: *The Best of Enemies: England v Germany* (Bloomsbury, 2000)

Dugdale, John: *Great Motor Sport of the Thirties* (Two Continents, 1977)

Edgar, Alfred: *Where the Cars Roar* (George G. Harrop, 1937)

Ferrari, Enzo: *My Terrible Joys* (Licino Cappelli, 1963)

Georgeano, G. N.: *Brooklands, A Personal History* (Beaulieu Books, 1978)

Green, Geoffrey: *Pardon Me for Living* (George Allen & Unwin, 1985)

Gregor, Neil: *Mercedes-Benz in the Third Reich* (Yale University Press, 1998)

Griffiths, Richard: *Fellow Travellers of the Right* (Constable, 1980/Faber Finds, 2010)

Hagen, Louis: *Autobiography* (unpublished manuscript)

Hilmes, Oliver: *Berlin 1936* (The Bodley Head, 2018)

Hilton, Christopher: *Hitler's Grands Prix in England* (Haynes, 1999)

Lang, Hermann: *Grand Prix Driver* (G. T. Foulis, 1953)

Lyndon, Barré: *Grand Prix* (John Miles, 1935)

May, Tim: *Francis Howe: Motor Man Par Excellence* (GMS Publications, 2014)

Mays, Raymond: *Split Seconds* (G. T. Foulis, 1951)

Monkhouse, George: *Grand Prix Racing* (G. T. Foulis, 1950/1953)

Monkhouse, George: *Motor Racing with Mercedes-Benz* (G. T. Foulis, 1948)

Monkhouse, George: *Mercedes-Benz: Grand Prix Racing 1934–55* (White Mouse Editions, 1984)

Neubauer, Alfred: *Speed Was My Lif*e (Barrie & Rockliff, 1960)

Nixon, Chris: *Racing the Silver Arrows* (Osprey, 1986)

Nixon, Chris: *The Robert Fellowes Collection: Grand Prix 1934–39* (Transport Bookman, 2001)

Perry, Roland: *Last of the Cold War Spies* (Da Capo, 2005)

Pritchard, Anthony: *Maserati: A History* (David & Charles, 1976)

Pritchard, Anthony: *Silver Arrows in Camera* (Haynes, 2008)

Purvis, Stewart and Jeff Hulbert: *Guy Burgess: The Spy Who Knew Everyone* (Biteback, 2016)

Reuss, Eberhard: *Hitler's Motor Racing Battles* (Haynes, 2008)

Roth, Joseph: *On the End of the World* (Pushkin Press, 2019)

Russell, Tony: *Out in Front: The Leslie Ballamy Story* (MRP, 2004)

Scheller, Wolfgang and Thomas Pollack: *Rudolf Uhlenhaut* (Dalton Watson, 2017)

Segrè, Claudio G.: *Italo Balbo: A Fascist Life* (University of California Press, 1990)

Sereny, Gitta: *Albert Speer: His Battle with Truth* (Macmillan, 1995)

Spurling, Hilary: *Anthony Powell: Dancing to the Music of Time* (Penguin, 2017)

Strachey, Lytton: *Eminent Victorians* (Chatto, 1918)

Straight, Michael: *After Long Silence* (W. W. Norton, 1983)

Tongue, Reggie (ed. Eric Dymock): *High Speed Diary* (Dove Publishing, 2002)

Urbach, Karina: *Go-Betweens for Hitler* (OUP, 2015)

Ustinov, Peter: *Dear Me* (Random House, 2011)

Venables, David: *Brooklands: The Official Centenary History* (Haynes, 2007)

Venables, David: *The Racing Fifteen-Hundreds* (Transport Bookman, 1984)

Walkerley, Rodney: *Grands Prix 1934–1939* (Motor Racing Publications, 1950)

Wasensteiner, Lucy and Martin Faass: *London 1938: Defending 'Degenerate' Art* (Nimbus, 2018)

Weguelin, David: *ERA* (White Mouse Editions, 1980)

Yates, Brock: *Vanderbilt Cup Race 1936 and 1937* (Iconografix, 1997)

Also consulted were articles by John Dugdale, Rodney Walkerley, William Boddy, Harold Nockolds, John Bridcutt and others in *The Autocar, Motor, Motor Sport, Speed* and the *VSCC Bulletin*, and film sources including Pathé News. And, of course, the edition of *Picture Post* published on 15 June 1939.

INDEX